OGDEN

Junction City

PICTORIAL RESEARCH BY JEROME BERNSTEIN
"PARTNERS IN PROGRESS" BY MURRAY M. MOLER

PRODUCED IN COOPERATION WITH
THE OGDEN AREA
CHAMBER OF COMMERCE

WINDSOR PUBLICATIONS, INC.
NORTHRIDGE, CALIFORNIA

OGDEN

Junction City

Richard C. Roberts & Richard W. Sadler

Windsor Publications, Inc.—History Book Division
Publisher: John M. Phillips
Editorial Director: Teri Davis Greenberg
Design Director: Alexander D'Anca

Staff for *Ogden: Junction City*
Senior Editor: Pamela Schroeder
Picture Editor: Laurel Paley
Text Editor: Karl Stull
Director, Corporate Biographies: Karen Story
Assistant Director, Corporate Biographies: Phyllis Gray
Editor, Corporate Biographies: Judith Hunter
Editorial Assistants: Kathy M. Brown, Patricia Cobb, Lonnie
   Pham, Patricia Pittman
Designer: Alexander D'Anca
Layout: Christina McKibbin

All color photographs by Grove Pashley unless otherwise
indicated

Library of Congress Cataloging in Publication Data
Roberts, Richard C., 1932-
   Ogden: Junction City.

   "Produced in cooperation with the Ogden Area
Chamber of Commerce."
   Bibliography: p. 277
   Includes index.
   1. Ogden (Utah)—History. 2. Ogden (Utah)—
Description. 3. Ogden (Utah)—Industries.
I. Sadler, Richard W., 1940-   . II. Moler,
Murray M.   Partners in progress. 1985.   III. Ogden
Area Chamber of Commerce.   IV. Title.
F834.03R63   1985   979.2′28   85-9540
ISBN 0-89781-154-2

Project Advisors
The publisher wishes to acknowledge the following individuals,
who lent valuable assistance in the preparation of this volume:

Rod Browning	William L. Garner
LaMar Buckner	Robert K. Eisleben
Richard Hemingway	Blaine Stewart
G.E. "Dutch" Belnap	Robert Hunter
Robert A. Madsen	Jay B. Taggart
H. Gary Pehrson	Rodney H. Brady
Steve Lawson	Kim D. Butters

Endpapers
This bird's-eye view depicts early Ogden.
Courtesy, Richard C. Roberts

Frontispiece
*Brown's Fort, depicted by noted Utah
painter Farrell R. Collett, was the new
name given to Fort Buenaventura after it
was purchased by the area's first Mormon
settler, Captain James Brown. Courtesy,
Weber State College*

Opposite
*The stagecoach remained the most common
form of area transportation through the
mid-1870s, when railroad branch lines began to radiate from the city. Courtesy, Utah
State Historical Society (USHS)*

Pages six and seven
*A familiar scene in rural Ogden, seagulls
look for tidbits as they follow a tractor
breaking ground for spring planting. Photo
by Barbara Parsons Bernstein*

CONTENTS

PROLOGUE

Throughout its rich history, Ogden has been the gateway city for America's Great Basin and Far West. The Indians who roamed the shores of the Great Salt Lake, centuries before the appearance of white settlers, favored the confluence of the Ogden and Weber rivers as a place to camp, meet, and trade. Mounds of artifacts near the juncture of the streams, and in several places within the boundaries of the city itself, testify to their contribution to the history of the Ogden area.

Early white explorers and traders also considered Ogden a major gateway. There were dreams that a river would be found flowing westward from the Great Salt Lake to the Pacific Ocean, providing a mid-continent version of the coveted Northwest Passage. Circumnavigation of the lake in the early nineteenth century disproved that theory, but other land routes were developed out of those explorations.

The railroads, binding the country together with bands of steel in 1869, met at Promontory Summit and drove the Golden Spike, but within a few years the junction of the Central Pacific and Union Pacific railroads was moved to Ogden. Ogden's location was important in its becoming the Junction City: thanks to the curvature of the Pacific coast, rarely noticed on flat maps, Ogden's main rail yards are within a few miles of being equidistant from Los Angeles, San Francisco, and Portland. Within a closer arc are Butte, Denver, and Phoenix.

The nation's generals and admirals knew about this geographical blessing for the Ogden area, and for the nation. As the clouds of war blackened in the late 1930s, the Ogden area was selected for development of a major air corps materiel handling and repair depot, for an army supply depot, and for a navy supply depot, in addition to enlargement of an existing arsenal.

The concept of Ogden as junction has had a tremendous influence on the development of the community and its people and on the establishment of spheres of commerce and industry to serve the needs of the city and its customers.

After the early trappers and traders gave way to Mormon agricultural settlement, Ogden seemed destined to be a farm-

ing town. The arrival of the railroads in 1869 diluted Mormon predominance in the population. World War II and the growth of defense establishments brought even greater numbers of non-Mormons, or Gentiles, into the Ogden area. The Church of Jesus Christ of Latter-day Saints is still strong in the Junction City, but other religious denominations are liberally represented, too. The growth of the city has brought it a unique diversity, including blacks, Hispanics, and Asians as well as descendants of immigrants from every nation in Europe, and this mix has paid dividends in enriching Ogden's history and in contributing to a better society.

Ogden has provided the nation with leaders in the fields of education, history, politics, firearms, banking, construction, agriculture, and recreation. Those contributions are certain to continue, thanks to the educational systems—from kindergarten through college—that flourish in Ogden's friendly climate. It is against this broadly outlined background that the history of Ogden, the Junction City, can be told.

—Murray M. Moler

CHAPTER ONE
EARLY OGDEN

Ogden—Junction City of the transcontinental railroad—stands at a natural point of convergence in the landscape with the Wasatch Mountains to its back and the Great Basin to its front, stretching westward to the Sierra Nevada. The site of Ogden was once covered by ancient Lake Bonneville, a huge freshwater lake whose levels can be traced in the mountains east of the city. The Great Salt Lake, the largest remnant of Lake Bonneville, dominates the western limits of Weber County.

The Weber River, for which the county is named, is born in the Uinta Mountains and plunges westward to the Great Salt Lake. The confluence of the Weber River and its sister stream, the Ogden, drew the earliest inhabitants to the area. The banks of these rivers became a home for Indians, who grew corn, made pottery, and fished. By the nineteenth century these sedentary bands had been succeeded by nomadic bands, many with horses, that crisscrossed the region. Shoshone and Ute, as well as other tribes, were the peoples who for a time called the area their home. The Shoshone and Ute Indians in particular developed trails up Weber and North Ogden canyons that would later be used by the mountain men and fur trappers.

Northern Utah, southern Idaho, and western Wyoming were hotly contested fur trapping areas in the early 1800s. Hudson's Bay trappers out of Fort Vancouver in the Oregon Country, Spanish and American trappers out of Taos, and mountain men out of Independence and St. Louis competed for the riches of the beaver country during the 1820s and the 1830s. A decisive figure in the Rocky Mountains fur trade, William Ashley organized several expeditions beginning in 1822. Some of his recruits went on to become celebrated explorers of the West. One was Jim Bridger, who was part of an Ashley expedition during the fall of 1824 when he sighted the Great Salt Lake.

The weather of 1824-1825 was so severe that Ashley's men changed their plans to pass the winter in Cache Valley and

Waterfall Canyon provided Ogden's settlers with water for irrigation of their crops. Waterfall Falls has been a natural attraction and picnic site since the earliest days of the city. Courtesy, Richard C. Roberts

9

Above
A bronze of Peter Skene Ogden stands in the center of the Newgate Mall on Wall Avenue. A Hudson's Bay Company brigade leader, Ogden explored the vicinity of Ogden in 1825. Photo by Grove Pashley. All color photographs by Grove Pashley unless otherwise indicated

Right
Rewarding the Waterfall Canyon hiker is Waterfall Falls. For over a century climbers have refreshed themselves with a drink cooled in late-season snowbanks at the base of the falls. During runoff, the fall's spume can be seen for miles across the Ogden plain.

Opposite page, top
Fort Buenaventura, depicted by Farrell R. Collett, was built in 1845 by Miles Goodyear, Utah's first permanent white citizen. Courtesy, Weber State College

Left
Modern day mountain men gather annually at Fort Buenaventura to relive the colorful past.

Above
Fort Buenaventura has been reconstructed on its original site along the Weber River. The site is now a state park.

Above
Mountain man Jim Bridger, who discovered the Great Salt Lake in 1824, was among the party of trappers and Indians who camped for the winter near the site of Ogden. An accomplished trapper and trader, he established Fort Bridger in southwestern Wyoming and was instrumental in opening Utah and the West to settlement. USHS

Above right
Ogden's link to the East, Weber Canyon, was a formidable barrier to the Western pioneer until the Union Pacific Railroad built through it in 1868-1869. Such geologic features as Devils Slide amazed travelers through the canyon. Courtesy, Ogden Chamber of Commerce

Right
Since prehistoric times, various Indian tribes have inhabited the Ogden area. The Shoshone and Ute, who prevailed in the years prior to white settlement, were attracted by an abundance of water, rich grassland, fish, fowl, and other game in the locale. USHS

Peter Skene Ogden, a brigade leader for the Hudson's Bay Company, came south from Cache Valley in 1825 to a place he called New Valley, known today as Ogden Valley. In his journal Ogden wrote, "I only wish we could find a dozen spots equal to it." USHS

instead established themselves in two camps by the Great Salt Lake—one at the mouth of the Bear River and the other at the mouth of the Weber River. Among other mountain men in the group were William Sublette, Daniel Potts, Johnson Gardner, and John H. Weber, for whom the Weber River was named. A number of Snake Indians stayed with the American fur trappers, who explored some of the lake shore. This area along the Wasatch front became a winter home over the next several years for fur trappers. In 1826 James Clyman, along with Louis Vasquez, Moses Black Harris, and Henry Fraeb, circumnavigated the Great Salt Lake in a bull boat; they were looking for beaver and an outlet to the Pacific.

Peter Skene Ogden, a British fur trapper for whom the Ogden River and eventually Ogden City were named, was born in Quebec in 1794, the son of Tory parents who had fled New York during the American Revolution. Ogden became a skilled fur trapper and valued leader for the North West Company (headquartered in Canada), which merged in 1821 with the British Hudson's Bay Company. As a brigade leader for the Hudson's Bay Company, he made several important discoveries, including the Humboldt River. During 1825 Ogden's Snake River Brigade—consisting of more than 70 trappers and their wives and children, equipped with 372 horses and 364 beaver traps—ventured through Idaho and into Cache Valley. In order to avoid American trappers, Ogden pushed southward to a place he called New Valley, known today as Ogden Valley.

During the middle of May, Ogden and his men spent a week in Ogden's Hole, where they trapped 590 beaver. In his journal Ogden noted that it appeared no whites had been there before. "I only wish we could find a dozen spots equal to it," he wrote. During the latter part of May, Ogden had a confrontation with a group of American trappers on the Weber River near Mountain Green. Under the leadership of Johnson Gardner, the Americans claimed the area belonged to the United States and induced twenty-three of Ogden's men to desert, taking with them about 700 beaver skins. The Snake River Brigade retraced their steps northward: Ogden Valley was the closest Peter Skene Ogden came to the site of the city that bears his name.

The most informative account of the area during the days

Above
Lorin Farr's gristmill, seen in a painting by Farrell R. Collett, was built in 1850. Courtesy, Weber State College

Right
The Old Mill dates back to the beginnings of Ogden City, when Lorin Farr supervised the building of the first sawmill and gristmill in northern Utah in 1850. The mill building survived until 1985.

The origins of the Continental Oil Company, which began in Ogden in 1875 with kerosene sales, are depicted in a painting by Ken Baxter. Courtesy, Weber State College

Above
The workshop of John M. Browning, the world's most famous gun inventor, has been preserved and can be seen at the Union Station, where a collection of original models for many of Browning's weapons is on exhibit. Courtesy, Golden Spike Empire

Left
A painting by Fred Hunger shows John M. Browning's gunsmith shop. In the 1880s the modest shop was located on the present site of Ogden's Orpheum Theatre. Courtesy, Weber State College

of the fur trade came from the pen of Osborne Russell, a trapper headquartered at Fort Hall on the Snake River. Russell's diary, published as *A Journal of a Trapper,* describes a journey south in late 1840 along the shore of the Great Salt Lake to the mouth of the Weber River, which he construed as "Weaver's river."

At this place the Valley is about 10 Mls wide intersected with numerous Springs of salt and fresh hot and cold water which rise at the foot of the Mountain and run thro. the Valley into the river and Lake—Weavers river is well timbered along its banks principally with Cottonwood and box elder—There are also large groves of sugar maple pine and some oak growing in the ravines about the Mountain—We also found large numbers of Elk which had left the Mountain to winter among the thickets of wood and brush along the river.

The entry for December 25, 1840, recounts the hospitality of a French Canadian and his Indian wife in an encampment which included "15 lodges of Snake Indians" and three families of mixed descent and tribe. A Christmas feast was served in the roomiest of the lodges, "being about 36 ft. in circumference at the base with a fire in the center." Tableware consisted of tin cups, large chips of bark for plates, and knives, and "the eating commenced at the word given by the landlady":

The first dish that came on was a large tin pan 18 inches in diameter round full of Stewed Elk meat. The next dish was similar to the first heaped up with boiled Deer meat (or as the whites would call it Venison a term not used in the Mountains). The 3d and 4th dishes were equal in size to the first containing a boiled flour pudding prepared with dried fruit accompanied by 4 quarts of sauce made of the juice of sour berries and sugar. Then came the cakes followed by about six gallons of strong Coffee already sweetened

Three people in this holiday company could speak English, "but very broken"; fortunately, Russell was "familiar with the Canadian French and Indian tongue":

as all dinners are accompanied with conversation this was not deficient in that respect. The principal topic which was discussed was the political affairs of the Rocky Mountains. The state of governments among the different tribes, the personal characters of the most distinguished warriors Chiefs etc.

A U.S. Topographical Bureau expedition ventured into the Ogden area in September 1843 under the command of John Charles Frémont. This was Frémont's second trip in search of an easy route for emigrants to the Pacific coast; in 1842 he had publicized South Pass, which became the gateway through the Rockies to Oregon and California. Reaching the mouth of the Weber River, approximately six miles west of the present city of Ogden, Frémont explored the Great Salt Lake in an "India-Rubber" boat. The island which bears his name today he named Disappointment Island. His report of this 1843-1844 expedition, published the following year, was studied extensively by many readers in the East who were eager to learn about the frontier—among them the Mormons in Nauvoo, Illinois. Frémont described the valleys of northern Utah as numerous and fertile.

By this time the fur trade had begun to dwindle. Trappers who wanted to stay in the West sought other ways to make their fortunes. Jim Bridger, for example, turned his attention to the trade in supplies for westward emigrants, establishing Fort Bridger in 1843. Miles Goodyear had much the same idea when he established Fort Buenaventura in 1845. Goodyear's post would become the nucleus for the oldest permanent settlement in Utah.

Goodyear, a red-headed Connecticut Yankee, was nineteen years old when he set out on the Oregon Trail in 1836. He became involved in the fur trade, trapping out of Fort Hall, but supplemented his income over the next decade by horse trading and horse racing. In 1839 he married Pomona, a daughter of the Ute Chief Pe-Teet-Neet, and by 1842 they had two children, William Miles and Mary Eliza. As the fur trade became less profitable, Goodyear looked for a place to develop as a supply station between St. Louis and the Pacific, a place where he could trap, trade horses and other goods, and raise his family. He chose a site on the lower Weber River near a large sandhill and in 1845 began to construct Fort Buenaventura. The compound was fenced by cottonwood pickets, form-

Explorer, soldier, and politician John Charles Frémont, the "Great Pathfinder," followed the paths established by mountain men to the Ogden area in 1843. From this site he made the first reliable maps of the Weber River and the Great Salt Lake. USHS

Above right
Evan DeBloois, a U.S. Forest Service archaeologist, helped survey the site of the original Fort Buenaventura. DeBloois is exposing a portion of the fort's original foundation, on which an exact duplicate was built in 1979-1980. The reconstructed fort is a state historical monument. Photo by Barbara Parsons Bernstein

Right
The Miles Goodyear Cabin was built in 1845 with cottonwood logs. A stockade enclosed the cabin, several other buildings, and a corral, all of which formed Fort Buenaventura. The cabin, whose roof and foundation have been replaced, is considered the oldest surviving pioneer dwelling in Utah. Courtesy, Ogden Chamber of Commerce

ing a rectangle about sixty by fifty-five feet. Cabins in each corner of the fort housed the Goodyears and the friends who helped build and sustain the fort. Goodyear kept goats, cattle, and horses. His garden included carrots, cabbages, radishes, and corn. Water for the crops had to be carried from the Weber River by bucket. From the top of the large sandy knoll, fifty yards southwest of the fort, it was possible to observe much of the valley both north and south.

Groups of emigrants traveled through the vicinity of Fort Buenaventura—west from Fort Bridger and down the Weber River—for the first time in 1846, when it was suggested that going around the south end of the Great Salt Lake would be a quicker way to California. Based on guesswork, this route proved tragic for the Donner party. Earlier in the year three other groups (the Bryant-Russell, Harlan-Young, and Leinhard parties) had used the Hastings cutoff down Weber Canyon, though we have no record of their visiting Goodyear's fort.

The first party of Mormons, seeking a haven in the West from religious persecution, became acquainted with Goodyear on July 10, 1847. Goodyear encouraged their leader Brigham Young to settle in the area, but the canyon of the Weber River was found to be too rugged. The Mormons settled instead in the locale that would become Salt Lake City. However, it was the counsel of Brigham Young to buy Goodyear's property as soon as possible. Captain James Brown, who had been a member of the Mormon Battalion during the Mexican War, was authorized by Mormon church leaders to negotiate with Goodyear for his "Mexican land grant," completing the sale late in November of 1847. In exchange for lands extending from the Wasatch Mountains to the Great Salt Lake and along the Weber River north to Ben Lomond Peak, Brown paid $1,950 in Mexican or Spanish gold coins. Goodyear moved out, taking his family and horses with him, and Brown moved his family in. Fort Buenaventura became known as Brown's Fort and then Brownsville over the next three years.

Goodyear's cattle and goats remained at the fort, becoming a significant source of milk and cheese not only for early Ogden but early Salt Lake City as well. By early 1848 the settlement at Brownsville included the Mormon families of James Brown, Henry Chilton, Louis Myers, George Thurlkill, Robert Crow, Reuben Henry, Artemus Sprague, Daniel Burch,

Brigham Young was instrumental in selecting the present site of Ogden and in encouraging families to settle there. In 1856 he predicted that where Ogden stands "a large city will be built up, and the railroad will make it a city of importance." Courtesy, Union Pacific Railroad Museum

William Stewart, Mrs. Ruth Stewart, and Urban Van Stewart. Two trappers and a Mexican boy remained from the Goodyear era and lived with the Mormons. Sprague, a blacksmith, made a plow out of wagon tire irons that was used by two of Brown's sons, Alexander and Jesse, to plow and plant five acres of wheat as well as patches of corn, turnips, cabbages, potatoes, and watermelons. The Brown brothers irrigated their crops through the summer by constructing a dam on Canfield Creek, which runs out of Waterfall Canyon. During 1848 and 1849 Ezra Chase, Charles Hubbard, and Ambrose and William Shaw settled with their families at Mound Fort, farming the land north of the Ogden River and using its water for irrigation.

In September 1849 the thirty families living in the Ogden area received a visit from Brigham Young and other Mormon leaders. Included in the delegation were members of a brass band, who entertained during several evenings of concerts and dancing. The hospitality of the settlement included dinners of goat meat, potatoes, pork, bread, and watermelon.

Young learned from settler Ezra Chase that his land was very productive in grain. But a short distance below, he said, drainage was so poor that it would "yield a hundred bushels of crickets to the acre and 50 bushels of mosquitoes." Young then gave his instructions as to how the town that would become Ogden should be laid out. Climbing to the top of the sandhill, he pointed to the bench land on the south side of the Ogden's fork, where the waters from the Ogden and Weber rivers could be brought together for irrigation and other purposes. Over the next two years settlers at the fort relocated to the east according to Young's guidance.

James Brown obtained permission to build bridges across the Weber and Ogden rivers and charge tolls to all who crossed. This improvement made it easier for settlers to get around in the Ogden area and, more important, also provided a means of making money from gold rushers traveling to California. Beginning in 1849 thousands crossed the continent in search of the yellow metal. About a third of them stopped in Salt Lake City, and many of those traveled north through Ogden, following a route around the northern end of the Great Salt Lake and along the Humboldt River. Ogden residents as well as those in Salt Lake City made a tidy profit selling supplies. Milk sold for 10 cents a quart. Butter, which was 20 cents a pound in 1849, jumped to 50 cents a pound in 1850. Gold rushers were particularly anxious for fresh garden vegetables and healthy livestock. Many traded away their goods at very low prices for these commodities. Because Brigham Young spoke firmly against involvement in the Gold Rush, most Mormons stayed within the Great Basin and continued their agriculture and merchandising.

Formalizing a plan for Mormon settlements, the General Church Conference voted in October 1849 to "lay off" a city in Captain James Brown's neighborhood (Ogden), one in Utah Valley (Provo), and one in Sanpete Valley (Manti). The name Ogden first came into use in January 1850, after which the town became the hub of the surrounding area as small forts and then other communities sprang up during the 1850s and 1860s. Mound Fort and Bingham's Fort (Lynne) had already been settled in 1848 and 1849, respectively. In 1850 the settlements of Harrisville, Marriott, Slaterville, West Weber, Wilson, North Ogden, Uintah, Burch Creek (South Ogden), and Riverdale were founded. In 1851 Farr West and South Weber were established, followed by Hooper (Muskrat Springs) in 1852. Subsequent years saw the founding of Plain City in 1859, Huntsville in 1860, and Roy in 1870. Many of

An illustration of early Ogden depicts the broad, straight streets laid out in typical Mormon geometrical style, based on the four points of the compass. Avenues lined with poplars, elms, and cottonwoods were the city's most distinctive feature. Courtesy, Richard C. Roberts

Lorin Farr came to Ogden in 1850 at the direction of Brigham Young. For two decades Farr was the town's leading citizen, serving as the first mayor and the first president of the Weber Stake of the Mormon Church. USHS

these communities succeeded, some failed, as Weber County developed. Ogden City prevailed as the political and social center.

Ogden City was laid out in a grid pattern under the direction of Henry Sherwood, William Lemon, William Dame, and Jesse Fox. City blocks were surveyed along with farmland. The city streets, from west to east, were: Franklin, Young, Main, Spring, Smith, Pearl, Green, and East. From north to south they were numbered one to nine. Main Street (today's Washington Boulevard) became the major thoroughfare of the town, which a visitor in this early period described as a "vast assemblage of log buildings, picketed, stockaded, and surrounded with out-buildings and cattle yards." By 1850 the population of Ogden and surrounding settlements was 1,141.

Much of the direction concerning the operation of the town continued to come from Brigham Young until, under an increasing workload as head of the church and government in Salt Lake City, he was at last obliged to delegate authority to administer the second-most important Mormon community. In January of 1850 he sent Lorin Farr to Ogden to become the community's political and ecclesiastical leader. A twenty-seven-year-old native of Vermont, Farr settled at Farr's Fort, located about one and one-half miles west of the mouth of Ogden Canyon on the north side of the Ogden River. Later he moved into a new home at First and Main streets (21st Street and Washington Boulevard).

One year after Farr's arrival the Weber Stake of the Church of Jesus Christ of Latter-day Saints was organized with Farr as president, a position he served in for nineteen years. Also in 1851 the first Ogden City officials were appointed by Young in his capacity as territorial governor. Farr was appointed mayor, an office he would hold for eleven consecutive two-year terms. Other city officers included four aldermen, nine councilors, a marshal, and a city recorder. All were appointed by Young and confirmed by a vote of the male population over twenty-one years of age. City elections for the next two decades would follow the same general pattern: a list of nominees was proposed, usually members of the Weber Stake hierarchy; voting was conducted by voice vote or uplifted hand; most voting was unanimous. Although ballot boxes were called for in the ordinances of Ogden City, written ballots were seldom cast, and the nominees were often elected by acclamation. Unanimous elections would later be cited as evidence of Mormon domination, leading to the struggle between church and federal authority that shaped Utah history until the turn of the century.

Over the next two decades this new municipality had plenty to contend with besides turning a frontier settlement into an orderly community. Even before Farr came into the Ogden scene, settlers and Indians had looked at each other with suspicion. The marginal land would not support all groups for long. Conflict erupted in September 1850, when a band of Shoshone Indians camped near the home of Urban Stewart on Four Mile Creek, near present-day Harrisville. Stewart ordered the Indians out of his cornfield. When the response to his request proved slow in coming, he shot Chief Terikee. The Shoshones burned Stewart's buildings and later threatened to burn Ogden unless Stewart was released to them. A group of Mormon militiamen from Salt Lake City came to aid Ogden, and Stewart fled for California.

Throughout the 1850s Indian troubles recurred sporadically. In 1854 James Brown recorded in his diary the difficulties involving Shoshones led by Chief Little Soldier. Events culminated at Mound Fort and Ogden City, where the Indians' guns were taken from them. One of the brothers of the chief said, "Here are my wife, my children, my horses and everything I have. Take it all and keep it, only give me back my gun and let me go free." Though the Indians felt helpless without their guns, Brown noted, it was better for them to live among the Ogdenites during the harsh winter. Posing little threat to the settlers, they could husk corn, chop wood, and do chores in return for board and room. Through the winter Brown gave lessons and preached to the Indians. And he taught the Shoshone dialect to groups of settlers in Weber County.

The incident of 1850 between Urban Stewart and the Shoshone stimulated the building of fortress walls in and around Ogden. The west side of Mound Fort (located on the west side of present-day Washington Boulevard between 9th and 12th streets) was cut back to create a steep and formidable face; a mud wall about nine feet high protected the other three sides. Bingham's Fort (a block and a half west of Washington Boulevard on 2nd Street) was surrounded by a twelve-foot-high mud wall reinforced with willows. Ogden City made

INDIANS OF WEBER COUNTY

A Shoshone chief for sixty years, Washakie was noted for his friendliness to the settlers. In 1866 Chief Washakie and 1,000 members of his tribe visited Huntsville in Ogden Valley, performing ceremonial dances in the town square. USHS

Indian presence in Weber County began as early as the fifth century B.C., when the Desert Archaic culture inhabited the area. By the seventh century A.D. the Fremont culture had moved into northern Utah. C. Melvin Aikens, an Ogden native and anthropologist at the University of Utah, studied structures and burial sites of the Fremont culture at Injun Creek, near Plain City, and concluded that the Fremont Indians stayed in the area until approximately 1400 A.D., when they were forced out by the northern Shoshones.

The Shoshones were the main tribe found in Weber County at the time of Mormon settlement, but other tribes, identified as Snakes, Utes, Crows, Blackfeet, Nez Perces, Flatheads, Arapahos, Commanches, Cheyennes, and Bannock Indians, had wandered through or made contact in the area at various times.

Although local Indians were usually friendly, early settlers recounted their visits with some anxiety because the Indians made demands, which were direct and often seemed threatening. In a report to the territorial legislature in 1854, Brigham Young stated that Weber County citizens had adopted a policy toward the small band of Indians "usually inhabiting" the area; this policy consisted of "distributing them out among the citizens, making for the Indians judicious selections, where they and their families may feel that they have a home and know that they can depend upon having food, shelter, and kind treatment in exchange for their labor."

There is no evidence that this policy was ever successfully carried out, and the relationship with the Indians remained uneasy. This uneasiness led to the building of nine forts in Weber County as protection against violent uprisings. Several incidents heightened fear among the settlers, particularly an 1850 confrontation that resulted in the killing of Chief Terikee and subsequent threats of wholesale reprisal against Ogden.

William Hall, a Huntsville settler, recounted an illuminating incident that took place on August 16, 1866. A group of 1,000 Shoshones, led by Washakie and other chiefs, camped in Ogden Valley, causing alarm in the community. Hoping to placate the Indians, Francis A. Hammond, Mormon leader of the Huntsville settlement, invited the chiefs and their followers to Sunday church services. Hammond then called for church members to bring donations to be presented as gifts to the Indians.

At the break of day the Indians assembled in the town square and formed a large circle. They danced for a considerable time, "always circling to the left." The Indians staged a mock-battle portraying a fight they had had with the Arapahos. President Hammond, in the shade of a bower freshly completed for the occasion, presented the Indians with gifts of four dressed beef, nine sheep, several sacks of flour, and more than fifty bushels of potatoes, carrots, beets, turnips, and other produce. The Indians accepted the gifts and departed for their winter camping grounds. Huntsville uttered a sigh of relief.

Tensions existed not only between Indians and settlers but between tribes as well. In 1861, Cheyennes pursued a band of Shoshones into the bottomlands of the Ogden River near Huntsville. Fifty Shoshone braves held off the Cheyennes, who approached "in single file and with faces and bodies gaudily painted and wearing war bonnets," according to Mary Jessop, a young eyewitness. The Cheyennes charged and appeared to be winning until their chief was killed. The Cheyennes retrieved his body and withdrew from the battlefield.

Most Indian matters were not as traumatic as these encounters. Typically, a small number of Indians would visit an isolated farm or home and make requests for food or other goods. Usually their demands were met. Overall, the trend was to avoid trouble, and in the long run relations with Indians became less threatening. Eventually, the increasing population of settlers put Indians in the minority, and government policy restricted them to reservation lands.

plans for a wall to be constructed of earth and stone—eight feet high with a width of six feet at the bottom and thirty inches at the top. Though construction along Wall Avenue was completed, the north and south walls remained unfinished. The completed portion is estimated to have cost the citizens of Ogden $40,000. To finance this and other municipal projects taxes were collected from property owners at the rate of ten dollars for each city lot; in addition, each able-bodied man over eighteen years of age was charged a ten-dollar tax. In lieu of cash, most men donated their labor in building walls, canals, ditches, and roads.

Canals were necessary for the survival of the community, and several small projects were begun in the area in 1851. Streams were dammed and ditches built to carry water for irrigation and household use and to supply power. The first large-scale project was begun in 1852; when completed the Weber Canal ran seven miles from Riverdale to lower Ogden. A number of settlers took advantage of the water power in the fourteen-foot-wide, five-foot-deep canal, among them Daniel Burch, who built a gristmill near its source. At 28th Street, Peter Boyle drew on the Weber Canal to turn a lathe for making furniture and to grind up sugar cane for sorghum molasses. At Wall Avenue and 24th Street, James Brown harnessed the power of this stream to turn a molasses mill. Tragically, an accident in this mill—his sleeve caught in the cogs of the rollers—cost Brown his life in September 1863.

The Ogden Bench Canal, begun in 1855 under the direction of Isaac Goodale, ran south and west from the mouth of Ogden Canyon to the developing community. Also notable, the canal known as Mill Creek was built in 1850 and 1851. In the same years Lorin Farr constructed a sawmill and a gristmill (about 225 yards northeast of Farr's Fort) powered by the water diverted from the Ogden River.

Water for drinking and cooking was taken from the rivers, ditches, and canals during the pioneer period. Usually, the water had to sit for some time to allow the sediment to settle. Although some wells were dug during this era, it was not until 1880 that the Ogden City Council began construction of a reservoir at the head of 24th Street to provide inhabitants with "good, pure water." The reservoir collected from the Ogden River as well as from Waterfall and Strong canyons. The original water lines were built of hollowed-out logs.

Ogden's link to Ogden Valley was a toll road, built in the 1860s. In this photograph the toll road is dwarfed by the rugged thrust of the Wasatch. Courtesy, Mr. and Mrs. Lowell Rowse

By the mid-1850s, Ogden's face had changed substantially under the influence of Lorin Farr. In December of 1854 Wilford Woodruff, traveling from Salt Lake City to observe and preach to the northern settlements, spent a week in the Ogden area:

This is the county seat of Weber County and is a flourishing

place containing some 150 families. . . . They have two schools
with about 120 scholars, one adobe school house 30 X 20.
There are many good dwellings in this city; also two stores,
one of which has been recently built by Captain James
Brown. They have raised during this past season about 10,000
bushels of wheat.

Woodruff visited Bingham's Fort, where he found 100 families (732 people), and North Ogden, which he called Ogden's
Hole, with 47 families. He noted that the farmland was good
and abundant. Hay and wheat seemed to be the major crops,
although sugar cane, potatoes, onions, cabbages, carrots,
beans, beets, and corn were also cultivated. Tithing and
other church donations were paid in wheat, hay, and cattle.
Woodruff noted further that the Shoshone Indians scattered
among the settlers did not like their situation.

In 1855 British traveler William Chandless stayed at the
home of James Brown. Chandless described Ogden City in
winter:

Ogden City was a specimen of the settlements of Utah on the
model of Salt Lake; part on the bench, part in the valley-
bottom, enclosed by an earthen wall, and laid out in "blocks";
a large portion was still unoccupied, but dobie-houses were
fast springing up. In the middle of the place was a school-
house, also used as a church, and its door plastered over with
parochial notices; near it were two small stores—few settle-
ments have as many and what people want they must get di-
rect from "the City" as best they can. The roads except on
the "bench," were a miserable alternation of mud and water,
and if not frozen over hardly passable for a foot traveller.
Several small mountain burns [creeks] ran through the place,
and to the north lay a small, deep, sluggish river, closed in by
Kinnik-Kinnik, and crossed by a substantial wooden bridge;
to this a list of tolls were affixed, but as far as I can see they
are never exacted. Cattle on all sides straggle about picking
up what they can find, and at night return, or are driven
within the walls; the cultivated land is necessarily more or
less distant, but danger gathers the inhabitants and their
stock to a single place.

By the time of Chandless' visit, James Brown had thirteen

THE MORRISITE CHALLENGE

For three days in mid-June 1862, scores of Utahns perched on steep Weber River bluffs a few miles southeast of Ogden to participate in a bizarre confrontation. At Kingston Fort the Morrisite sect made its stand, defying both the LDS Church and territorial authority.

As a youthful coal miner in Burswardly, England, Joseph Morris had been badly burned in an accident, and after recovering he was baptized into the LDS Church. In 1853, when he was twenty-eight, he emigrated to Utah.

He settled first in Sanpete County in central Utah, where he began promulgating what he called "advanced doctrines." His theories were so contrary to approved Mormon teaching that his wife left him. He wandered to Salt Lake City, Provo, and then Slaterville but in each community was soon asked to leave. In October 1860, he made his final move—to Kingston Fort at South Weber, located in the river bottomlands just west of the mouth of Weber Canyon. The fort had been named for James Kingston, a Mormon bishop who directed its construction seven years earlier. Its low adobe walls enclosed a ten-acre square.

Morris strengthened the fort to accommodate his small band of followers until his colony comprised about 140 men and their wives and children—a total that never exceeded about 500 baptized persons. He issued a steady stream of proclamations, some of which described LDS President Brigham Young as a "blasphemer" and "deceiver." He also asserted that polygamy was not acceptable to God, that women should be allowed to hold the Mormon priesthood, and that all property should be shared by the community.

As a result the Morrisites were socially and economically ostracized by their orthodox Mormon neighbors. In February 1861 Kingston Fort was visited by Mormon Apostles John Taylor and Wilford Woodruff, who formally excommunicated several of Morris' followers. Times became ever more difficult for the Morrisites, as a severe winter cut into their food supply. They could not find a miller who would grind flour for the apostate community.

Early in 1862 Morris predicted that the Second Coming of Christ was imminent—so close that there was no point in planting crops that year. He set aside May 30 as "Foreshadowing Day" to prepare for the Savior's arrival and the end of the world. Some of the Morrisites were so alarmed that they attempted to leave the community, taking their property with them. When Morris refused to let them go, several of the dissidents obtained court orders permitting them to depart Kingston Fort with their possessions.

Morris ignored the court orders. Warrants for the arrest of Morris and four of his lieutenants were issued, but Morris warned he would fight rather than surrender to federal marshals. Tension built until the court sent two deputy territorial marshals, Robert T. Burton and Theodore McKean, to gather a posse and assume control of the fort.

The deputy marshals, taking no chances, formed a small army of around 500 men. The force included a 200-man infantry company from the territorial militia, an artillery battery, and a number of mounted and well armed volunteers.

On June 13, as Burton's forces occupied the bluffs to the South of the fort, Burton sent a message to the community giving Morris thirty minutes to surrender himself and his key aides. When the Morrisite chieftain rebuffed the deputy marshal, Burton shouted a warning for women and children to leave the fort because "forcible measures" were about to be taken. The gates to Kingston Fort remained closed. Morris secluded himself in his private quarters to pray.

After meditation, Morris told his followers that they were safe and that their enemies would be destroyed. An account in Dale L. Morgan's *History of Ogden* (1940) relates that "his words were given a terrible punctuation; no sooner had he finished speaking than a cannon ball entered the fort, struck down two women, injuring a third." Two hours had passed since Burton's ultimatum.

"A three-day battle ensued," Morgan continues. "The militia accomplished nothing whatever, despite their numerical superiority. . . . On the 15th, however, the Morrisites were put into a panic by the approach of a rolling battery which they imagined to be an 'infernal machine.' They stacked their arms and surrendered, and a body of the militia entered the fort." Burton called for Morris, John Banks, Richard Cook, John Parson, and Peter Klemgaard to present themselves for arrest.

Accounts differ as to what happened next, but a Morris disciple, quoted in Morgan, said Burton was "so enraged" at the lack of immediate compliance that he attempted to run Morris down with his horse. Morris reportedly grabbed the bridle and reins and sent the horse back upon his haunches, and then went to the western part of the fort, opposite the schoolhouse. Burton followed and again demanded complete surrender "in the name of Lord Jesus Christ and by the authority of the United States."

"Brother Joseph stood firmly, and looking up at Burton replied 'Never! No, never! No, never!' Then Burton fired five shots at him. At the fifth shot Joseph reeled and was caught in the arms of John Eames, who laid him down gently on the ground. Such was the earthly end of Joseph Morris. . . ."

More than 5,000 rounds and 100 cannonballs had been fired into the fort. Besides Morris, casualties among the defenders included four women and a man. Two militiamen died in the siege.

Surviving Morrisite leaders were tried on various charges. Seven were convicted of second-degree murder; another sixty-six were found guilty on lesser counts. Despite protests from Mormon authorities, Governor Stephen S. Harding released all on probation and remitted their fines.

The Morrisites scattered throughout the West. The largest segment moved to Soda Springs, Idaho, and later to Deer Lodge, Montana, where they continued as a group until the 1950s. Locally, a headstone in a small South Weber cemetery is all that remains from this conflict. The headstone identifies the occupant of the grave only as "a Morrisite."

—Murray M. Moler

wives, and Mormon polygamy had become the most prominent issue in a growing antagonism between the U.S. government and the Church of Jesus Christ of Latter-day Saints. From the federal government's perspective, the political and economic control exercised by the church—as seen in the unanimity of voting and in the closed system of Mormon trade—posed a threat to U.S. sovereignty in the territory. In 1857 President James Buchanan, alarmed by rumors of treacherous behavior, attempted to wrest control of the territory from the Mormons. Buchanan replaced Brigham Young as territorial governor with Alfred Cumming and sent federal troops to enforce the appointment. The result was the Utah War.

Under the direction of Brigham Young the Mormons prepared to fight. The Mormon militia, called the Nauvoo Legion, drilled and prepared to stop the federal army, under Colonel Albert Sidney Johnston, from entering the territory either from the east through Echo Canyon or from the north via the Bear River. Ogden troops participated in both areas.

In the spring of 1858, Young ordered Mormons throughout northern Utah to leave their homes and move southward to Utah County. Ogdenites took as many of their goods as they could carry and camped near Provo, Springville, and Payson. Their homes were left filled with straw, ready to be set afire as the army approached. Though tensions were high, some of the men returned to tend their crops.

A peace settlement was reached by the end of June. As part of the agreement Brigham Young stepped down as territorial governor and the troops under Johnston's command were to be stationed south and west of Salt Lake City at the new Camp Floyd.

With the return of peace Ogdenites moved back to their homes. The 1858 harvest was very successful in Weber County, and with the encouragement of Brigham Young new emigrants continued to arrive in Ogden. The years following brought quiet growth and prosperity, far removed from the ravages of the Civil War. However, the relative isolation of the pioneer era was soon to end as the transcontinental railroad stretched to connect the Union with the western territories, and Ogden was directly in its path.

CHAPTER TWO

JUNCTION CITY OF THE TRANSCONTINENTAL RAILROAD

The building of a transcontinental railroad had been long talked of as the United States expanded its boundaries and the need to connect the East and West became a national interest. As early as 1844 promoter Asa Whitney had petitioned Congress to support a transcontinental railroad. These efforts came to fruition with the signing of the Pacific Railroad Act in July 1862 by Abraham Lincoln. The project languished through the Civil War but was resumed afterward with greater public and congressional interest.

The Union Pacific Railroad received subsidies for laying the track from Omaha westward, and the Central Pacific had a similar contract to build from Sacramento eastward. The Union Pacific built the rail line through Ogden and joined with the Central Pacific fifty-seven miles to the northwest at Promontory, Utah, on May 10, 1869. This meeting of the rails was celebrated by the entire nation. A telegraph message to the east and west coasts announced the completion of the first transcontinental railroad and the driving of the Golden Spike.

The approach of the railroad construction toward Ogden was followed in the newspaper by local residents. On March 2, 1869, a Tuesday, *The Deseret News* reported that "the rails were down over the bridge at Devil's Gate on Sunday evening, and they were scattered along the line to the mouth of the canyon. There is little doubt but today the locomotive will enter this valley, and at the close of this week it cannot be far from Ogden."

By the following Monday, March 8, 1869, anticipation had the entire town in its grip, as described by Joseph Hall, correspondent of the *Salt Lake Telegraph:* "At 11:20 a.m. on that day, the Union Pacific track layers hove in sight of Ogden and from that time continued their march with great rapid-

On May 10, 1869, the East and West were joined at Promontory, Utah. This photograph was taken just after the ceremonies had concluded and the crews could take a break from the earlier tumult. Courtesy, Union Pacific Railroad Museum

Above
By March 1869 the Union Pacific Railroad had broached Weber Canyon, the most formidable obstacle along the right-of-way. The railroad overcame the canyon's barriers with bridges and tunnels. UHS

Left
The construction of railroad track through Weber Canyon was accomplished mostly by laborers recruited from the Ogden area. Mormon leaders Lorin Farr and Chauncey West contracted to build the line through the canyon. USHS

Left
The "1,000-Mile Tree" in Weber Canyon marked the construction of 1,000 miles of railroad track from Omaha, Nebraska, toward the eventual transcontinental link-up with the Central Pacific Railroad at Promontory Summit. USHS

Below
The first locomotive arrived in Ogden on March 8, 1869. The entire population turned out to greet the long-awaited Black Hawk, whose appearance heralded the day when Ogden would become the Junction City. USHS

Grenville M. Dodge, a major-general of Union volunteers during the Civil War, displayed brilliance in quickly rebuilding bridges and railroads destroyed by the Confederate armies. He put his wartime experience to work as superintendent of operations for the Union Pacific, rapidly completing the transcontinental railroad from Omaha to Promontory Summit. USHS

ity." Mormon crews toiled on this stretch under Union Pacific contracts with Mormon leaders Lorin Farr and Chauncey West. Hall saw large crowds of citizens from Ogden and surrounding areas gather to watch the progress of the line toward the city from Weber Canyon. The onlookers stood on the high bluffs and "feasted their eyes and ears with the sight and sound of the long expected and anxiously looked for fiery steed."

At approximately 2:30 in the afternoon the Union Pacific locomotive Black Hawk steamed into Ogden City. Amid the waving of flags, a military brass band under the direction of Captain William Pugh "enlivened the occasion with music; and a salute was fired by the artillery of Captain T.S. Wadsworth." A stand had been erected near the track at the bottom of 4th Street (24th Street today), and a procession including the mayor, city councilmen, teachers, schoolchildren, and citizens marched with banners bearing salutations such as "Hail to the Highway of Nations: Utah Bids You Welcome." At some point during the procession the locomotive sounded its whistle and frightened the young children, sending them running in disarray into the slough near the tracks and soiling their best clothes.

Mayor Lorin Farr presided over the ceremonies of the day. Franklin D. Richards, Mormon Church Apostle and community leader, delivered an eloquent and stirring address welcoming the representatives of the railroad and offering them congratulations: "An enterprise of such magnitude calls forth our admiration and gratitude. It is impossible for any people to hail this auspicious event with greater joy than we do." Richards went on to point out that the railroad would permit "the world's great men—of wisdom, science and intellect to visit . . . our mountain homes and to form a true estimate of our character and position."

The railroad would indeed bring travelers to Ogden, in greater numbers than anyone could have anticipated on this day of festivity. The coming of the railroad to Ogden had in fact already challenged Mormon dominance in the affairs of Utah.

Brigham Young was upset with the Union Pacific for having turned the railroad north through Ogden rather than south through Salt Lake City. As late as November 1868 the proposed route for the transcontinental line was to run south of the Great Salt Lake and through the territorial capital. However, after making a survey of the region in 1867, Grenville M. Dodge, the chief engineer of the Union Pacific, had concluded that "a careful examination convinced me that our true line west is north of Salt Lake. ... " Brigham Young appealed this decision to the company directors and even threatened a Mormon boycott, but reason and Dodge and thus Ogden won out. Lorin Farr attended the Golden Spike ceremonies in place of Brigham Young. While the Golden Spike was being driven, Brigham Young was in Salt Lake City planning the construction of a rail line, the Utah Central, from Ogden to Salt Lake City.

On completion of the transcontinental line, a question vital to the economic and political development of the region had yet to be answered: Which town would finally be designated as the junction for the transfer of freight and passengers between the Union Pacific and the Central Pacific? The original Pacific Railroad Act, as signed by Lincoln, specified that the Union Pacific would build to the California-Nevada line, but this provision was changed in 1866 to allow the two companies to build until they met. This meeting point, however, was not agreed upon until the Union Pacific had surveyed some 225 miles of track across the Nevada flats, parallel to the work Central Pacific crews were doing for a road up Weber Canyon. Rejecting this parallel track-building, the government forced the companies to agree on the summit of the mountain range at Promontory. This agreement, made on April 10, 1869, added "that the common terminus of the Union Pacific and the Central Pacific Railroad shall be at or near Ogden." The two railroad companies used Promontory as the transfer point until December 1869, when the exchange was moved to Ogden.

There was one other important matter to be settled before Ogden would become known as the Junction City: that was the issue of where the north-south line would traverse the east-west transcontinental line. Other settlements along the transcontinental line vied with Ogden for that distinction, primarily Evanston, Uintah, Taylor's Switch, Harrisville, Bonneville, Corinne, and Promontory. Of all of these, Corinne gave Ogden its greatest competition.

As a north-south junction, Corinne had the advantage of terrain, being on a "natural highway" to the north into Idaho

THIS TRAIN

STOPS

20 Minutes for Supper at the

Golden Hotel

PROMONTORY, UTAH.

FIRST-CLASS MEALS, 50 CENTS.

THE GOLDEN SPIKE

Completing the first Trans-continental Railroad was driven at this point May 10, 1869. Don't fail to treat yourself to a first class meal at this celebrated point.

T. G. BROWN, Prop.

Above
In its brief heyday Promontory Summit featured saloons, pool halls, and the Golden Spike Hotel, for the relaxation of weary railroad crews and passengers. Courtesy, James A. Dolph

Opposite page, top
South of Ogden at the mouth of Weber Canyon lies Unitah, which boomed briefly as a transshipment point to Salt Lake City until the Utah Central Railroad bypassed it in 1870. Courtesy, Ogden Chamber of Commerce

Opposite
Promontory Summit flourished until the railroad terminus was moved to Ogden. Once the center of national attention, Promontory soon became just a way station where helper engines were hooked on to drive trains up the steep slopes of the Promontory Mountains. Photograph by A.C. Hull. Courtesy, Union Pacific Railroad Museum

and Montana. Historians Brigham D. and Betty M. Madsen, in their article "Corinne, the Fair: Gateway to Montana Mines," said that Corinne was able to establish itself as a center for wagon traffic because it "offered a dry firm road straight up Malad Valley. . . . Ogden, two days of heavy travel away, did not have a chance with the teamster who measured his profits on the road." Prospects looked bright for Corinne as the community continued to grow. On February 18, 1870, the legislature of the Territory of Utah approved a charter for the City of Corinne. Bernice Gibbs Anderson, in her article "The Gentile City of Corinne," wrote that by 1872 the town had a variety of businesses, including "wholesale and retail liquor dealers, cigar and tobacco dealers, billiard tables, banking houses, job wagons, ice cream and soda fountains, breweries, livery stables, auctioneers, and Chinese work houses."

But Corinne was a Gentile town in Mormon territory. The threat it posed to Mormon politics and Mormon morality was a decisive factor in the competition to become the Junction City. For Corinne, as Brigham and Betty Madsen concluded on this subject, "The only obstacle on the road to success

When it was decided that the transcontinental railroad would run north of the Great Salt Lake, Brigham Young began making plans for the Utah Central Railroad, which would assure Salt Lake City's access to the transcontinental line. Courtesy, Ogden Chamber of Commerce

Left
The Utah Central Railroad, the first line west of the Mississippi River to be built without government subsidies, began service January 10, 1870, connecting Salt Lake City to the transcontinental junction in Ogden. From the Browning Collection. Courtesy, Union Station

Below
Corinne vied with Ogden for the title "Junction City." Corinne had already achieved fame as the first Gentile city in the Mormon territory of Utah. Courtesy, Union Pacific Railroad Museum

OGDEN'S UNION STATION

The venerable Ogden Union Station deserves its place on the National Register of Historic Sites for past service during the halcyon days of railroad travel and its new role as a multi-purpose community center and museum. Ogden has in fact had three different stations since Union Pacific track crews entered the city on March 8, 1869, on their way toward Promontory Summit and the historic meeting with the Central Pacific to complete the nation's first transcontinental railroad.

The first station was built along the right-of-way at the foot of 4th Street (now 24th), just west of Wall Avenue. It was a typical early depot: two stories high, of wooden frame construction, and painted a gaudy red. A boardwalk kept pedestrians out of the mud as they walked to nearby hotels, cafes, saloons, bakeries, curio shops, and other establishments catering to travelers.

As railroad traffic through Ogden increased, so did demands for a better depot. Ogdenites complained that the deteriorating old station gave visitors an erroneous

impression of their city.

LDS Church President Brigham Young had sparked the drive by donating 131 acres of privately owned land to the railroad companies. Subsequently the Ogden Union Railroad and Depot Company, jointly owned by the Union Pacific (U.P.) and the Southern Pacific (S.P.), was organized to operate the station and yards. Henry Van Brunt, a friend of U.P. president Charles Adams, was selected as architect.

The cornerstone of the second station was laid November 5, 1888, at Wall Avenue and 5th Street (now 25th). Mayor David Eccles proclaimed a holiday. Bars closed for the afternoon. A crowd of more than 5,000 braved a light snowstorm to hear attorney Parley L. Williams deliver the keynote address. He declared, "this structure, now begun, will in years to come offer its hospitable roof to travelers from all lands and will be a medium through which strangers within your gates will receive their impression of your people, your city and your country."

The Ogden *Standard* described

the new station as "a symbol of the dawn of the bright days of prosperity which from this time is assured to Ogden, the most promising city in the West."

The structure had two-story north and south wings and a three-story center section that included more than thirty hotel rooms. A large electric clock, donated by Ogden jeweler J.S. Lewis, was installed in the tower below an elaborate weathervane. The waiting room, ticket windows, and a cafe were on the main floor, with railroad offices filling the second level.

The second station, which went into operation early in 1889, served admirably for thirty-four years, until it was destroyed by fire on the evening of February 13, 1923. The blaze originated in the hotel room of a Pullman porter who, af-

The Union Depot tower was adorned by a large electric clock donated by Ogden jeweler J.S. Lewis. Ogden set its time by this clock for thirty-four years. From the Church Archives. Courtesy, The Church of Jesus Christ of Latter-day Saints

The Union Depot Hotel, built in 1869, offered hospitality to cross-country travelers, who could also choose to stay at the Ogden House, the White House (later Junction House), or the Keeney House. Courtesy, Weber State College

ter pressing his uniform, failed to unplug the electric iron on his way out. It took several hours to control the fire. There were no casualties that night because telephone operator Fannie McCarty remained at her switchboard until all occupants had been alerted and evacuated.

Only a few offices and the ticket counter were still fit for use. The clock tower stood amidst the blackened stone and brick walls but was toppled two weeks later by a severe wind. Falling bricks killed clerk Frank Yentzer.

Los Angeles architects John and Donald Parkinson were commissioned to design a new station, using the old foundation. It opened May 22, 1924, with bands playing and orators praising crews for the rapid reconstruction.

The two-story structure was 374 feet long and averaged 88 feet wide. Its roof was of Spanish tile, the walls of Ogden-made buff-pink brick. Reflecting an Italian Renaissance style, its four Wall Avenue doorways were trimmed with carved Boise sandstone and wrought-iron embellishments. A main floor restaurant had 51 counter seats and tables for 100 patrons. There was a large baggage room, barber shop, men's smoking room, women's rest area, and an emergency medical facility.

The main lobby was 60 by 112 feet and 56 feet from floor to ridgepole. High crossbeams were made from massive fir timbers. The ticket counter was on the east side; Western Union telegraph and stationmaster offices were at the south end; and the Union Newsstand was situated along the west wall. Big doors opened onto the waiting platform and a subway connecting eight shedded tracks.

Railroad offices occupied the second floor; a closed passageway above the ticket counters connected Union Pacific and Southern Pacific operations. A U.S. Mail terminal was housed in a brick building north of the main depot. Railway Express and the U.P. commissary and laundry were in buildings to the south.

This basic configuration was retained through the hectic days of World War II, when thousands of GIs stopped in Ogden to enjoy the hospitality provided by the local U.S.O. However, by the time of the 1969 celebration of the Golden Spike centennial it had become apparent that the future of Union Station was threatened. The express office and commissary had been demolished; the dining room, newsstand, laundry, and mail terminal were closed. The railroads discussed plans for a smaller, makeshift structure in the Riverdale Yards to handle the few remaining passenger trains.

The Ogden *Standard-Examiner* began an editorial campaign to save the station and convert it into a convention center and museum. Civic and governmental leaders enthusiastically rallied to the cause. After months of negotiation, the Ogden Union Railroad and Depot Company agreed to give the depot to the city, although retaining ownership of the land.

The Union Station Development Corporation was formed as a unit of the municipal government to carry out redevelopment. Architects Ronald D. Hales and Steven T. Baird drew imaginative, practical plans. Mrs. Teddy Griffith became executive director. Campaigns for private and public funding were eminently successful.

Viability of the project was assured when Val A. Browning, chairman of the Browning Company, donated to the station his priceless collection of inventor and production models of sporting and military firearms. Most were invented by his father, John M. Browning, working closely with brother Matthew. Families of both John and Matthew Browning made many other valuable contributions to the station, including the theater and vintage car collection housed in the former mail terminal. Also popular are the model railroad exhibit and meeting rooms provided by the Dumke and Wattis families.

Ceremonies on October 21, 1978, rededicated Ogden Union Station to its new role as depot, museum, community center, and symbol of Ogden's contributions to the growth and prosperity of the state and nation as the West's Junction City.

—Murray M. Moler

The rail link to Idaho and Montana, the Utah Northern Railroad, bypassed Corinne and helped establish Ogden as Junction City in a network of east-west and north-south trade routes. Courtesy, Ogden Chamber of Commerce

was expressed by the editor of the local paper: 'We have the banded influence of Mormonism against us on three sides.'"

Brigham Young took action in Ogden's favor, building the Utah Central Railroad, which connected Ogden to Salt Lake City. Conspicuously absent during the Golden Spike ceremony a few days before, Young attended the Utah Central ground-breaking ceremony near the Weber River on May 17, 1869. The Utah Central Railroad began service the following January 10, and the Union Pacific over the years allowed its passengers to make sideline trips from Ogden to Salt Lake City without any additional increase in their fares. The Utah Central constructed a depot conveniently north and east of the Union Depot, making easy railroad-car exchanges by use of the Y of the tracks.

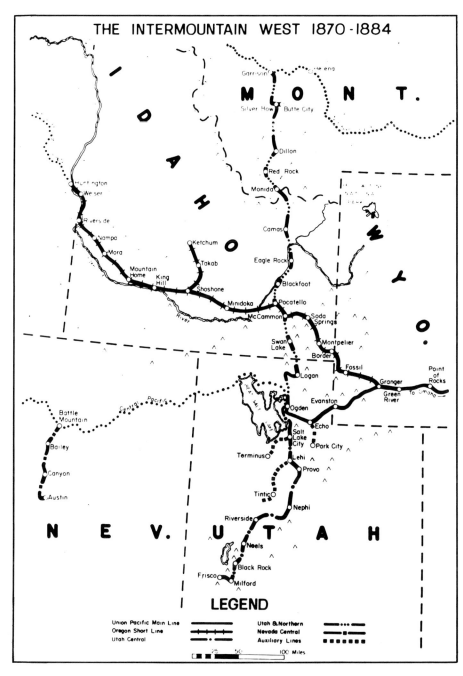

THE INTERMOUNTAIN WEST 1870-1884

LEGEND

Union Pacific Main Line		Utah & Northern	
Oregon Short Line		Nevada Central	
Utah Central		Auxiliary Lines	

25 50 100 Miles

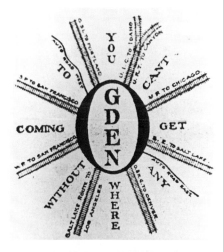

Above
During Ogden's early turbulent development, Aaron Ross, a longtime resident, worked as an express messenger for the Wells Fargo Company and as a driver for Alex Toponce, who hauled freight between Montana and Ogden. From the Browning Collection. Courtesy, Union Station

Above
In the last thirty years of the nineteenth century, Ogden became the hub for rail-roading in the Intermountain West. With its large switching yards and impressive depot, Ogden came into its own as the Junction City. Courtesy, Union Pacific Railroad Museum

Top right
An Ogden Chamber of Commerce logo promoted the theme of Ogden's importance as the center for Western rail traffic. Courtesy, Richard C. Roberts

Another line gave Ogden another edge. The Utah Northern Railroad established a northward route to Brigham City and Logan, bypassing Corinne. Organized on August 23, 1871, this railroad completed its track to Logan by 1878. By 1884 it connected with the Northern Pacific at Garrison, Montana, putting Ogden into a network of east-west and north-south trade lines.

To ensure the victory of Ogden over Corinne, Brigham Young offered land to the Union Pacific and Central Pacific railroads for a depot and shops. As early as January 1869, he met with property owners in the western part of Ogden. Church records say that "all consented to let him have their land at $50 per acre, provided the property was for a railroad town. . . . Brigham Young showed Dr. Durrant (of the Union Pacific) a fine place for railroad work shops, a short distance above the site of Elder Taylor's mill, a few miles south of Ogden."

The Weber County property records books indicate that on October 6, 1874, Young deeded 131 acres to the Union Pacific and Central Pacific Railroad companies on the condition that

this grant of the land herein described is made on the express consideration on condition that the said Union Pacific and Central Railroad Companies, will make the city of Ogden and the land herein granted the permanent Junction of the two roads.

The Ogden City Council followed with a resolution that appropriated "Five Thousand ($5000.00) Dollars for the purpose of securing the location of the Junction of the U.P., C.P., U.C., and U.N. Railroads in Ogden City."

By 1878 the battle between Ogden and Corinne was over. Ogden City was the junction. The *Salt Lake Independent* reported that "Corinne is one of the things of the past. It will in another year be simply a way station on the Central Pacific Railroad." In fact, many Corinne citizens moved to Ogden, where they opened businesses and became community leaders. With the completion of the Lucin Cutoff in 1904, Corinne was no longer on the transcontinental line.

The Junction City—Ogden has used this title in directories, gazetteers, tourist guides, and chamber of commerce brochures. As Junction City, Ogden thrived as the volume of

IRON AND SILVER: THE BRIEF HISTORY OF OGDEN MINING

On two occasions—in 1873 and in 1891—Ogden had hopes of becoming a major mining center. Both booms were short, however. The long-term growth and prosperity of the city, its destiny, lay with the railroad that carried the ore dug up elsewhere.

Israel Elliott Brown opened a small iron mine on the west flank of Willard Peak, about ten miles north of Ogden, in 1873. His Ogden Iron Manufacturing Company built a blast furnace on a thirty-acre tract at 21st Street and Wall Avenue, between the Central Pacific and Utah Northern railroads. When the initial batch of iron was tapped, Brown was optimistic. Watching the molten metal pour into a sand mold, he predicted that Ogden would become a leader in the manufacture of stoves and other wrought-iron products. But after only a small quantity of ore had been smelted, the furnace blew up, wrecking the $120,000 ironworks. Attempts to revive the enterprise failed, and the company was dissolved.

The silver boom that began in 1891 lasted somewhat longer—a little more than two years. A prospector whose name is not recorded in history made a strike on Ant Flats, a bowl-like depression and meadow at an altitude of around 8,000 feet. The vein he found was so rich he called his mining camp "La Plata," Spanish for "silver."

Within a few months, hundreds of prospectors and camp followers had flocked to La Plata, about twenty-five miles northeast of Ogden, on the north side of the Weber-Cache county line. Some reports place the peak population at 1,500, others as high as 5,000. A couple of primitive hotels were built, along with a few stores, a small bank, and a newspaper.

Roads were improved to Ogden and to Logan, as these cities competed for the anticipated commercial benefit from the newest Utah bonanza. While the ore was rich in silver, the "pay dirt" proved to be unfortunately shallow, and by late 1893 the excitement was over.

William Hope "Coin" Harvey became prominent during Ogden's silver experience. He arrived in the Junction City from West Virginia in 1888 to practice law and deal in real estate. By the time he had begun to build an ostentatious mansion on the east slope of Little Mountain, it had become apparent that Harvey had a flair for promotion. He organized a boosters group called the Order of Monte Cristo, which advertised Ogden as a mining center and livestock center. Through the magazine *Coin,* the source of his nickname, Harvey attained national attention as a leading advocate of the free coinage of silver, the hottest political issue of the 1890s. In 1932, at the age of eighty, Harvey ran for the presidency of the United States as an independent.

David O. McKay, one-time Ogden educator and popular president for many years of the Church of Jesus Christ of Latter-day Saints, had fond memories of La Plata. The strike came while he was in his teens, and carrying the mail to and from the mining camp on horseback provided him with his first paying job.

"I'd saddle up in Huntsville, get the mail from our post office, and head up the canyon and over the hills to the flat," he told an interviewer. "Sometimes I had a light load, other times my saddle bags were filled. I made the trip three times a week and enjoyed it, except in the snow."

There are only a few traces left of once-prosperous Plata, which is now private property—rotted wooden walls, piles of stone and waste ore, and caved-in shafts and tunnels.

—Murray M. Moler

Right
The apparent calm of this turn-of-the-century view of the Union Station belies the constant activity of the 200 train crews needed to handle the freight and passenger business that passed through the yards. The engine and repair shops were maintained by 800 additional workers, making the station and yard Ogden's major employer. Courtesy, Ogden Chamber of Commerce

Below
In the early 1900s more than seventy passenger trains were being serviced daily in the Ogden yards. Most were through-trains with connections made in Ogden. From the Church Archives. Courtesy, The Church of Jesus Christ of Latter-day Saints

Below
Although the Union Pacific Railroad had constructed its first roundhouse in Ogden as early as 1870, the development of extensive railroad shops began in the 1890s, when the Union Pacific and Southern Pacific railroads constructed major facilities. From the Heber H. Thomas Collection. Courtesy, Harold B. Lee Library, Brigham Young University

freight business increased tremendously in the 1870s and 1880s. The Central Pacific carried 80,000 tons in its Utah trade in 1871. By 1884 it reported an annual average of 125,000 tons. About half of this cargo was related to mining, being mostly ores and machinery shipped to and from Montana. Imports to Utah accounted for about two-thirds of the freight, including merchandise, building material, lumber, railroad material, and produce. Sundries included wagons, livestock, wool, hides, dried fruit, salt, hay, and other items.

Passenger service was also on the increase. Three transcontinental trains per day were making stops at the Ogden depot in 1878. Timetables show several daily arrivals and departures on the Utah Central line to Salt Lake City as well as a daily run on the Utah Northern line to the north.

The rapid growth of the railroad continued through to the twentieth century, influencing Ogden's development more than any other single factor. By 1910 the Utah Central, the Oregon Short Line (earlier the Utah Northern), the Southern Pacific, the Denver and Rio Grande, the San Pedro, Los Angeles and Salt Lake, and the Union Pacific were all routing both passengers and freight through the Junction City. In that year railroad payrolls pumped about four million dollars into the local economy; a quarter of the total came from Southern Pacific, the area's leading employer with about 1,000 residents in its work force. In 1913 the Ogden railroad yards handled more than 500,000 freight cars; about seventy passenger trains passed through the city on a daily basis.

During this era of cross-country trains, a street-rail system

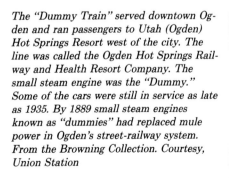

The "Dummy Train" served downtown Ogden and ran passengers to Utah (Ogden) Hot Springs Resort west of the city. The line was called the Ogden Hot Springs Railway and Health Resort Company. The small steam engine was the "Dummy." Some of the cars were still in service as late as 1935. By 1889 small steam engines known as "dummies" had replaced mule power in Ogden's street-railway system. From the Browning Collection. Courtesy, Union Station

provided transportation in and around town. The Ogden City Railway Company had its beginning in 1883. Originally the cars were mule drawn, but by 1889 small steam engines known as "dummies" were in use. During the 1890s, when lines were extended to the Ogden Hot Springs Resort and to Brigham City, electricity became the source of power. The local railway reached its peak of service in the first decades of the twentieth century, including a line up Ogden Canyon to Huntsville. Ridership declined with the popularization of the automobile, and the street railway system was replaced during the 1930s by buses.

The railroad changed Ogden—economically, politically, and socially. No longer a pioneer village, the Junction City had to deal with a huge influx of non-Mormons, who competed with established residents for control. Thus Ogden became a prize sought by Mormon and Gentile political groups. The decades of the 1870s and 1880s saw political parties in Utah organized along religious lines. The People's party encompassed most Mormon voters while the Liberal party was organized by and for non-Mormon voters. The Liberal party, with its strongholds in Corinne and Salt Lake City, sought to expand its influence by capitalizing on the U.S. government's campaign against polygamy.

The affairs of the People's party in Ogden were tightly controlled by the Weber Stake hierarchy, headed by Franklin D. Richards. A member of the Quorum of Twelve Apostles, he had moved to Ogden in 1869 to ensure that the city would stay within the Mormon fold. Richards became probate and county judge of Weber County, serving from 1869 until 1883, and in 1870 he established the *Ogden Junction,* a newspaper which for eleven years ardently defended the Mormon Church and plural marriage.

In the heat of nationwide controversy plural marriage came to be perceived as the reigning characteristic of the Mormon Church, though only about 20 percent of adult Mormons engaged in the practice. The vast majority of Ogden's men were monogamous. About two-thirds of the men in plural marriages had only two wives. Polygamy was most often practiced by the male leadership of the Church. Lorin Farr had six wives and thirty-four children while Franklin D. Richards had eleven wives and twenty-eight children. In an 1880 interview Jane S. Richards, Franklin's first wife, spoke with Mrs. Hubert Howe Bancroft, wife of the famous historian, concern-

Franklin D. Richards, a prominent leader in the Mormon Church and in Ogden politics, served as probate and county judge for Weber County and as a member of the territorial legislature. He was the first president of the Utah State Historical Society. USHS

ing her experience in plural marriage. She reflected that a plural wife necessarily saw her husband less than a woman living in a monogamous marriage, and this allowed her to develop more independence. Though they did not all live in Ogden, Jane Richards' account suggests that her husband's wives (including two sisters and their niece) generally made the effort to get along with one another and that on the whole polygamy was not too dissimilar in most respects to the conventional form of marriage.

Congressional passage of the Edmunds Act in 1882 and the Edmunds-Tucker Act in 1887 put teeth into the anti-polygamy movement with provisions for fines and confiscation of property as well as imprisonment. Between 1884 and 1893 there were more than a thousand convictions for unlawful cohabitation under these laws. The Edmunds Act stipulated that polygamous men could not vote or hold political office, and this had a decided impact on Ogden politics. With the passage of the law, Mayor Lester J. Herrick and members of the Ogden City Council and Weber County Court (similar to the County Commission) resigned.

The disenfranchisement of polygamists under the Edmunds Act stirred the hopes of the Liberal party for political victory

Opposite page
The majesty of David H. Peery's home "The Virginia," which was located at Adams and 24th Street, complemented his career as a businessman, church leader, publisher, and mayor of Ogden. USHS

A cobblestone mansion, constructed by prominent Ogden booster, mayoral candidate, and jeweler J.S. Lewis, dominates Ogden Canyon. Lewis donated the Union Station clock and was instrumental in the development of the canyon. Courtesy, Richard C. Roberts

in Ogden. In 1880 Weber County had 2,779 registered voters (1,473 males and 1,300 females) and Ogden had 1,168 registered voters (602 males and 566 females). Women had been allowed to vote in the Utah Territory for more than a decade. City elections were hotly contested, as evidenced by bands, parades, and occasional counterfeit ballots. In the 1883 mayoral election, the first after passage of the Edmunds Act, the People's party held on narrowly as David H. Peery, a former Mormon Stake president, defeated Liberal party candidate John S. Lewis 1,059 votes to 818. Peery won again in 1885 by a slimmer margin of 1,129 to 946.

Feelings of both Mormons and non-Mormons became very tender when their politics and religion were attacked by the other camp. Ogden newspapers fanned the partisan fires from both sides, and violence was not unheard of. An 1872 incident reported in the *Salt Lake Herald* is illustrative of this era:

Yesterday afternoon, as C.W. Penrose, Esquire, Editor of the Ogden Junction *was proceeding down East Temple Street, he was hailed by some person walking behind him; and upon halting, was accosted by a petti fogging lawyer named W.R. Keithly, who grabbed him by the coat collar and muttered with an oath, something about taking something back. Mr. Penrose, whose left hand was encumbered with a small box, demanded Keithly to take away his hand, at the same time disengaging himself from him. Keithly then drew back and struck Penrose a heavy blow with a cane he carried, the blow taking effect on the cords of the neck behind the left ear, the force breaking off the head of the cane. This stunned Penrose and rendered him measurably helpless. But the brute, not satisfied, struck him another heavy blow with the stick, across the left temple, this time breaking it in two, and leaving a rather ugly gash. . . . We understand Keithly took umbrage at an article recently published in the* Junction *supposed to reflect on him.*

Another Ogden newspaperman was involved in an altercation when Mormon Church leader George Q. Cannon was arrested in 1886 under the Edmunds Act. During the trial in Salt Lake City, Martha Cannon, one of his wives, was interrogated in a relentless fashion. George Q. Cannon's sons Frank and Hugh and their cousin Angus were offended at the dis-

Below
In 1888 the newly completed Ogden City Hall and the Broom Hotel graced Washington Boulevard, which was wide enough to turn a horse and wagon around easily. Stately trees shaded the downtown area's dusty streets. USHS

The Ogden landscape east beyond Monroe Avenue was still bleak prior to the turn of the century, punctuated only sporadically by stately homes. From the Heber H. Thomas Collection. Courtesy, Harold B. Lee Library, Brigham Young University

Victorious at last over the Mormon-dominated People's party, the Liberal party won every seat on the Ogden City Council in the election of 1889. USHS

trict attorney's behavior and physically assaulted him as he was leaving the Continental Hotel. For this attack Frank Cannon, editor of the influential Ogden *Herald,* served briefly in jail.

Although tempers and emotions were running high through the 1880s, some cooperation between Mormons and Gentiles began to occur, notably in April 1887 when the Ogden Chamber of Commerce was organized. David Peery served as president for the first year and Judge Philip H. Emerson, a non-Mormon, served the second year. The chamber acted in support of economic development throughout the community and was the first broadly based commercial organization in Utah. It became a significant conciliatory influence, though partisanship continued to dominate at election time.

A founding member of the chamber, David Eccles, was the People's party candidate for mayor in 1887. Eccles had two wives and was therefore technically ineligible to hold office. However, like most Mormon men who practiced plural marriage, he did so in secret and had already served a term as one of the five Ogden city councilmen. His Liberal party opponent in the mayoral race was Fred J. Kiesel. Kiesel, who had been defeated for that office by David Peery in 1885, lost again to Eccles by only 110 votes—1,364 to 1,254.

Vehemently opposed to the union of church and state under the People's party, Kiesel ran again in 1889. The People's party nominated John Boyle. Voting took place at the recently completed city hall amid the usual excitement of an election day, heightened by challenges to the eligibility of individual voters and by charges of stuffing the ballot box. There was an intense effort on both sides to obtain the maximum turnout for their party. Railroad men at work were rushed into the city to do their duty. Crowds milled around the city hall and the Broom Hotel until late in the evening, when it was announced that the Liberal party had won every municipal office. Mayor Kiesel had defeated his opponent by 391 votes. Ogden was the first major Utah city to be captured by the Liberal party. The headline in the *Utah Daily Union* read: "OGDEN AMERICANIZED."

Within two months of their election the new mayor and council recast the street plan that had been in existence for nearly four decades. Except for Wall Avenue, the north-south streets—Franklin, Young, Main, Spring, Smith, Pearl, Green,

and East—were renamed for U.S. presidents. To allow for municipal growth, the city's northern boundary was moved twenty blocks up from the Ogden River, and the east-west streets were renumbered accordingly. Old 5th Street, for example, became 25th Street.

The rivalry of the 1870s and 1880s did not die easily, but Mormons and non-Mormons became more cooperative in politics as well as in business. Statehood was a goal that both sides wanted to achieve, and in the years leading to 1896, when Utah became the forty-fifth state, several changes toward that end came about. Polygamy, the most prominent obstacle to statehood, was abandoned in Mormon Church President Wilford Woodruff's Manifesto of 1890. Furthermore, there was a decided effort to reorganize territorial politics along national party lines rather than along Mormon and Gentile lines. In Ogden Republican and Democratic party mass meetings were held in 1891. The People's party faded out of existence in that year, and the Liberal party had disappeared by 1893. Frank J. Cannon, by that time editor of the Ogden *Standard,* declared that his paper would advocate

Above
Ogden's east bench in 1940, seen from the same locale as the 1872 view opposite, shows the city's irrepressible advance toward the foothills. The mountains show the impact of the clear-cutting logging operations of the previous century. USHS

Opposite page
This 1872 photograph of Ogden's east bench by William H. Jackson reveals that the city was confined mostly to the vicinity of Main Street (Washington Boulevard) and the Wall Avenue railroad depot. USHS

the interests of the Republican party. In 1894 Cannon cam-
paigned as a Republican and was elected as Utah's last territorial delegate to the United States Congress, serving from
1895 to 1896.

The railroad, which transformed Ogden politics, encouraging emigration from the populous East, also brought religious
diversity to the community. The first Roman Catholic Mass
in Ogden was celebrated during Christmas week in 1871 at
the home of Michael Maguire, located on the south side
of 25th Street between Lincoln and Grant. Father Patrick
Walsh and his successors traveled from Salt Lake City to perform services for the mostly Irish congregation in Ogden until
1878. Then Father Lawrence Scanlon took up residence as
pastor of St. Joseph's, a new wooden frame structure on the
south side of 25th Street between Lincoln and Grant. By
1881 there were 150 Catholics in Ogden, and by 1884 this
number had increased to 400. Father Patrick M. Cushanhan,

Above
*Ogden observed the Fourth of July, 1896,
with parades, speeches, and festivities. Giving the day special significance was the entrance of Utah into the Union as the forty-
fifth state just six months prior to the national holiday. Courtesy, Ogden Chamber of
Commerce*

Opposite page
*The population of Ogden lined 25th Street
on January 4, 1896, for a Statehood Day
parade. From the Browning Collection.
Courtesy, Union Station*

Where the ZCMI parking center and the Eagles Lodge now stand, the courthouse and the First Methodist Episcopal Church formerly held sway. The cornerstone of the church was laid in 1890. USHS

arriving from Ireland in 1881, spearheaded the building of a larger church, completed in 1902 and dedicated as St. Joseph's by Bishop Scanlon.

The waiting room of the Union Depot was blessed by the first Episcopal services in Ogden, held on July 17, 1870. The Reverend James L. Gillogly and his wife lived in a boxcar in the railroad yards for several months, awaiting the purchase of a church site. The Episcopal Church of the Good Shepherd, which is admired today for its substantial Gothic design, was completed in 1874 at a cost of $11,000. From the 1870s to the 1890s a school was conducted on the grounds of the church, with yearly enrollment during the 1880s averaging 175 students. Tuition ranged from one to two dollars a month. Church membership grew from 95 members in 1883 to 600 by 1915.

Presbyterian worship in Ogden began in 1878 under the direction of the Reverend G.W. Gallagher. During the 1880s services were held in a building at Lincoln and 24th streets, and by 1906 a new building was completed on the corner of

24th and Adams. The Central Park Presbyterian Church was organized in 1890 by C.N. Strevell, who later became head of the Strevell-Patterson Hardware Company of Salt Lake City.

Congregationalists held services in Ogden as early as 1876, though they did not formally organize until 1884. By 1895 the membership had grown to 137. The educational arm of the Congregational Church, the New West Educational Commission, constructed a two-story brick schoolhouse on the corner of 25th and Adams. The Ogden Academy remained in operation for a decade; in 1896 it was leased to the Ogden City Schools. The New West Educational Commission also maintained schools in Hooper, Lynne, and South Weber.

Numerous other Protestant denominations founded congregations in Ogden during the late 1800s and early 1900s, including the Spiritualists (1874), Baptists (1881), Lutherans (1888), African Methodist Episcopalians (1908), and International Bible Students/Jehovah's Witnesses (1909).

The Jewish congregation Brith Sholem began in 1890 as Ohab Sholem in Ben Oppman's clothing store at 352 25th Street, with Sam Rosenbluth as president. A branch of the Holy Trinity (Greek Orthodox) Church was organized in Ogden in 1905 by Parthenios Lemberopulos, a priest of the Salt Lake City church. Japanese residents opened the Ogden Buddhist Temple in 1913.

Serving the religious majority of Ogden, a Mormon tabernacle at the corner of 22nd and Washington was dedicated in 1869. Begun in 1855 under the direction of William N. Fife, its construction was distinguished by arches fastened with wooden pegs. The foundation was of rock, and the two-foot-thick walls were adobe. It had a seating capacity of 1,200. Ornately remodeled in 1896, this beautiful pioneer building was razed during the 1960s to make way for the Ogden Temple of the Church of Jesus Christ of Latter-day Saints, dedicated on January 18, 1972.

Though the strong Mormon influence remained, the diverse religions and ethnic groups that came to Ogden because of the transcontinental railroad would change forever the social fabric of the city. More than the steel rails and powerful steam engines of the converging lines, it was this diversity of cultures that transformed Ogden from a homogenous agricultural village to a multi-faceted city fortuitously located at the crossroads of the continent.

CHAPTER THREE
RIDING THE RAILS INTO THE TWENTIETH CENTURY

At the time of the completion of the transcontinental railroad Ogden was a small agricultural community. Irrigation canals and ditches bounded the city blocks—essentially the region west of Washington Boulevard from Ogden River to 28th Street. A few houses were scattered to the south beyond 28th Street and some on the "bench" above Adams Avenue, but most houses and businesses lined the streets between Washington Boulevard and the Wall Avenue slough. These streets were dusty during the dry seasons and muddy in wet weather, prompting one observer to write in 1860 that the mud came up to the eyes of the cattle; the "road was made of mud just as soft as a pot of mush." Board sidewalks connecting one business to another were a necessity on the main streets.

By the beginning of World War I, according to a chamber of commerce publication, Ogden had 8.5 miles of paved streets (the total for Utah during this period was 34 miles) and almost 100 miles of paved sidewalks. The street-railway service had about 100 miles of track. To provide the city with culinary water, 64 miles in water mains had been installed and 38.5 miles of pipe had been laid in the sewer system. The city also had three public parks.

As a result of the railroad Ogden had grown from an "inland town" into a major city of commerce and trade to outside areas.

In 1860 there were 1,463 people in Ogden; in 1870, the year after the arrival of the railroad, there were 3,127; in 1880, 6,069; and in 1890, 12,889. These population increases reflected vigorous economic growth in the area.

In 1889 the *Ogden Directory* listed five major flour milling concerns in the city. Other industries listed were Farr's Woolen Mills, the Ogden Broom Factory, the Vinegar Works, Utah Powder Company, the Ogden Iron Works, and three brew-

Visitors stopping in Ogden in the early 1870s enjoyed the comforts of the Keeney House on Wall Avenue. A quarter-mile boardwalk saved them from sinking into a sea of mud as they trekked from the depot to the hotel. From the Church Archives. Courtesy, The Church of Jesus Christ of Latter-day Saints

65

Above
Through the first decade of the twentieth century, Ogden streets above Washington Boulevard were still hard-packed dirt, but progress demanded paved sidewalks and water and sewer lines. In the background of this 25th Street scene is the Ogden Academy, which later became Central Junior High School. *USHS*

Right
The Phoenix, Eagle, and Advance Roller mills were consolidated in the late 1880s by David Eccles into the Ogden Milling and Elevator Company. By the turn of the century, milling had risen to an annual 30,000 bushels of wheat, most of which was grown by Weber County farmers. *Courtesy, Richard C. Roberts*

eries. The directory also cited the establishment of a city water company, the installation of telephone service, and the founding of several banks, marking the transition from barter to a money economy.

The businesses and industries that came to Ogden with the railroad built on the foundation laid by pioneer industries. Brick making, for example, thrived in the latter half of the nineteenth century: at one time, Weber County had thirty separate brick manufacturers.

Flour milling, another pioneer industry, was begun in Ogden in 1850 by Lorin Farr, and over the next several decades eleven mills were spread throughout Weber County. David Eccles consolidated much of the milling in the area into the Ogden Milling and Elevator Company in 1886, appointing James Mack as president. The combined operation included the Advance Roller Mill (earlier a Farr mill), the Phoenix Mills (which had been operated by Mack and David Peery for more than a decade), and the Eagle Mills (earlier the Stevens and Stone Mills). During the early 1890s, the Taylor Mills built in 1853 by Daniel Burch in Riverdale were added to Eccles' Ogden Milling Company. By the turn of the century the company was purchasing and milling 30,000 bushels of wheat, most of which came from local farmers. The leading

Below
Ogden industrialist David Eccles' business empire began with the establishment of the Eccles Lumber Yard at 24th Street and Lincoln Avenue. The company later became the Stoddard, and then the Anderson Lumber Yard. USHS

brands of flour included "Phoenix," "Ogden's Best," and "Straight Grade."

Sawmills and lumberyards contributed significantly to Ogden's growth. As noted in the diary of Charles Middleton, an early Ogden resident, in the pioneer period trees were felled in Ogden Canyon near the river so that the spring runoff would float the logs down to the mill. Timber became more accessible in 1862 with the building of a road through Ogden Canyon. Sawmills were then constructed in the canyon as well as at its mouth, and logging expanded into all the canyons east of Ogden and up to Monte Cristo. The first lumberyards in Ogden were established in 1869 by Barnard White and Joshua Williams. David Eccles became a leader in the lumber business during the 1880s. By 1888 the Eccles Lumber Company was doing $100,000 in trade annually.

As the volume of railroad traffic grew, so did the need for travelers' accommodations. The city's first hotels anticipated the arrival of the transcontinental railroad, opening their doors in 1868: the Ogden House at the southeast corner of 24th and Washington, and the White House (later called the Junction House) on the southeast corner of 25th and Washington. The Union Depot Hotel was constructed in 1869, the Keeney House in 1870. The Beardsley Hotel and the City Hotel were both completed during the 1870s. Ogden welcomed tourists as well as those traveling on business to the Junction City. The 1878-1879 edition of the *New Overland Tourist and Pacific Coast Guide* described the contrasting majestic and pastoral scenery to be enjoyed nearby:

The Wasatch Mountains rise some thousands of feet above the city, and the tourist would find much of interest in a stroll up the mountain side and along the canyons. Ogden Canyon is about five miles long, and from its mouth to its source, from plain to mountain top, the scenery is grand and imposing. In places the granite walls rise on each side 1,500 feet high, and for a considerable distance not more than 150 feet apart. About six miles from Ogden, up in the mountains behind the town is a lovely little valley called "The Basin," watered by mountain streams and covered with a luxuriant growth of grass.

Many of the tourists who visited Ogden and the "luxu-

Above
A hot springs resort west of Ogden was developed during the 1880s by Ranson H. Slater. Hotel guests arrived on a branch line of the city's railway system. USHS

Left
At its peak of popularity the Hot Springs resort attracted visitors from all over the Intermountain area. Eventually public tastes turned away from the hot "medicinal" baths, saloons, and horse-racing that were its highlights, and the resort faded away. Photo by Barbara Parsons Bernstein

THE WORLD'S GREATEST FIREARMS INVENTOR

When Jonathan Browning settled in Ogden in 1852, he was already well known as a gunsmith. He invented two rifles that earned a reputation for reliability. USHS

Jonathan Browning, who bartered with John Broom for a wagonload of iron, opened for business as a blacksmith and gunsmith in Ogden in 1852. His son John Moses Browning, born January 23, 1855, was destined to become the world's greatest firearms inventor.

As a boy John showed an interest in the craft of gunmaking, fashioning a makeshift weapon from odds and ends in his father's shop at the age of ten. Through his teenage years he continued and refined his experiments, aided by younger brother Matthew, who was John's constant companion and, eventually, business partner.

In 1879 John M. Browning received his first patent. This design for a single-shot rifle became the Model 1885 Winchester. Sale of the manufacturing rights brought in $8,000, prompting him in later years to call it his most profitable invention. Though he earned far

more later patents, Browning averred:

But it was a big eight thousand . . . They don't come that big anymore. A check that size wasn't often deposited in the local bank; it made me so rich that I've never worried about money since. It gave me eight thousand dollars worth of certainty that I could invent things for which people would pay large prices.

His independence assured, Browning went on to patent more than 100 original models of firearms, including rifles, shotguns, automatic pistols, machine guns, and aircraft cannon. Browning's .45 caliber automatic pistol became the official U.S. military sidearm in 1911, and it was not until 1985 that the Army switched, amid controversy, to another lighter weapon. The famous Browning Automatic Rifle (B.A.R.) first saw action in World War I, and from that time through the Korean War all machine guns used by U.S. troops were of Browning design.

By the time of his death in 1926,

John M. Browning was recognized worldwide as preeminent in his field. But his reputation was made first in Ogden with a hefty $8,000 bank deposit.

Bottom
At the top of this picture is the lathe Jonathan Browning hauled by wagon from Council Bluffs in 1851, the first lathe in the territory. In the foreground is the workbench where his son John M. Browning fashioned many of the weapons that became standards for the world. From the Browning Collection. Courtesy, Union Station

Below
John M. Browning took keen delight in test firing his new weapons. He is shown here posing for a formal portrait behind his Model 1917—Caliber 30, Water-Cooled Machine Gun. From the Browning Collection. Courtesy, Union Station

One of the first banks in Ogden, the First National Bank was established in the southeast corner of the ZCMI Building. USHS

riant" Ogden Valley stayed at the equally luxuriant Broom Hotel. John Broom, a native of England and convert to the Mormon Church, arrived in Ogden in 1851 and dabbled in a variety of businesses before he gave a thought to building a grand hotel. He once sold a wagonload of molasses and dairy supplies to a detachment of U.S. troops and, while leaving their camp, happened to notice the charred remains of an Army wagon train, which had been burned during the Utah War. He loaded his wagon with old iron tires, spindles, and other iron parts, which he then traded to gunsmith Jonathan Browning (father of the legendary firearms inventor) for the lot on the northwest corner of Main and 5th streets (Washington and 25th streets). This would become the site of the Broom Hotel, but not for another twenty-four years. Meanwhile Broom acquired more land, including sugar cane holdings that he sold in order to invest in a gold mining enterprise, which made $70,000. The idea to build a first-rate hotel came when he heard travelers talk of poor hotel accom-

modations. At a cost of $70,000 construction began in 1882, and the Broom Hotel opened for business on January 15, 1883. It was three stories high, with a floor plan 66 by 160 feet. An additional $25,000 was expended for furniture. The second floor included a large dining room and thirty-four elegant parlors with bay windows; there were thirty-five third-floor rooms. Contemporary advertisements noted the suites were all equipped with bathrooms and other modern conveniences. The elegant main floor featured tonsorial establishments, bathhouses, a billiard hall, reception rooms, and offices of the hotel. The Broom Hotel remained a landmark of the city for more than half a century.

In 1875 John E. Dooly founded Ogden's first bank; in 1883 this institution became the Utah National Bank. The Deseret National Bank of Salt Lake City organized the Ogden First National Bank in 1881 with H.S. Eldredge as president. In 1890 David Peery was installed as president of the new Ogden Savings Bank. The Utah Loan and Trust Company was established in 1888 by the Richards brothers—Charles Comstock and Franklin S.—sons of the Mormon Apostle Franklin D. Richards. This institution experienced extreme financial difficulty during the 1890s but was saved from failure late in the decade through the efforts of another Mormon Apostle, Heber J. Grant.

More than fifty newspapers have been established in Ogden since the coming of the railroad. Most of them died almost before being born, leading some to call Ogden "the graveyard of Western journalism." Ogden's first newspaper was published in 1869 by T.B.H. Stenhouse, but the *Telegraph and Commercial Advertiser* lasted for only a couple of months. The *Ogden Junction* was the leading newspaper from 1870 until 1881 under the direction of Franklin D. Richards and Charles W. Penrose. Its successor, the *Ogden Daily Herald*, was issued from 1881 to 1887. The *Standard* began publication in 1888 under the editorial leadership of Frank J. Cannon; William Glasmann took over as editor and publisher from 1894 until 1916. The *Morning Examiner,* first published in 1904 under the editorship of Frank Francis, merged with the *Standard* in 1920, becoming the *Standard-Examiner* with J.U. Eldredge, Jr., and A.L. Glasmann as publishers.

In the early period Ogden journalism was decidedly two-fisted, as political battles were fought in the newspapers. The

Above
William Glasmann was the editor and publisher of the Ogden Standard *from 1894 until his death in 1916. In 1920 the* Standard *merged with the* Morning Examiner. *From the Browning Collection. Courtesy, Union Station*

Opposite page
Although the Standard-Examiner *eventually became the dominant newspaper in the Ogden area, it faced competition over the years from Salt Lake City's two major dailies, the* Tribune *and the* Deseret News, *whose advertising enticed the Ogden shopper to make the short trip to the "Big City." Pictured is Ogden's Deseret News office. Courtesy,* Deseret News

A microcosm of nineteenth-century Ogden society is captured in this photograph of 25th Street. The figure on the left is Joe Hall, former Pony Express rider; on the right is watchmaker, sheepman, and chemist Herman Kuchler. USHS

sensational *Ogden Freeman,* published sporadically during the latter 1870s, advertised itself as "aggressive and progressive and Anti-Mormon, Anti-Chinese, and Anti-Indian." Personal attacks were not uncommon and not without consequences for the editor. Charles Penrose was cudgeled by a cane-wielding lawyer who took extreme exception to a reference to himself in the *Junction.* Charles Hemenway of the *Herald* had his life threatened on numerous occasions. Charles King, editor of the *Morning Rustler,* was tarred and feathered by a mob in 1880. King moved on to the *Utah Daily Union* but apparently did not learn to temper his journalistic style. In 1889 he was shot in the throat and leg by Edward W. Exum, who was enraged about an article that tarnished the reputation of his wife.

Aside from controversy, the newspapers offered information relating to the everyday concerns of Ogden residents. A look at the January 1, 1870, issue of the *Junction* shows that a ride on the Gilmer and Salisbury Stage Line to Salt Lake City cost three dollars. The Railroad Saloon on Main Street (Washington Boulevard) advertised fresh oysters, received daily from Baltimore, by the case, can, or plate. C.B. McGregor's Ogden Circulating Library charged a five dollar life membership fee or ten cents per volume per week.

The newspapers and city directories advertised businesses and services of many kinds—attorneys, dentists, doctors, undertakers, saloons, shooting galleries, midwives, hotels, eating establishments, shoemakers, tailors, and medicine dealers, as well as dealers in coal, ice, furniture, and general merchandise. Dr. A. Lepper advertised a bathhouse where

hot, cold, medicated, and electric baths can be obtained, and all chronic diseases can be treated without medicine. I will diagnose any disease without asking any questions, locate the symptoms, and tell the cause. Those who are suffering with disease of the heart, lungs, liver, spleen, kidneys, deafness, or diseases of the eye, etc., would do well to call and find out their true condition.

Sharp Brothers Dentists promised painless extraction of teeth, modest terms, and a neatly furnished private room for ladies. P.J. Barratt, attorney and counselor at law, announced collections as his specialty. James Allen's Staple and Fancy

Opposite
The cigar-store Indian outside of Barney's on 24th Street was a traditional ornament in the days when Americans still could enjoy a good five-cent cigar.

Opposite page, top
Late nineteenth-century Ogden barber shops located at the Broom Hotel, the depot, and along 25th Street offered a haircut for 35 cents, a shave for 15 cents, and a bath for 50 cents.

Above
The Saddle Rock Restaurant on 24th Street featured "Oysters in Every Style" as a specialty of nineteenth-century cuisine in Ogden. Photos from the Hebert H. Thomas Collection. Courtesy, Harold B. Lee Library, Brigham Young University

Dry Goods advertised free delivery within the city or to the depot as well as "a magnificent assortment of gent's underwear for all seasons." The U.P. Brewery and Malting House offered beer at fifty cents a gallon for both saloons and families. Gibson and Eccles Lumber Yard noted "our prices defy competition." H.J. Powers, M.D., advertised his specialties as venereal diseases and diseases of the throat and lungs.

The 1883 directory of Ogden City and Weber County declared that the railroad brought with it business, enterprise, capital, life, and enhanced prosperity . . . though not unmixed with some "evils." These evils appeared most conspicuously on 25th Street. For three-quarters of a century (1875-1950) Ogden's "two-bit street" would be notorious for saloons, opium dens, prostitution, gambling, and violence. Prominent madams such as "Gentile Kate" and "Belle London" controlled prostitution along the "Electric Alley." The contrast between the new city, represented by 25th Street, and the pioneer lifestyle troubled residents (this change was explored in Bernard DeVoto's "Sin Comes to Ogden"). Many blamed the entrenchment of vice on minority groups, but it appears to have involved all segments of the population. Criticism was leveled at city officials and police for tacit or active complic-

An impending water shortage prompted the building of an artesian waterworks in 1914, when thirteen wells were drilled in Ogden Valley. These and later wells are now submerged under Pineview Reservoir. Courtesy, Ogden Chamber of Commerce

ity in the continuation of criminal activities. By the end of World War II the public outcry was so great that cleanup of "two-bit street" became a civic priority over the next decade. In the 1970s and 1980s the renovation of 25th Street and downtown Ogden has brought about increased commercial activity and local pride.

In making the transition from pioneer village to railroad town and then to modern city, Ogden had to establish utility services for its growing population. In 1881 the Ogden Water Company was formed by the city. In 1888 the city purchased the waters of Strong and Waterfall canyons to ensure an adequate supply for municipal development. Water was taken from the Ogden River, Wheeler Creek, Cold Water, Waterfall, Strong, and Warm Creek canyons. In 1914 Ogden City began to use water from artesian wells located in Ogden Valley.

Ogden's first electricity system was run by the privately owned Ogden Electric Light Company. In the first attempt at lighting the city by electricity, a high steel tower was erected on the corner of Adams Avenue and 24th Street, and four large light bulbs were hooked up in a way that would illuminate a good portion of the area below the bluff of the hill. The electricity was turned on with a great deal of fanfare

Above left
Workers building the pipeline from Pioneer Power Plant Dam enjoyed a spectacular view while riding the tramway above the mouth of Ogden Canyon. Courtesy, Richard C. Roberts

Left
Six-foot-diameter steel pipe was used to connect the Pioneer Power Plant Dam at Wheeler Canyon to the wooden pipeline that carried water on a six-mile course from the rim of Ogden Canyon to the city. Courtesy, Weber State College

Left
The Pioneer Power Station at 12th Street and Harrison Boulevard was the first installation of its kind in Utah. A generating capacity of 10,000 horsepower fed electricity to the area's growing industrial base and to the city's network of electric railroads. Courtesy, Ogden Chamber of Commerce

Below
The dam on the Ogden River near Wheeler Canyon helped provide power for the Pioneer Power Station, located near the mouth of Ogden Canyon. The dam was completed in 1898 at the cost of a quarter of a million dollars. Courtesy, Ogden Chamber of Commerce

and excitement from the crowd, as reported in the Ogden *Standard* of May 19, 1881. The light burned brightly for a few seconds, and then fizzled. The crowd went home disappointed. However, on June 20, 1881, stores were lighted by electricity supplied by a steam generating plant; this was replaced in 1883 by a hydroelectric plant, located near the mouth of Ogden Canyon. The fee charged to Ogden store owners was seventeen dollars a month for one light. Each owner could have only one light, which was turned on at dusk and off at midnight from a central switch at the powerhouse. Service was extended soon afterward to residences.

The George A. Lowe Company of Ogden installed the first telephones in the state in 1879, running a private wire between its warehouse and store. Within a year public telephone service was being provided by the Ogden Telephone Exchange Company and several other small telephone companies in Ogden, which were consolidated in 1883 into the Rocky Mountain Bell Telephone Company.

The telegraph was the most important means of long-distance communication until well into the twentieth century. The Deseret Telegraph line, a Mormon cooperative system completed in 1867, served towns from St. George to Logan. As the railroad advanced, Western Union extended its network, and by the end of 1869 Ogden had two telegraph offices. As the Junction City, Ogden became the most important relay between Chicago and San Francisco: by 1885 Western Union employed thirty telegraph operators in the local office. By 1903 the relay office had been moved to Salt Lake City.

The need for hospital and medical services became acute during the railroad era. Some "physicians" called themselves medical doctors but had no training. Smallpox, diphtheria, scarlet fever, and typhoid fever were prevalent. In 1879 sixty Huntsville children died of smallpox; Ogden had suffered a similar epidemic three years earlier. In 1882 the Ogden City Council funded a six-room isolation facility for smallpox patients south of the city on Burch Creek. In 1883 the Union Pacific Railroad Company purchased a two-story adobe building at 28th and Adams and converted it into a hospital. A city hospital built in 1892 at 651 28th Street was turned over to private management in 1897. The Thomas D. Dee Memorial Hospital was opened at 24th Street and Harrison Boule-

Telephone poles became part of the Ogden skyline in 1880. Hand-crank phones remained in use until 1940, and, in the early years of long-distance service, the operator often assisted by repeating portions of the conversation. USHS

Left
To provide a Catholic education for young women, the Sacred Heart Academy was opened by the Sisters of the Holy Cross in 1878. Housed originally in a two-story wood-en-frame building at 26th and Washington, the school had a faculty of seven sisters. By 1883 enrollment had reached 200. From the Heber H. Thomas Collection. Courtesy, Harold B. Lee Library, Brigham Young University

Left
In 1892 the Sacred Heart Academy moved to a new building, located on a five-acre plot at 25th and Quincy, that could accommodate 600 boarding students and a faculty of twenty-one sisters. A sad moment in Ogden history came when the school closed in 1938 and this cherished building was razed. From the Browning Collection. Courtesy, Union Station

Right
Between 1880 and 1910 Ogden's "show school" was Central School at 25th Street and Grant. Since 1911 the building has served as the home of the Ogden lodge of the Benevolent and Protective Order of Elk. From the Browning Collection. Courtesy, Union Station

Opposite
By 1900 graduating high school seniors had benefited from a half-century of active support for education in Ogden. Courtesy, Mr. and Mrs. Lowell Rowse

Above
The Weber Stake Academy, which eventually became Weber State College, was founded by the LDS Church in 1889 at 2445 Jefferson Avenue. In 1933 it was donated to the state. The school moved to the Harrison Boulevard campus during the 1950s. Courtesy, Ogden Chamber of Commerce

Right
While not yet a national basketball power, the 1902 Weber Stake Academy girls' basketball team struck fear into the hearts of their opponents. Courtesy, Ogden Chamber of Commerce

vard in 1910 and served the residents of Ogden for nearly six decades. Today the site continues to serve Ogden as a city park.

Education was under the direction of churches until 1890, when territorial law and community effort combined to strengthen public schools. In that year there were 3,296 children in Ogden of school age (six to eighteen) with 1,751 attending public schools, 961 attending parochial schools, and 584 not attending school. Ogden voters approved a $150,000 bond for construction of new buildings. The original Ogden High School was completed in 1909 at 25th Street and Monroe Avenue.

New industries and new businesses multiplied in Ogden as the turn of the century drew near. Ogden's sugar industry began during the fall of 1898 with David Eccles' Ogden Sugar Company. Production of sugar from beets rapidly increased, and later the Ogden and Logan factories were combined to

"UTAH HAS 46 CANNERIES WITH OGDEN AS INDUSTRY CENTER"

The above headline appeared in a special ten-page section of the Ogden *Examiner* on December 14, 1919. It demonstrates how important the canning industry once was to the Ogden area.

Preserving food has always been of utmost importance in Utah, as maintenance of a two-year emergency supply has long been the policy of the Church of Jesus Christ of Latter-day Saints. Accordingly, Mormon pioneers who settled in Ogden began immediately to preserve fruits and vegetables—by drying or bottling—for use in winter or when harvests were poor.

Commercial preservation of tomatoes began in 1888 when the Utah Canning Company of Ogden was formed with Thomas D. Dee as president and Isaac N. Pierce as manager. The plant—an unpainted board structure at 29th and Pacific, near the railroad tracks—canned 8,000 cases during its initial season.

As other vegetables and fruit were added to the list of crops grown locally or imported for processing, many more canning com-

Above
Started by Thomas D. Dee and managed by Isaac N. Pierce, the Utah Canning Company was best known for the Pierce brand, which promised: "Un-adulterated satisfaction is sealed up under the label of Pierce's pure food products." USHS

Left
Two turn-of-the-century Ogdenites enjoy a "tailgate lunch." They can choose from copious fare ranging from Hooper Tomatoes to NBC (Nabisco) Uneedum Crackers. Courtesy, Brad Larson

panies formed. Hundreds of Utah residents found employment in the industry, particularly during the seasonal peak.

By 1919, when the canneries section was published in the *Examiner,* the list of firms was headed by the Utah Packing Corporation, with plants in Ogden, Wasatch, Riverdale, Hooper, and West Weber. Woods Cross Canning had four Davis County factories. William Craig Canning Company boasted three—in Roy, Five Points, and North Ogden. The world's largest pea cannery was in

PIERCES PURE FOOD CATSUP.
Good To Taste! Without An Equal!

Morgan. Other firms in the area carried the names of Van Allen, Goddard, Kaysville, Brigham City, Wright-Wittier, Jones, North Ogden, Uintah, Willard, Perry, Honest Pack, and the Golden West Marmalade Company.

The Utah Canners' Association, with offices in downtown Ogden's old Colonel Hudson Building, represented forty of the state's forty-six canneries.

In that heyday peas and tomatoes remained the principal canning crops. Other products included pork and beans, green and wax beans, lima beans, and thirty varieties of pickles, as well as asparagus, catsup, tomato sauce, chili sauce, Worcestershire sauce, spaghetti, syrup, molasses, horseradish, pumpkin, squash, hominy, sauerkraut, beef steak, sausage, beets, peanut butter, condensed or evaporated milk, apples, peaches, pears, figs, cherries, rhubarb, strawberries, dewberries, plums, prunes, apricots, raspberries, blackberries, grapes, soups, mincemeat, honey, and many flavors of jams and jellies.

Ogden-canned foodstuffs could have filled just about any grocer's shelves.

Utah cannery production in 1918, much of it going overseas because of World War I, totaled 30 million cans of milk and 1,954,825 cases of fruit, vegetables, and other products. Average-size cans were packed 24 to a case, small cans were 36 to 72 to a case, and large restaurant-size cans were 6 to a case.

To serve the growing industry the American Can Company built a huge factory, on 20th Street between Grant and Lincoln, that could manufacture 70 billion cans annually. In its factory on 31st Street, near Lincoln, the Kieckhefer Paper Box Company made the cases in which the cans were shipped. The Ogden Iron Works specialized in making machines for all phases of the farming and canning industries.

The Utah canneries reached their peak during World War II, when around 5 million cases of foodstuffs were processed. Crews in Weber County alone grew to more than 600 workers at the seasonal peak, most of them women, and hundreds more workers were needed to handle the harvest.

Then came the decline.

Thomas D. Dee II, grandson of Utah Canning Company's first president and himself a former president of the Utah Canners' Association, attributes the virtual demise of the industry in the Beehive State to changing economics and technologies that favored California. Supporting this view are Grant Rounds, retired superintendent for the Del Monte Canning Company, and Fred Montmorency, former mayor of South Ogden and former Del Monte quality-control supervisor. In an interview they pointed out that most of Utah's

fruit and vegetables came from small garden plots and family orchards. Suppliers who lived near a cannery would bring pole beans to be processed in children's wagons and even baby buggies.

California took over the top place in food processing after the development of large-scale farms, which devoted multi-acre fields to a single crop that could be easily worked and harvested with machinery. Another setback was the introduction of a tomato species that ripened all at once, producing fruit of uniform size and density. These were highly marketable, although, as Tom Dee insists, "not nearly as flavorsome as Utah tomatoes."

California's longer growing season also lowered its production cost per acre, enhancing the efficiency of volume farming. At the same time Utah canners were faced with increasing freight costs to ship their produce to more populated sections of the country. "After the Second World War," Dee said, "it simply cost more to produce and can foods in Utah than their selling price at the stores."

The Utah Canning Company, when it merged with a pleasant Grove canner in 1960, sold its far-famed Pierce Pork and Beans label to a California market, and it is still readily available, although no longer an Ogden product.

The LDS Church's unique welfare program now operates the only cannery in Ogden. Its modern plant, on 17th Street near Wall Avenue, was visited by President Ronald Reagan a few years ago. Its wide variety of products, canned mostly by volunteer church members, are not sold to the public but are available to the needy only through bishops' warehouses.

—Murray M. Moler

form the Amalgamated Sugar Company.

Canning companies began in Utah and Ogden in 1888 with the organization of the Utah and Colorado Canning Company under the leadership of Isaac N. Pierce. By 1897 three canning companies were operating in the city; by the beginning of the First World War eighteen canneries dotted Weber County, including the Utah Packing Corporation, the William Craig Company, Goddard Pickle and Preserve Company, Banner Canning Company, and the North Ogden Canning Company.

Sidney Stevens was the owner of a large wagon manufacturing plant centered in Ogden during the last part of the nineteenth century. ZCMI (Zion's Co-operative Mercantile In-

At right in this 1892 scene of Washington Boulevard is Boyle's Furniture Store. Peter A. Boyle began making furniture in Ogden in 1862. USHS

Opposite page
Zion's Co-operative Mercantile Institution (ZCMI) began operations in Ogden in 1869, a year after it had first opened its doors in Salt Lake City. David H. Peery was the first manager. Over the years, the store has occupied three of the four corner sites at Washington and 24th Street, the heart of downtown Ogden. From the Church Archives. Courtesy, The Church of Jesus Christ of Latter-day Saints

stitution) opened its doors in Ogden in 1869, and 1885 saw the founding of J.G. Read and Bros. Company, manufacturers of leather goods, with wholesale and retail outlets.

John Scowcroft, emigrating from England in 1880, started a confectionery that formed the basis of the John Scowcroft and Sons Company, a diversified manufacturing and wholesale concern that encompassed clothing, canning, and knitting factories, a food and spice processing plant, and American Food Stores. The firm's Never-Rip overalls were advertised widely in the West. By 1914 the clothing factory employed 250 people, who made 1,500 pairs of overalls and work pants and 450 work shirts each day.

The Utah Construction Company was organized in 1900 with capital of $200,000. The beginnings of this wide-reaching firm are found in the railroad construction company founded by W.W., C.J., and A.B. Corey in 1881. In 1887 E.O. and

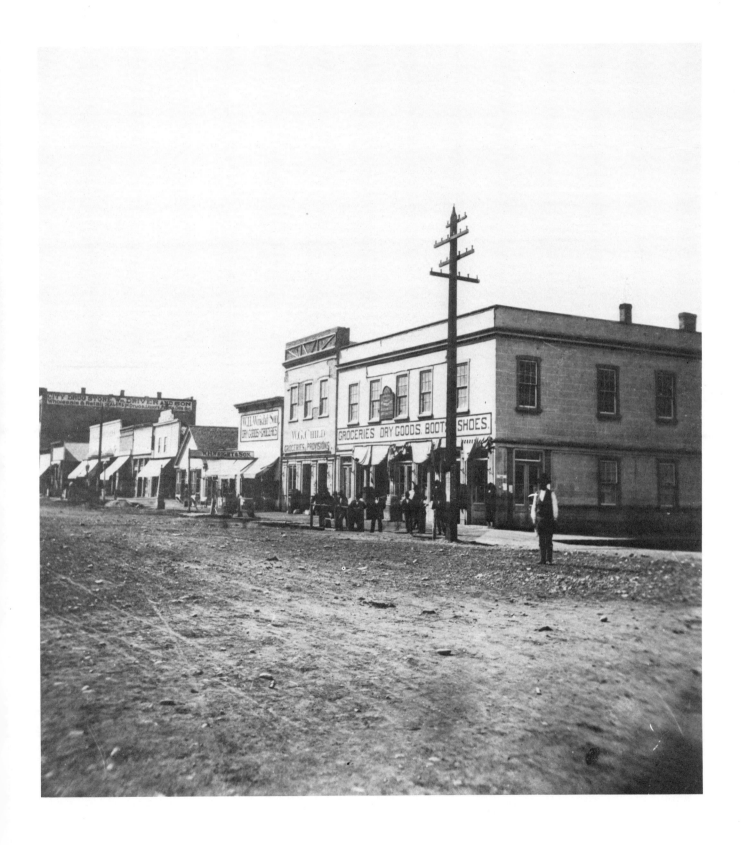

W.H. Wattis became partners in the firm. The company experienced financial difficulties during the decade of the 1890s and was reorganized in 1900 under the leadership of David Eccles. During the next half century the firm would complete numerous railroad lines and participate in the six-company consortium that built Boulder Dam.

Most of Ogden's residents during the pioneer era had their roots in the British Isles or northern Europe. The railroad brought people with many different ethnic backgrounds, some as emigrants and some as laborers. Many of the Chinese workers who had built the Central Pacific railroad stayed on to maintain that route, establishing small communities in Corinne and in Ogden. In 1880 Ogden had 33 Chinese resi-

John Scowcroft's Never-Rip overalls were in constant demand. The Scowcroft business empire got its start in 1880 in a small bakery and candy store on Washington Boulevard. From the Browning Collection. Courtesy, Union Station

dents; this figure had grown to 106 by 1890. During this era of intense anti-Asian prejudice, the Chinese stayed in their section of town (along lower 25th Street between the Broom Hotel and the depot), and a few set up businesses, including several laundries and Sing Lung Store, a grocery owned and operated by Wong Leung Ka. Until the first decade of the twentieth century Ogden's Chinese were for the most part single men; the arrival of families brought stability to the Chinese community, which branched out to the north of 25th Street.

Some Italians, as Mormon converts, migrated to the Ogden area prior to 1869. The Italian population grew as others came to seek work with the railroad. Also seeking work, Greek

emigrants began to arrive in the Ogden area, largely after the turn of the century.

Blacks began to settle in Ogden with the arrival of the railroad, some as laborers, but most as porters, waiters, and cooks. As Ogden's black community developed, an important element was the Porters and Waiters Club on lower 25th Street, managed for a number of years by Billy Weekly. From the beginning, blacks as well as other minorities experienced discrimination, segregation, and sometimes worse. As early as 1869, racial violence took the life of a black railroad employee at a station forty miles east of Ogden. The incident received no more official notice than an entry by paymaster O.C. Smith: "There was a man shot and hung at Wasatch tonight. . . . "

Ogden's darkest hour, the lynching of George Segal, occurred on Sunday, April 20, 1884. Segal, a twenty-seven-year-old Japanese emigrant, had been arrested the night before for shooting Elizabeth Gudgell, owner of the Gem Restaurant on lower 24th Street. At about 4 a.m., police officers manning the city jail at 25th and Washington saw an armed mob of masked and disguised men approaching. By force the mob gained entrance to the jail and sledgehammered open Segal's cell door, which was made of boiler iron. Segal was dragged outside and hanged from the south end of the fire-bell tower. No indictments were issued by a special fifteen-member grand jury that was asked to investigate the lynching.

Ten years later, social unrest would again come to Ogden in the form of "Kelley's Army," one of several such groups marching and riding the rails to Washington, D.C., to protest the depression and unemployment caused by the Panic of 1893. Ogden and Salt Lake units of the Utah National Guard (formed only three weeks earlier on March 27, 1894) were called into service to control the protestors. Organized by Charles H. Kelley of San Francisco, this "Industrial Army" had traveled as far as Ogden in very crowded boxcars furnished by the Southern Pacific Railroad. However, the Union Pacific and Denver and Rio Grande railroads refused to carry them further east. Ogden thus became the temporary home for the 1,200 men of Kelley's Army. During the three days that the Industrial Army was in Ogden (April 9 to April 11, 1894) the men were confined to the Southern Pacific Railroad yards and cars and were closely guarded by five companies of

Above
An "Industrial Army" of unemployed workers led by "General" Charles H. Kelley of San Francisco were detained in Ogden railroad yards for three days in 1894. Militia and police were called up to safeguard frightened residents, but soon the city's sympathy turned in favor of Kelley's men. Courtesy, Richard C. Roberts

Opposite page
Although Ogden's finest seem to resemble the "Keystone Cops," theirs was a proud heritage of keeping the peace. From the Browning Collection. Courtesy, Union Station

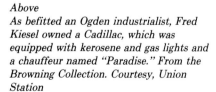

Above
As befitted an Ogden industrialist, Fred Kiesel owned a Cadillac, which was equipped with kerosene and gas lights and a chauffeur named "Paradise." From the Browning Collection. Courtesy, Union Station

Top
Dorothy Browning is reputed to have been Ogden's first woman to drive an automobile. She is pictured here after having shot a badger in the sagebrush. From the Browning Collection. Courtesy, Union Station

Left

Orlando J. Stillwell owned Ogden's first automobile, which he purchased in 1902. Within a short time the improved road to Ogden Valley lured Sunday drivers to attempt the journey. However, the majority preferred the traditional horse and buggy. In the upper right can be seen the pipe carrying the city's water supply. From the Church Archives. Courtesy, The Church of Jesus Christ of Latter-day Saints

Below left

The Maxwell Agency in Ogden would soon be overshadowed by sales of the more popular Ford. USHS

Below

The advent of the automobile did not diminish Ogden's wagon and carriage business in the early years of the twentieth century. Asail Ipson continued a thriving trade at 2220 Washington Boulevard until World War I. Courtesy, Weber State College

the militia as well as policemen from both Ogden and Salt Lake City.

Ogden appeared as an armed camp. Initially there was much fear of the "Industrials," but soon it was apparent that many were sick and weak, and the community's sympathy turned toward Kelley's men. In addition to providing the men with food, some local residents formed a parade of protest, with banners and slogans denouncing the use of the militia. The Ogden *Standard* was particularly outspoken in its criticism of Governor Caleb West. Finally on April 11 the Industrial Army, under police and militia guard, marched from the Southern Pacific Railroad yards up Washington Boulevard while an Ogden band played "Marching Through Georgia." Kelley's Army moved peacefully out of Ogden to Uintah, where they boarded a Union Pacific train headed eastward.

Within a matter of months Ogden was again involved in labor unrest. During the summer of 1894 local railway workers voted to join with the American Railway Union in the nationwide Pullman strike. Strikers refused to allow any trains to move that included Pullman cars. Trains that were stopped in Ogden stranded 300 passengers. Some fighting broke out, but the most serious problem was a series of twelve separate fires, beginning on July 8, 1894, that caused a total of $135,000 damage in the heart of Ogden's business district. Although the charge was never proven, many Junction City residents believed the fires were started by union members. By July 13 the trains began to move as the federal government intervened to end the strike.

In spite of the problems associated with its sudden growth as the Junction City, citizens of Ogden have always enjoyed their recreation. In the nineteenth century summer activities were often held along the Ogden River at one of the groves, such as Jones', Kay's, or the Hermitage. In 1879 the Ogden Driving Park opened at Monroe Avenue and 20th Street for horse racing. Baseball has long been a favorite in Ogden, which was the site for the deciding game of the 1870 territorial championship between the Corinne city team and the Enneas from Salt Lake City. The Corinne team won 12 to 8. In 1871 the Ogden Echoes played Corinne for the territorial championship, losing the first game 81 to 9. The Echoes won the second game 54 to 38 but lost the third 65 to 31. Swimming was enjoyed at the Utah Hot Springs and at the Syra-

Left
A popular sylvan retreat for residents of Ogden was the Hermitage, located halfway up Ogden Canyon in Winslow's Grove. Boating and fishing were among the many attractions of the hotel, which was eventually destroyed by fire. Courtesy, Ogden Chamber of Commerce

Below
The pond at the Hermitage Hotel was photographed around the turn of the century. From the Church Archives. Courtesy, The Church of Jesus Christ of Latter-day Saints

Right
Elaborate floats mounted on wagons delighted the crowds in front of the Orpheum Theater during the 1896 Fourth of July parade. Courtesy, Ogden Chamber of Commerce

Left
The 1896 Fourth of July parade was a representative highlight of summer activities in nineteenth-century Ogden. Courtesy, Ogden Chamber of Commerce

Above
Civil War veterans of the Grand Army of the Republic (GAR) on 24th Street get ready to join the Memorial Day parade down Washington Boulevard. USHS

Left
Ogdenites gaze upon a Memorial Day parade passing the Boyle Furniture Company on dirt-packed Washington Boulevard. The marchers included representatives of the GAR, Masonic lodges, the Ogden Fire Department, the Knights of Pythius, and various civic groups. From the Heber H. Thomas Collection. Courtesy, Harold B. Lee Library, Brigham Young University

Above
The ride from the east end of 25th Street to Malan's Heights was "wild and woolly" and put guests in great appetite for the immense meals served at the resort. From the Browning Collection. Courtesy, Union Station

Above right
President William Howard Taft was an occasional visitor to Ogden. In the fall of 1909, he visited the city on his way to Salt Lake City to confer with western Republican leaders and meet the leaders of the Mormon Church. Courtesy, W. Mack Stuart

cuse Resort on the Great Salt Lake. The Ogden Rifle Club held weekly shoots at their course along the Weber River during the 1890s.

For a decade, beginning in 1894, Ogdenites and visitors enjoyed the hospitality of the Tim Malan family at the family-built rustic hotel called The Heights. The road wound up Taylor's Canyon to Malan's Basin, where a visitor could enjoy the sights with board and room costing only six dollars a week. Round-trip transportation from upper 25th Street was one dollar.

Ogden hosted Utah's first chautauqua, a program of education and entertainment for which townspeople would gather, often outdoors or in a large tent, to hear lectures by celebrities, scholars, and world travelers. Held in July 1911, this whole-hearted community effort included camping along the Ogden River, as well as lectures from "the men of the hour, the leading statesmen and orators." It was embellished also with singers, pageants, and outdoor demonstrations. Speeches touched on religion, history, geography, and evolution. Special attention was given to farming and agriculture, and junior chautauqua programs were organized for children. The success of this event made the Junction City a regular stop on the chautauqua circuit.

The railroad had brought culture as well as conflict to Ogden, prosperity as well as diversity. Ogdenites had learned to compromise in politics and to accommodate new inventions to old lifestyles. Commercial expansion and war in the twentieth century would change Ogden further.

Left
Enjoying a family gathering, the Belnaps pose around the turn of the century outside their home at 2155 Madison Avenue in Ogden. Courtesy, Richard C. Roberts

Right
During the election of 1912, Progressive party candidate Theodore Roosevelt stopped in Ogden to campaign and to visit the Hermitage resort. Roosevelt can be seen at the rear of a cavalcade of Sunday drivers, who prevailed upon him to pose with them at the mouth of Ogden Canyon. From the Browning Collection. Courtesy, Union Station

CHAPTER FOUR
OGDEN GOES TO WAR

There has long been a perception of Ogden as a community with a federal and military orientation. While not the predominant aspect, the U.S. government presence has been a strong influence on the economic and social history of the city. The procession of countless American soldiers through Ogden on the railroad, on their way to fight in the Spanish-American War, the Mexican Border Incident of 1916, World War I, and World War II, stands out in the memory of many long-time residents.

Ogden has contributed its share of soldiers to the procession, beginning in 1898. Batteries A and B of the Utah Artillery saw action in the Philippines, returning in August 1899 to a jubilant welcome at the depot from a crowd of 10,000. In 1916 Troop B, First Squadron, Utah Cavalry, was dispatched to the Mexican border to protect against raids by the revolutionist Pancho Villa. By March 1917 the last units had returned from patrol duty near Nogales, Arizona; many Ogden veterans of this campaign went on soon afterward to serve in World War I.

In World War I a number of Ogden volunteers and conscripts were assigned to the 362nd Regiment and other regiments of the 91st Division, which fought in the Argonne-Meuse campaign in France and in the Ypres-Lys sector in Belgium. Approximately sixty citizens of Ogden served in Battery B, 145th Field Artillery Regiment of Utah, which was an element of the 40th Division (Sunshine Division), made up of troops from California, Nevada, and Utah. The 145th Field Artillery trained at Camp Kearney, near San Diego, then shipped overseas to Camp De Souge, near Bordeaux. As the regiment prepared to move to the front lines, the armistice was declared. Ironically this unit was to receive the heroes' welcome on its return to Ogden. The combat veterans of the

In 1920 Ogden observed Armistice Day, a time to recall America's efforts in the "War to End All Wars." USHS

Right
Members of the Utah Battery fought during the waning days of the Spanish-American War. Subsequently, in February 1899 the Utah Battery saw action against the forces of Emilio Aguinaldo, the leader of the Filipino Insurrection. Here they engage units of Filipino infantry at Chinese Church, Manila. USHS

Opposite
Utah volunteers of Battery B stand by their field pieces during exercises at Camp Merritt, San Francisco, in preparation for shipping out to the Philippines during the Spanish-American War. The trees in the background are part of Golden Gate Park. USHS

Right
On August 19, 1899, the population of Ogden turned out to welcome the Utah Battery returning from the Philippines. From the Browning Collection. Courtesy, Union Station

Below
Utah cavalry patrolled the Mexican border near Nogales, Arizona, to deter Pancho Villa's irregulars from raiding into the United States. Courtesy, Richard C. Roberts

362nd Regiment were released from the Army at Fort Russell, Wyoming, and returned as private citizens.

The 145th Field Artillery Regiment arrived at the Ogden Depot on January 17, 1919. There was much concern on the part of Utah officials about the mixing of soldiers with the crowds, because of the threat of an influenza epidemic in the community. The orders were that the troops would march on parade—from the depot up 25th Street, along Washington Boulevard between 28th and 21st streets, and again down 25th Street—but that no crowds were to gather at the station and there would be no speaking with the troops, nor would the soldiers be allowed to break ranks. But the jubilation of the Ogden crowd altered the orders. At the depot, families and friends clamored to greet their returning soldiers, and these homecomings were left uninterrupted by officials. Governor Simon Bamberger and state officials led the 1,117-man regiment in the biggest military parade in the history of the city of Ogden. After the parade the soldiers returned to the train and proceeded to Logan, where they were mustered out of federal service.

In the period between World War I and World War II, several federal and military installations were established in the Ogden area. Several advantages—such as inland location (less vulnerable to possible enemy attacks than a coastal site), an

Opposite page
During World War I Ogden enthusiastically supported the numerous home-front programs. Gene Browning (right) and Cary Browning (left) urged Ogdenites to purchase Victory Bonds to finance the war effort. From the Browning Collection. Courtesy, Union Station

Below
In preparation for combat in France, the 145th Field Artillery completed a march from Camp Kearney, outside San Diego, to Poway Valley, south of Los Angeles, in six days, which was acclaimed as record time by the area commander. Courtesy, Richard C. Roberts

Above
Ogden advertising assured motorists that "you can get there from here." Courtesy, Ogden Chamber of Commerce

Left
Spectators survey the damage after the Arlington Hotel blaze in 1923, which gutted Washington Boulevard between 24th and 25th streets. The Egyptian Theatre later occupied this site. Courtesy, Mr. and Mrs. Lowell Rowse

Opposite page, top
Ogden welcomed the 145th Field Artillery upon its return from France in 1919 with the biggest military parade in the city's history. Courtesy, Richard C. Roberts

Opposite page, bottom
During the 1920s heavyweight champion Jack Dempsey, seen here at the Ogden Union Station, had a large following in Utah because of his Mormon origins and because his early career centered in the Ogden/Salt Lake City area. From the Browning Collection. Courtesy, Union Station

established railroad system, and a sufficient work force—did much to attract government interest, but another significant factor was the leadership of the community. The Ogden Chamber of Commerce was especially active in soliciting federal agencies to bring their business to Ogden, ensuring that needed land, equipment, and funds were available. Leading these efforts in the 1920s and 1930s were chairman of the Military Affairs Committee Frank M. Browning and chamber members Marriner Browning, E.G. Bennett, L.M. Nims, H.A. Benning, Val Browning, S.C. Powell, J.A. Howell, Ora Bundy, A.L. Levin, chamber president Heber Scowcroft, and chamber secretary E.J. Fjeldsted.

The Ogden Arsenal was the first military installation in the area. In early 1920 the War Department purchased approximately 1,200 acres in Sunset, six miles south of Ogden, and commenced construction. By 1923 there were thirty-five magazines for storing ammunition. An administration building and other service buildings, street and railroad access, and a water supply system had also been completed. The facility was neglected for several years, however, until a storm destroyed thirty of the magazines, causing damage estimated at $600,000.

In 1935 an appropriation of $300,000 went to the Works Progress Administration (WPA) to rehabilitate the depot, and in the following year a permanent crew was assigned to begin restoration and regular military work there. A bomb-loading plant was added for the Army and the Army Air Force. Between 1940 and 1942 the Ogden Arsenal was expanded to include facilities for loading and storing small-caliber artillery shells. At the height of World War II the arsenal served as a master depot for storing and shipping vehicles, ammunition, small arms and artillery pieces, and employed approximately 6,000 persons.

WPA and other federally sponsored projects had become especially important to Ogden during the 1930s as a traumatic experience for all America, the Great Depression, throttled the economy. Utah suffered earlier and more deeply from the downturn than parts of the nation that had greater economic diversification. Hard times in Utah had actually begun in the 1920s when adverse freight rates, the decline of markets for food products, the lack of expansion markets for processed minerals, and the virtual destruction of the sugar beet indus-

The Pingree National Bank, located on Washington Boulevard, was forced to close, a victim of the Great Depression. From the Ernst Dahline Collection. Courtesy, Mr. and Mrs. Lowell Rowse

try all combined to depress the state's economy. Utah fell ever deeper into economic decline during the 1930s.

Weber County, an agricultural region producing wheat and grains, cattle, sheep, truck-garden vegetables, and sugar beets, was particularly hard hit during this period. Ogden, with grain milling, stockyards and meat packing, canning, and a railroad industry that depended on transportation of those products, suffered the same fate. The spiral effect of the Depression had an impact on almost all aspects of Ogden and Weber County life.

Weber County agriculture felt the decline shortly after World War I. Overproduction by American farms and loss of government markets combined to produce disastrous effects. Mack S. Taft, in *The Great Depression in Weber County, Utah: An Exercise in Oral History,* interviewed farmers who remembered the hard times. J. Levi Beus of Hooper said, "the trouble was to get cash. Our potatoes just stayed in the pit. . . . " Beus also lost money on a herd of sheep, which he bought at the beginning of the Depression, as the price "went down and down, and they were very cheap. In fact, the by-products [company] wouldn't come and get them hardly." Vern C. Parker of Hooper, who raised chickens and sold eggs, had a hard time getting enough money to buy gas to take the eggs to market in his Model T Ford. Parker said, "we just couldn't pay our taxes with no money available. You couldn't borrow it; you couldn't sell an animal for anything. You'd have a nice cow that was worth between $50.00 and $60.00 and $75.00 and sell it for $10.00 or $15.00 or $20.00. . . . "

Farmers in Huntsville, in a meeting in November 1932, launched a campaign to get county commissioners, state legislators, and congressmen to take action to give them relief. "Is it fair," one farmer asked, "that we pay the same high taxes when it takes practically all that is raised on our farms to pay the taxes? Our land values have shrunk at least two-thirds. Our taxes remain the same. How long can we survive?"

Weber County led the way in organizing Utah farmers to obtain better tax rates, marketing practices, and prices for their commodities. The Farm Bureau, organized as early as 1916 with D.D. McKay of Huntsville as the president, federated in 1925 and assisted in the organization of other cooperatives, such as the Utah Canning Crops Growers Asso-

Above
Even the Depression could not dampen the
1931 New Year's Eve celebration at the Ogden Depot. USHS

Opposite page
Life in Ogden between the wars was a mon-
tage of everyday life in America—enjoying
watermelon (bottom right), listening to
afternoon serials on the radio (top), and
visiting the Jardine Juniper in nearby Logan Canyon (bottom left). Courtesy, Mr.
and Mrs. Lowell Rowse

ciation, Weber Central Dairy, Wool Marketing Committee,
and Utah Sugar Beet Cooperative Association. As bad as
conditions were for Weber County farmers, Mack Taft concluded from his studies that they were better off than most
others in the area. Generally the farm families were "fed,
clothed and cared for."

On August 31, 1931, the Ogden State Bank could not open
its doors. The fall of this major Ogden financial institution
shook the confidence of the local business world. Many farm
and business loans were lost. Foreclosures left herds of sheep
wandering untended on Ogden hillsides after the failure of
the bank.

Although there was no Federal Deposit Insurance Corporation then, eventually some 67 percent of bank losses were returned to the investors. In addition to the financial losses,
there were personal costs to reckon. Archie P. Bigelow, president of the Ogden State Bank, was economically and emo-
tionally destroyed by the bank failure. Cecil Tucker, court
clerk in the bankruptcy proceedings, recalled that during the
trial Bigelow, a prominent, respected businessman known for
generosity in his business dealings in Ogden, was asked on
the stand if he had any money. When Bigelow produced a
five-dollar bill from his pocket, the lawyer took it from him,
leaving the banker completely broke. Bigelow left Ogden for
California, where he died "shattered" and "heartbroken." The

In this circa 1938 photograph, crowds cheer on competitors in the local soapbox derby. Courtesy, Ogden Chamber of Commerce

An advertisement in a corner drugstore window reminds the onlooker of the state of the economy at the time this Depression-era photograph was taken. Courtesy, Mr. and Mrs. Lowell Rowse

Pingree National Bank also failed. But the Commercial Security Bank and the First Security Bank Corporation weathered the depositor run caused by the closure of the Ogden State Bank. William Budge, who worked for Commercial Security Bank, remembered the people who came in and wanted their money: "We stayed open. We didn't close at the regular banking hours; we stayed open just as long as the people came in." The Commercial Security Bank prepared scrip to be issued if the government so ordered, but the currency system stabilized in time.

Businessmen George T. Frost, Brad Paul, Stanley Robbins, and Hyrum Wheelwright have spoken of these difficult times. Frost recalled starting a Hudson automobile dealership on the corner of 27th Street and Washington Boulevard with only a $250 investment. A little money went a long way in buying equipment and services. Mr. and Mrs. Brad Paul ran a small grocery store, remaining open from eight o'clock in the morning until eleven o'clock at night to break even. In addition Paul worked a second job to keep his family afloat. Stanley Robbins managed the David H. Peery and the Fred J. Kiesel estates. The Peery enterprises included the Egyptian Theatre, the Ogden Theatre, and the White City Ballroom, which made a good profit during the Depression years by holding drawings for expensive prizes. During the summer months crowds of up to 5,000 people attended the White City Ballroom dances. Where else could they be entertained at a nominal price, relieve their minds of the cares of the real world, and have a chance to win a new car? Hyrum Wheelwright said that during the depths of the Depression the Wheelwright lumber business suffered badly, surviving only because of surpluses built up earlier. In February 1932, total lumber sales in all of Weber County amounted to only $7,000, and the Wheelwrights' business accounted for $2,800 of that amount. In some months, however, they went into debt at a rate of $500 a month.

In the professions, too, the Depression was a difficult time. Attorney Ira Huggins recalled that "there was plenty of legal business, but there was no money to pay fees with." David J. Wilson said, "I think everybody ran into the question of collections. Of course if the people didn't have the money, they couldn't pay you. So many of us carried a great many unpaid fees on our books. These never were paid . . . . But in the question of foreclosures, we were paid by the institution that employed us, and there was no difficulty on that score."

Medical doctors faced the same situation: having plenty of work, but collecting less than 30 percent of their fees. Physicians remained true to their Hippocratic oath during the Depression, among them Dr. Frank K. Bartlett. "I was a young man, anxious to build up my business, and if anyone called me at three o'clock in the morning, if he lived across the tracks, I went whether I got my money or not. A lot of people didn't get anything to me because they didn't have it. But that didn't make any difference." Dr. Junior Edward Rich, son of Dr. Edward I. Rich (father and son served in Weber County as physicians for a span of seventy-one years), stated that the Depression was a trying time for doctors, because they had continuing costs to meet while fees dropped off radically. "In fact, some months I had difficulty paying my nurse and paying my overhead."

Thus it was among professional people, independent businessmen, and farmers, but it was the wage earner and laborer who suffered the most in Ogden. In December 1929 the Ogden *Standard* reported on the plight in the homes of working families: "They are homes that do not know the continual pinch of poverty, but which, through sickness or sudden lack of employment, are in need."

Curtis II. Marshall, who worked for the American Pack and Provisions Company, remembered that "sometimes we only got four days a week during the depression years. . . . We did cut down to probably 75 percent of our usual volume, which showed that people had cut down on their meat consumption." Mrs. Curtis Marshall remembered "making over old clothes" for the family. "Lots of times we'd go to the Deseret Industries and get old clothes, even other people's old clothes, and . . . make them into clothes for our children . . . . We'd make a big pot of soup or a pot of beans, and we could feed them a lot cheaper than feeding them on beef steak, that's for sure."

Angus C. Richardson, who was one of the fortunate in being employed throughout the Depression, said he lived within his means, attending the movies for entertainment. He went on Thursday nights because that was Grocery Night. "They used to give away groceries, and those theaters were just filled to the top [with people] trying to win those groceries. . . . A lot of people that went would just hope and pray, and they depended on something like that." Even those who did not have steady work "always found enough money to buy a ticket to the show and they killed two birds with one stone. They had a chance for a little entertainment and they had an opportunity of getting their groceries, not for a week, but for two or three weeks. We used to go to the dances all the time, and they had good crowds. They used to have a prize dance and give away candy and things of that sort to induce you to come."

Generally, railroad workers with seniority were employed throughout the Depression, but part-time workers and those with fewer years of service were laid off when the volume of business declined. Thor Blair, newsstand agent at the Ogden Depot, remembered that during the 1930s the trains were "sporadically" ridden by "gaunt men led by a faint hope of finding some employment." A friend told him, "I've been riding this railroad for many, many years and that's the first

Torn down in 1942-1943 to make room for the present Municipal Building, Ogden's old City Hall was constructed in 1888-1889 from stone quarried at Thistle in Spanish Fork Canyon. From the Church Archives. Courtesy, The Church of Jesus Christ of Latter-day Saints

time in my life that I have had a private car on a regular ticket."

People made major changes in their life plans and took new directions because of the Depression. Joseph W. Brewer, leaving the University of Chicago because of a lack of money to continue his education, came home to work in his father's dairy equipment business. As business dropped off, Joe Brewer began to carry automobile tires in the store. The tire business increased, and Brewer later organized the J.W. Brewer Tire Company with outlets throughout the Intermountain West. A similar story comes from J. Willard Marriott. Helping his father with a sheep drive in the winter of 1924-1925 made him realize the desperate condition of the sheep industry in Weber County and led young Marriott to invest in an A & W Root Beer franchise in Washington, D.C. This was the beginning of a business career that culminated in the Marriott Corporation.

As the Depression deepened, city and county budget cuts threatened repayment of the Echo Dam debt, the Ogden Stadium project, completion of the El Monte golf course, and construction of the Ogden Airport—all of which represented much-needed jobs. In addition, the budgets called for a 10 percent reduction in appointive city and county employee wages and a slight reduction in the county poor fund, which was under more pressure all the time. The Utah state budget was not sufficient to take up the slack.

Church relief was helpful. Each denomination tried to take care of its members, but resources were scant. The bishops of the Church of Jesus Christ of Latter-day Saints provided some local relief. In the 17th Ward, Bishop Earl Stanley Paul devised a wood-gathering project to keep men employed and to provide fuel for homes that would otherwise be unheated. The unemployed men of the ward were also contracted as a group to harvest fruit on a share basis, and in that way they were able to get fruit for their families. They also harvested beets for cash. The Mormon welfare program did not come into effect throughout the Church until after 1936, and its benefits were realized late in the Depression.

Marriner S. Eccles, successful financier and president of the First Security Corporation, left Ogden to serve as Franklin D. Roosevelt's chairman of the Federal Reserve Board and as a major formulator of the deficit spending and

government-assistance approach of the New Deal. In Ogden the relief programs of the federal administration came none too soon: the Federal Emergency Relief Administration (FERA), Public Works Administration (PWA), Works Progress Administration (WPA), National Youth Administration (NYA), and Civilian Conservation Corps (CCC).

FERA brought relief to needy families in Ogden City and Weber County. A study of 169 families in the program showed that they experienced significant improvements in terms of health and having the necessities to survive on. The CCC had several projects in Weber County, including the building of recreational campsites and roads in Ogden Canyon and up to Monte Cristo. The CCC also developed the Ogden Bird Refuge. Many city and county youths continued their studies at Ogden High, Weber High, and Weber College because of the National Youth Administration work programs.

More significant for employment purposes, however, were

Above
During the New Deal era thirteen federal projects were undertaken in Weber County, including Ogden High School and the Municipal Building, which can be seen rising up behind the old Ogden City Hall. From the Browning Collection. Courtesy, Union Station

Opposite page, top
Construction of Pine View Dam was begun in 1936 to provide supplementary irrigation to more than 60,000 acres between Brigham City and South Ogden. Courtesy, Mr. and Mrs. Lowell Rowse

Opposite
The Civilian Conservation Corps aided in the construction of Pine View Dam and the irrigation pipeline. Pictured is the CCC camp that housed these workers. Courtesy, Jerome Bernstein

A bleak January day culminated a dream for Ogden area boosters, as ground was broken at Hill Field. Courtesy, Ogden Chamber of Commerce

the projects of the Public Works Administration and the Works Progress Administration. There were thirteen federal projects in Weber County during the New Deal era. The Public Works Administration employed local workers in 1933 for construction of a new U.S. Forest Service building at Adams and 25th Street. Since 1908 the Ogden office had served as the headquarters of District Four, which encompassed the territory of the Intermountain states. Other major construction projects undertaken by the PWA included the twelve-story Municipal Building at 25th Street and Washington Boulevard and the Ogden High School on Harrison Boulevard. Built on a cost-sharing basis with local and federal funding, the school was called the "Million Dollar High School" because of its price tag and because of its fine construction, which was of brick with terra cotta trim.

The PWA also supported the building of the Pine View Reservoir, which provided water for Weber and south Box Elder counties and hydroelectric power. Completed in 1937, this project cost a total of $4 million. Also significant were the road built through North Ogden Pass to the upper Ogden Valley, the construction of a rock wall in Ogden Canyon, work in several public parks, and a Federal Writers' project, which produced a survey of public records and a *History of Ogden* by Dale Morgan. These various projects represented a considerable investment of the federal government in the Ogden area. But, as in other parts of the United States, it was the build-up for World War II that brought real prosperity back to the area.

Above
When its construction was completed, the Utah General Depot was the largest of the country's eight general depots supplying the armed services. USHS

Left
During World War II the Utah General Depot employed 7,000 Ogden-area residents. The depot stored munitions and supplied the armed forces with a galaxy of materials, ranging from C-rations to trucks. The depot also housed the only U.S. Army Repair Railway Shop in the United States. Courtesy, Ogden Chamber of Commerce

Above
While encamped at Cape Gloucester, New Britain, in preparation for landing in the Philippines, Ogden men serving with the 40th Division encountered terrible winds, often of hurricane strength, and volcanic dust that penetrated every pore. Courtesy, Richard C. Roberts

Above right and opposite page
In action against Japanese forces during the Philippine Islands campaign, men of the 222nd Field Artillery from the Ogden area fired more than 13,000 rounds from their 155-millimeter howitzers in artillery engagements on Luzon, Panay, and Negros islands. Courtesy, Richard C. Roberts

Hill Air Force Base was established in nearby north Davis County, thanks to the determined efforts of the Ogden Chamber of Commerce, which arranged for a substantial donation of property for the base. Initial construction was begun in 1938 by the WPA. The Ogden Air Depot served as a major supply and maintenance depot for air bases in Utah and the Pacific Northwest and as an auxiliary depot controlled by Sacramento Air Depot until 1943, when it was upgraded as a separate command. At that time the mission of the base shifted from distribution of supplies to repair of aircraft engines, parachutes, radios, bombsights, and other components and winterization of aircraft such as the P-39, P-40, and B-24 Liberator. By 1943 approximately 22,000 people were employed at the base, a large share of them women who performed sheet metal work, welding, and aircraft engine repair.

Defense Depot Ogden, first known as Utah General Depot, was established as a general warehousing facility in 1940. Eventually it became the largest quartermaster depot in the United States, with 5 million square feet of enclosed warehouse space and 13 billion square feet of open storage space. At its peak in 1943 the depot employed 7,700 civilians and shipped 200 carloads of materiel per day to support the war effort.

In 1942 the Clearfield Naval Supply Depot was constructed twelve miles south of Ogden. Its mission as a conduit of sup-

The Ogden railroad yards handled as many as 120 passenger trains each day during the war. Courtesy, Ogden Chamber of Commerce

plies to West Coast and Pacific Fleet stations made Clearfield one of the most significant inland bases. By the end of World War II the base required a civilian work force of 7,600 to handle an inventory of more than 500,000 different items with a value of almost $600 million—nearly three times the total value of all assessed property in the state of Utah at the time.

Prior to World War II the National Guard had several units stationed in Ogden: the 115th Medical Detachment; 115th Ordnance Company; Battery B, 145th Field Artillery; Battery B, 222nd Field Artillery; and the 222nd Field Artillery Band. These National Guard units (approximately 324 men from Ogden) went on active service for a one-year training period beginning March 3, 1941; this turned out to be a call up for the duration of the war. Most of Ogden's National Guard troops served in the Pacific.

After the declaration of war, Weber County citizens entered all the services and served in all the major areas of combat. A total of 7,723 Weber County residents (4,765 from Ogden) were in uniform during the war; when it was over, 161 were counted among the dead or missing.

On the home front more than 50,000 civilians worked at federal and military installations in the Ogden area. The railroads, too, operated at full capacity. The Ogden depot handled as many as 120 passenger trains each day on its seventeen tracks. Angus Hansen, a Union Pacific car man and welder, recalled the crowds that seemed to jam the station continually: "I don't think you could go down to the depot any time, night or day, that you didn't find that depot full of people . . . . " Railroad worker Tom Zito remembered soldiers who were so tired from traveling on the trains they would "just go outside in the summertime and drop anywhere they could get a little sleep . . . . For a long time during the war [there was] a passenger train in and out of the depot every five minutes around the clock." Lamar Belnap was another eyewitness as to how the war years affected the city: "These troop trains would come in, the soldiers had been confined to the trains and were anxious to get out of it. They'd head up 25th Street and find a bottle or drink."

The hectic railroad travel was interrupted by tragedy on December 31, 1944. On that date the "Pacific Limited," as it stopped for a freight train, was struck from the rear by a

The Pacific Limited wreck on the Lucin
Cutoff made a tragedy of New Year's Eve,
1944. The injured, including a large number
of servicemen in transit, were brought to
Ogden for medical treatment. From the
Browning Collection. Courtesy, Union
Station

fast-moving mail train at Bagley, seventeen miles west of Ogden on the Lucin Cutoff track; 48 died and 79 were injured. As the injured were brought into Ogden for medical treatment, the community did what it could to help and afterward mourned for those who lost their lives in this disaster.

Community sentiment during the war was not always as kind. Japanese residents of Weber County, including several farmers and business people, suffered financial loss, public humiliation, and violation of their constitutional rights. Many Japanese-Americans, upon being released from relocation camps after the war, settled in Weber County and made significant contributions to the community.

A number of Italians, former prisoners of war, also settled in the Ogden area when peace came. Approximately 7,000 POWs were incarcerated at camps at Hill Air Force Base and Ogden General Depot. The prisoners worked in various farm, construction, and food-processing jobs in Weber, Davis, and Box Elder counties. When Italy became an ally to the United States in 1943, the Italians performed work supporting the war effort. Some returned to Ogden, married Ogden girls, and established their homes in the community.

In several ways the war years had a tremendous impact on Ogden. Those years brought to a climax the era of federal and military involvement in the economy of the area, tipping the balance from agriculture to industry and commerce. It might be said that during the war years Ogden left its age of innocence and entered into a new and more challenging age.

During World War II thousands of German and Italian prisoners of war were held at the Utah General Depot. Some were put to work as farm laborers, while others worked in local canning factories. (The Italian POWs organized an orchestra that performed at the Ogden railroad depot on Sundays.) USHS

CHAPTER FIVE
OGDEN'S SECOND CENTURY

The end of World War II brought Ogden to its centennial and a new phase of its history. Railroads, which had carried Ogden to a summit as the Junction City, experienced an inexorable decline in passenger business. The resulting cutbacks in operations and facilities, combined with a shift of Weber County land-use from agriculture toward residential development, forced Ogden to search for new industries to keep the growing population employed.

In 1940 Ogden had a population of 43,688; in 1950—57,112; in 1960—70,797; in 1970—69,478. The 1980 census showed a drop to 64,407. As the population increased, residential areas expanded to the city limits with development of Nob Hill on the east, Eyrie Meadow and Ron Clare Village on the north, and Nelson Park Addition, College Heights, Forest Green Estates Subdivision, and Shadow Valley on the south.

The drop in the population of Ogden from 1970 to 1980 reflected a shift from the city to the suburbs, as county population went up from 126,278 in 1970 to 151,700 in 1980. As new housing developments flourished, areas that prior to World War II had been small agricultural communities underwent a change that affected the agricultural base of the regional economy. In Weber County in 1964 there were 927 farms; in 1969 there were 765 farms; in 1974 there were 712 farms.

One of the critical changes in Ogden's economy after World War II accompanied the severe erosion of passenger railroad service. In 1944 the railroads were running 120 passenger trains through the station every twenty-four hours. The Korean War period maintained some of that activity, and as late as 1959 railroad worker Clarence Werner remembered that there were still thirty to fifty trains a day going out of Ogden: "Any direction you wanted to go, you could catch a passenger out of here." Within a few years, however, passen-

At midnight Junction City shone like a beacon. From the Browning Collection. Courtesy, Union Station

Left
Much of the Ogden area's dairy production was processed at Cream O' Weber, which has since been replaced by the new state office complex. USHS

Above
Harold George, tour conductor, shows the multitude of passenger trains that passed through Ogden's Union Station in its glory days. Photo by Barbara Parsons Bernstein

A CENTURY IN THE LIVESTOCK TRADE

Ogden was the livestock capital of the Intermountain West for more than a century. Millions of head of cattle, sheep, and hogs were bought and sold annually at the bustling Ogden Livestock Yards and processed by local slaughterhouses and packing plants. Full trains of livestock cars had top traffic priority on railroads.

No more. Giant stock trucks now handle transportation. Family pastures have, for the most part, been replaced by mass-production feedlots. Only a couple of small slaughter facilities remain in or near Ogden. The Ogden Livestock Yards have auctions just once a week.

That same pattern has been repeated across the country. Chicago's yards, once the nation's busiest, have long been closed. So have those in many other metropolitan centers.

Miles Goodyear was Ogden's

first white settler and also the area's first livestockman, raising cattle and horses.

As pioneer livestock herds increased, Ogden youths found employment during the summers watching over the animals that browsed on community pastures. Boys were paid one dollar per animal each month. In the early era meat dealers included Chauncey W. West, Matthew Biel, Robert Hall, the Wright brothers, William Kendall, Henry Hill, and Ambrose Greenwell.

Opening of the transcontinental and north-south railroads accelerated the growth of the industry: Ogden, as Junction City, was the logical place for transshipment of livestock. Commission buyers opened offices in Ogden, and large-scale packing plants were built. The first U.S. Cattlemen's Congress was held in Ogden on April 29, 1892.

Ogden's Mayor Harmon Peery built the Ogden Livestock show into an event of major importance, making the city a center for Western stockmen. From the Browning Collection. Courtesy, Union Station

The annual Golden Spike National Livestock Show drew so many visitors to Ogden that the Golden Spike Coliseum was constructed in 1926 at a cost of $100,000 to house it and other industry events.

Garth Peck of Ogden, one of Utah's most active livestock buyers, remembers well the peak—and decline—of the industry to which he devoted his life. His father Leo and uncle Roy established Peck Brothers' Livestock Company in 1922. Garth, who had worked in the stockyards as a boy, joined the firm upon graduation from college.

"At its prime Ogden was the twelfth largest livestock yard in the country," Garth Peck recalled in a 1985 interview. "As many as three million sheep a year went through here, along with thousands of cattle and hogs. I drove 150,000 miles a year in Utah, Nevada, Idaho, and Wyoming buying stock. It was exciting. I loved it. So did my father . . . . "

Replacement of the railroad cars by trucks as the primary transportation method was inevitable, he explained, because the trucks could load livestock right at the farmyards and unload at the feedlots or packing plants.

Commission agents closed their operations in the Ogden Livestock Yards on December 18, 1967. Thus deals by "private treaty"—a direct negotiation between seller and buyer, rather than a public auction—came to an end at that facility as Garth Peck completed the last sale, a pair of Holsteins.

The Weber Livestock Auction Company was formed to conduct Tuesday-only auctions. Manager Richard Widdison and associates handle 600 to 700 head of cattle and 80 to 100 hogs weekly; during the fall 400 to 500 sheep add to the business at each auction.

Despite the decline of the yards, livestock is still a multimillion dollar industry in Weber County. Scores of farmers still breed and raise stock. Many calves and lambs are sold to out-of-state feeders. At Hyrum, Utah, about fifty miles north of Ogden, large feeding and packing operations—Tri-Miller specializing in hogs and E.A. Miller and Sons in cattle—supply a significant percentage of Utah consumers with meat. Miller trucks, loaded with processed meat or with live animals, are a common sight on the highways of the West.

In the era when Ogden was the "Hog Butcher of Northern Utah," the Douglass Brothers Meat Market at 2321 Washington Boulevard displayed dressed poultry and game and hung freshly slaughtered carcasses of pork and beef. The shopper chose a cut, and the butcher sawed it off on the spot. From the Heber H. Thomas Collection. Courtesy, Harold B. Lee Library, Brigham Young University

After hauling cattle to eastern markets, these trucks usually are filled with hogs on the return run.

Lynn Richardson, recently retired as division vice-president of marketing at the First Security Bank, recalls the best years of the Ogden Livestock Yards and the Golden Spike National Livestock Show. "In the early 1960s we figured that the livestock industry brought $40 million to $45 million a year to Ogden," Richardson calculated. "That would be around $120 million a year at today's prices. Ranchers bringing stock to the market would load their trucks with hay, grain, fencing, clothes, food, machinery and gas—all bought in Ogden—for the drive back home. Livestock formed Ogden's financial backbone."

—Murray M. Moler

ger service was discontinued by the private companies because of overwhelming competition from automobile, bus, and air travel. On May 1, 1971, the U.S. government-sponsored National Passenger Railroad Corporation (Railpax), which later became AMTRAK, took over the management of passenger service nationwide, curtailing many existing routes. Only limited traffic came through Ogden.

With the drop in business the railroad companies were forced to lay off or transfer many of their operations. In 1970 the Union Pacific closed its Ogden laundry plant, razed the commissary building at 25th Street and Wall Avenue, and shut down its telephone-switchboard facility. When the station ticket office was turned over to Railpax, the Railway Express Agency was demolished, and all but two of the passenger-line tracks were torn up and removed. Marking the end of an era, in 1972 the long familiar Barkalow Brothers newsstand and snack bar was closed down.

In the same year the Union Pacific-Southern Pacific freight office building, located near 24th and Wall Avenue, was torn down, one of many facilities to fall victim as the railroad companies streamlined and modernized over the years. The roundhouses, which had handled the steam engines, were no longer needed and they had been destroyed. Many of the repair shops were no longer necessary because improved equipment required less maintenance and because of reduced traffic. The ice plant at 33rd Street and Riverdale was obsolete because of new refrigerator cars. In 1972 the railroads built a "run around track" that allowed traffic to pass through Ogden to Salt Lake without stopping, minimizing the importance of the Ogden facility.

Many prominent community leaders and residents who had seen or had been involved in the history of railroading in Ogden recognized that the same fate might be in store for the Union Station. Their efforts to prevent the loss of this historic structure were successful. On October 21, 1978, with proper ceremony the Union Station was dedicated by Ogden City and the railroad companies to serve as a multi-purpose community center. While continuing to house the station for AMTRAK and Southern Pacific and Union Pacific offices, this community center now also contains the Browning Theatre, the Browning Firearms Museum, and a historic model-railroad display, and it affords space for development as a commercial facility with businesses and shops. In this way the Ogden Station remains an important monument reflecting the history and traditions of the Ogden community.

Trends in industries associated with railroad traffic were keenly felt in the Junction City. For example, meat-packing companies began to consolidate operations in plants on the West Coast and in the Midwest, obtaining their livestock near their plants or using trucks for transportation. There was no longer any need to ship livestock by rail along the routes that passed through Ogden; thus the Ogden Livestock Yards, which had been used to feed and water stock in transit, lost that business and closed on January 31, 1971. In April 1973 the Southern Pacific hauled its last load of sheep to the winter range.

Meat-packing in Ogden was another casualty of the industry-wide shift to other areas. On November 14, 1970, Swift and Company closed its local plant, taking approximately 1,000 jobs out of the Ogden economy. Also shutting down during the 1970s were Wilson and Company and William C. Parke and Sons. These blows to the livestock and meat-packing business in Ogden had the effect of devaluing the annual Golden Spike National Livestock Show. Begun in 1918 as the Ogden Livestock Show, this event grew in importance through the years. In 1923 the Golden Spike Coliseum was built to accommodate as many as 3,000 entries of the best breeds of cattle, sheep, and horses from fifteen states and Canada. By the 1970s it had lost its national appeal, becoming a local show and auction.

Additional pressure on the economy of modern Ogden resulted from the loss of major businesses originally established in the heyday of the railroad, among them the Scowcroft industries and the Shupe-Williams Candy Company. The sugar manufacturing ended in 1941 with the closing of Ogden's Amalgamated Sugar Company plant, though the main offices remained. The canning industry declined with the county's agricultural base. The American Can Company factory, located at 20th Street and Lincoln Avenue since 1914, closed its doors in December 1979.

Government and military facilities and their contractors continued to play an important role in Ogden's economy. The Ogden Arsenal doubled its work force during the Korean War to 3,000, producing armaments. In a 1955 reorganization the

Above
Hill Air Force Base has played host to myriad aircraft, from RB-71s to mock-ups of the space shuttle Columbia. Courtesy, Ogden Chamber of Commerce

Right
As a major logistics center, Hill Air Force Base makes a significant contribution to employment in the state. Aircraft and missiles are serviced at the base. Shown here is an F-4 production line. Courtesy, Hill Air Force Base Historical Archives

Arsenal was disbanded; its munitions inventory, valued at $17 million, was moved to Hill Air Force Base, and its ordnance functions were transferred to the Tooele Army Depot and Defense Depot Ogden.

Hill AFB maintained a significant place in the nation's military establishment, with increased activity during the Korean and Vietnam conflicts. After World War II civilian employment dropped to 2,300 but rose to more than 16,000 in 1952, when an expansion and modernization program was initiated. The Cold War era expanded the mission of Ogden Air Materiel Area to worldwide scope and stabilized the work force at approximately 12,000 people.

After 1957 missiles became an important part of Hill AFB operations. To carry out these responsibilities a $3 million facility was constructed on the base. In 1964 the Department of Defense authorized another expansion, which added some 5,500 civilians to the payroll and made Hill the largest employer in the Ogden area. In 1981 there were 19,260 civilians employed at Hill in support of the Atlas, Titan, Minuteman, and other missile programs and the fighter-interceptors of the Air Force and Air Force Reserve, including the F-4, and F-16.

Defense Depot Ogden continued its important contributions to the military after World War II. During the Korean War the depot shipped an average of 37,000 tons of war materiel per month and employed around 4,000 people. In 1981 the work force was 1,500 employees.

In 1963 the Clearfield Naval Supply Depot was turned into a private development as the Freeport Center, a seven-million-square-foot manufacturing and distribution facility with approximately seventy major companies housed in more than sixty spacious buildings.

Hill AFB's assignment in missile defense brought several manufacturers to Ogden. The first of these was the Marquardt Corporation, a pioneer in high-performance ramjet engines. In 1956-1957, Marquardt spent $3 million to construct a 250,000 square-foot production plant (now occupied by Volvo-White Truck Corporation). At its peak in 1959 the company employed 1,700 workers in the production of ramjet engines to power the Bomarc missile. As this missile was phased out, Marquardt secured other contracts, notably for production of the rocket nozzle for the nose cone of the Polaris missile and control rockets for the Apollo vehicles in the space program. Marquardt also established the Air Force-Marquardt Jet Laboratory at Little Mountain, fifteen miles west of Ogden. This test facility, completed in 1959 at a cost of $14 million, employed some 175 persons at the site.

In 1961 Thiokol Chemical Corporation moved into its new $335,000 offices at its Aerospace Center in Ogden. This center was built to coordinate the firm's work on the Atlas ICBM and later the Minuteman missile programs, which included construction and testing at a site twenty-seven miles west of Brigham City. In 1962 Thiokol established at Ogden the Astro-Met Division to direct data-gathering probes of the upper atmosphere for such clients as the Atomic Energy Commission.

In 1960 the Boeing Company of Seattle constructed a missile operation in the west section of Hill Air Force Base, in the area of the old Ogden Arsenal. Named Air Force Plant 77 this $12 million project required the modification of fifty-seven buildings and construction of nine new buildings. The plant assembled Minuteman missiles for deployment to sites in Wyoming, Montana, North and South Dakota, and Missouri. In 1963 Boeing employed 900 Utah workers but later cut back to 150 workers.

Federal employment in Ogden gained again by the establishment of an Internal Revenue Service branch. In December

In 1979 the energy crisis and heating cutbacks had an impact even on the Ogden IRS Service Center. The fragile computers were kept at prescribed temperatures, but the employees felt the bite and had to bundle up. Photo by Barbara Parsons Bernstein

Opposite page
As the "melting pot" of Utah, Ogden continues to grow and improve by assimilating what is good from every part of the world. Here new citizens are welcomed in naturalization ceremonies.

Left
Heirs to the American dream, Melvin Dummar and his wife Bonnie assumed an "American Gothic" pose on the porch of their Ogden home while hoping that the country's ultimate rich uncle, Howard Hughes, had remembered them in his will.

Below left
The proposed Equal Rights Amendment occupied the hearts and minds of Ogden citizens and was given a thorough airing in the community. Pictured is a pro-ERA demonstration in front of the Municipal Building. Photos by Barbara Parsons Bernstein

1956, the IRS began development of the Western Internal Revenue Center at the Utah General Depot (later known as Defense Depot Ogden). By the end of 1957 there were 360 employed at this Western Service Center, which processed individual tax returns from eight Western states. As this operation expanded, construction of a second IRS building was completed in early 1970 at 1200 West 12th Street. With this new complex, in addition to Building 3-B at Defense Depot Ogden, the IRS Service Center makes a major contribution to the Ogden economy, employing up to 3,900 workers, almost half on a full-time year-round basis. The other half are employed seasonally to process tax returns. In its first twenty-five years of operation the IRS Center processed over 358 million tax returns and put more than $525 million into the local economy in salary and local purchases.

By the 1950s it was evident that changing economic times had left Ogden overly dependent on government projects. Business and community leaders resolved to build a sound economic base in the private sector, attracting industries that could keep pace with the rapidly changing economic world. Several community organizations participated in realizing this goal.

A leader in this movement was the Ogden Chamber of Commerce (now known as the Ogden Area Chamber of Commerce). The chamber had played an important role prior to World War II in attracting military and government agencies to Ogden; from the 1950s onward it spearheaded the drive to bring in new private industry. Today the chamber has a membership of some 800 Ogden business and industrial organizations. Among its councils and committees are the Committee of 100, which raises money for various chamber projects; the Spikers, a group of ambassadors for the community; the Military Affairs Committee; the Women in Management Committee; and the Education Committee, which participates in various school and college projects.

In 1969 the Chamber of Commerce formed a committee to investigate the possibility of developing an industrial park in Weber County. After a study of similar projects in Denver and Wichita Falls, the decision was made to raise money for its construction. In just twenty-two weeks the Ogden Industrial Development Fund climbed to $1,320,900 with donations from more than 500 firms and individuals who supported this

Political upheavals and economic dislocations may disturb Ogden, but it remains a community where neighbors will lend a helping hand. Photo by Barbara Parsons Bernstein

plan "to finance the rebirth of Ogden's economic growth." On November 9, 1971, the Ogden Industrial Development Corporation was created to oversee the distribution of the monies. Ground-breaking ceremonies for the Weber County Industrial Park took place on June 28, 1972, on a 476-acre tract of land in northwest Weber County. In August 1972 the Bradley Corporation of Menomonee Falls, Wisconsin, became the first company to decide to build in the park, constructing an 80,000-square-foot heating and plumbing manufacturing facility. Since that time the industrial park has attracted several important companies. With the development of Kimberly-Clarke's $100 million plant for manufacturing baby-care products, the industrial park has filled nearly to capacity.

Since its inception on January 2, 1964, the Weber County Industrial Development Bureau (now known as the Weber Industrial Development Corporation) has been instrumental in the relocation of several new industries to the industrial park, including Bourns, Inc., an electronics firm that manufactures potentiometers for computers; Parker-Bertea Corporation, manufacturer of hydraulic flight-controls; Pacific Chromalox Corporation, producer of electric heating elements; Vermont American Corporation, distributor of power and hand tools; and Aviation Materials Management, Inc. (AVMAT), supplier of aviation equipment.

Other Weber County locations also attracted important business, such as Great Salt Lake Minerals and Chemicals Corp.; Williams International (producer of jet engines); Colorado Milling Company (flour milling); Jetway (passenger loading bridges); Levolor Lorentzen, Inc. (window blinds); IOMEGA Corporation (disc-drive subsystems for computers); Thiokol—Utah Division (flares and auto air bags); and Western Zirconium Corporation, a division of Westinghouse that prepares metals used in the nuclear power and chemical industries.

After 1975 the Ogden Commercial and Industrial Park, managed by the Ogden Business Development Department, further broadened the economic base of the city, providing sites for Golden State Casting, which manufactures precision castings for aircraft, firearms, and other commercial uses; Kremco, which does heavy steel work mainly for oil rig equipment; Young Electric Sign Company; Beehive Bottling; Pacific Intermountain Express; Interwest Veterinary Supply;

Halverson Plumbing; Mountain Bell; Wells Cargo: and Richards Sheet Metal.

The success in bringing new industry to Ogden was due not only to the efforts of the Chamber of Commerce, the Weber County Industrial Development Corporation, and the Ogden Industrial Development Corporation, but also to many other community groups supporting the development of new business and employment opportunities, in addition to cultural and civic improvement programs. Among these groups were Golden Spike Empire, Inc., which was established in 1969 with the objective of promoting local tourism, and the Junior League of Ogden, founded in 1953. The Junior League has a long history of community service, with antecedents in the Martha Society (1926 to 1934) and the Welfare League of Ogden (1934 to 1953). The Junior League has supported projects such as the Volunteer Service Bureau, Golden Hours Center, Community Arts Council, Union Station, Nature Center, Family Support Center, and Positive Image for Ogden Committee. Other community-oriented organizations include the Kiwanis, Rotary, Lions, Elks, and Exchange clubs.

Several public officials have worked to answer the needs of the community. Among the notable Weber County commissioners are Boyd Storey and Robert A. Hunter, who took the lead in programs to promote county growth. Harmon W. Peery, the flamboyant "Cowboy Mayor," used the Pioneer Day Rodeo to draw attention to Ogden during his two terms in office (1942-1943 and 1948-1949). The administration of Mayor Bart Wolthius, from 1966 to 1973, emphasized integration of ethnic groups into the mainstream of the community as well as developing support for industrial growth and downtown revitalization. The Marshall White Center and the industrial park were major projects of his era. A. Stephen Dirks, mayor from 1973 to 1983, counted as his major achievement the "Renaissance of Ogden," which stressed community development, housing rehabilitation, and completion of the Ogden Mall and the Hilton Hotel. Mayor Robert A. Madsen, elected in 1983, uses "Ogden Now" as a motto for economic growth and revitalization of the downtown district.

Weber State College has been another factor in Ogden's growth and progress. Established in 1889 as a Mormon Church Academy, the school became a state-supported junior college in 1933. In the 1950s the institution began its move

Preacher, legislator, grocer, restauranteur, columnist, and barbecue-sauce inventor, the Reverend Robert Harris has focused public attention on many causes as one of Ogden's most noted social activists.

A. Stephen Dirks, who served four terms as mayor and promoted the "Renaissance of Ogden," greets Thomas P. "Tip" O'Neill during the House Speaker's visit to Ogden in 1980. Photos by Barbara Parsons Bernstein

Governor Scott Matheson presents an award for long and distinguished service within the Democratic party to Mrs. Alberta West of Ogden. Photo by Barbara Parsons Bernstein

Right
Publisher Abe Glasmann and general editor Joseph Breeze long presided over Ogden's most influential newspaper. In recent years the Standard-Examiner *led the campaign to save the Union Station. From the Browning Collection. Courtesy, Union Station*

Above
Mayor Harmon Peery is shown entertaining film stars Abbott and Costello at Ogden's Old Mill. The revitalization of the Pioneer Days celebration was Peery's unique contribution and won national attention for the city. From the Browning Collection. Courtesy, Union Station

Opposite
The cleanup and redevelopment of Ogden's "two-bit street" featured refurbished storefronts, shade trees and benches, and decorative lamp posts. From the Browning Collection. Courtesy, Union Station

Left
Making room for the new state office building complex at the city center, workmen topple the chimney of the Ben Lomond Hotel, which became the Radisson Towers. Photo by Barbara Parsons Bernstein

Above
In an effort to revitalize downtown retailing, several blocks of old business buildings were razed to make way for the Ogden Mall. Photo by Barbara Parsons Bernstein

from the original downtown site on Jefferson and 25th streets to the new location on Harrison Boulevard; the campus has become a beautiful part of the community. In 1959 it became Weber State College, a four-year institution. With an enrollment of nearly 11,000 students the college is one of the largest undergraduate schools in the United States, offering a balanced curriculum of teacher training, liberal arts, and technology programs. The Utah Schools for the Deaf and the Blind are located in Ogden, and the Utah State Industrial School was located in Ogden for nearly a century.

The old St. Benedict's Hospital, constructed at the end of World War II on Ogden's east bench, was a focal point for residential development. After the hospital moved to South Ogden in 1979, these buildings were converted into a low-cost retirement complex. Courtesy, Ogden Chamber of Commerce

Other resources contributing to the resurgence of the community include the new McKay-Dee (1971) and Saint Benedict's (1979) hospitals and new schools such as Bonneville High, Ben Lomond High, and Weber High. The old Weber High was converted into the Ogden-Weber Vocational Center, and the Stevens Henager Business College also developed facilities in Ogden. A new county library (1968) with branches in Roy (1976) and North Ogden (1982) replaced the Carnegie Free Library, which had served the area since 1903. The Ogden and Newgate malls and the downtown and 25th Street

Opposite
Ogden policeman and firefighters braved flame and smoke to save Reed Hotel patrons, but this 1979 fire proved one of the costliest in terms of lives lost in the history of the city. Photo by Barbara Parsons Bernstein

Above
Excess ground water raised havoc with Ogden's northeast bench, resulting in costly damage to homes and personal property in the early 1980s. Photo by Barbara Parsons Bernstein

RECREATION IN OGDEN

The Ogden area has been a favorite attraction since the days when travelers had to ride horses or walk. Today's recreation-seekers arrive by auto, airplane, motorhome, train, or bus and stay in modern motels and hotels. According to the Utah Travel Council 315,000 out-of-state visitors to the four-county Golden Spike Empire spent an estimated $55 million in 1984, making tourism a major industry in Weber, Box Elder, Morgan, and Davis counties.

Utah residents spend additional millions on leisure-time activities of their own, enjoying a wide variety of participant and spectator sports, cultural events, and community attractions available in northern Utah. Recreation is one important reason many newcomers decide to make their permanent homes in the area.

Tourists and residents alike fish in rivers and streams in the Wasatch Mountains; in Pineview Reservoir, ten miles east of Ogden; and in Willard Bay, a large artificial lake just north of the Weber-Box Elder county boundary. Sailing, swimming, water skiing, para-gliding, and power boating are also popular on both Pineview Reservoir and Willard Bay. Swimmers are welcome at six public pools in and around Ogden. Several water slides have been built.

Marshes along the eastern shores of the Great Salt Lake have long provided abundant flocks of duck and geese during hunting seasons, even during periods of high water. There are pheasant, quail, grouse, sagehen, and other game birds in the fields, open ranges, and foothills. Deer, elk, and moose thrive in the nearby mountains.

The winter sports centers at Snowbasin, Powder Mountain, and Nordic Valley—all only a few miles east of Ogden—are constantly being improved for skiers. There are miles of groomed snowmobile trails.

Horseback riding is the number-one recreation for hundreds of Utahns and visitors, who may trot around pastures or take to the mountain trails. The six-day Pioneer Days Rodeo every July is one of America's best-attended, highest-paying rodeos. Chariot racing, winter and summer, is a thrilling sport.

Hiking, backpacking, jogging, and distance running are increasing in popularity. So are biking, mountain climbing, bird watching, and tennis. There are ten public and three private golf courses in Ogden and adjacent communities. With U.S. Forest Service facilities plentiful, families can picnic or camp along the lakes and streams.

The annual show put on by the Golden Spike Mineral and Gem Society proves the popularity of rockhounding in Utah, where the geology is varied and unique. Antique car fans have an annual Liberty Park show, and the permanent Browning-Kimball exhibit at Union Station features rare motor vehicles. There is an annual contest at Weber State College for high school bands. WSC and area high schools provide a menu of spectator sports almost year-round—football, basketball (the WSC Wildcats have won many Big Sky Conference championships), golf, and baseball.

Art galleries at Weber State College, Union Station, and the Bertha Eccles Community Art Center offer frequent shows, in addition to the outdoor show during Pioneer Days. The Utah Symphony Orchestra and Ballet West perform

often in WSC's Austaad Auditorium at the Browning Fine Arts Center, which is also the scene of frequent top-rated plays, musicals, and lectures. An Autumnfest each fall at Union Station includes an opportunity to sample a variety of ethnic foods. This follows the chili-cooking contest of the late-July holidays, when sections of Washington Boulevard are cordoned off for the Ogden Area Chamber of Commerce Street Festival.

The Union Station museums display the inventors' collection of Browning firearms and an elaborate model-train exhibit depicting construction of the transcontinental railroad. Weber State College has a well-equipped natural history museum and planetarium. Fort Buenaventura, a state park on the south side of the Weber River, features a re-creation of Miles Goodyear's pioneer settlement. The Ogden Nature Center on 12th

Above
Two skiers inaugurate the opening of Snow Basin Ski Resort in 1946 with a team jump off Bjoangaord Hill. Courtesy, Ogden Chamber of Commerce

Above right
Generosity characterizes Ogdenites Donnell and Elizabeth Dee Shaw Stewart. Their donations made possible, among many other things, the Dee Events Center, the Stewart Library, and the Stewart Bell Tower. Courtesy, Weber State College

Street is the home for scores of birds and animals and has delightful nature walks. So does the Forest Service trail along South Fork, where special signs guide sightless visitors.

A new venture is an annual Western Film Fair at Union Station. An aircraft and missile museum is being planned for Hill Air Force Base.

—Murray M. Moler

Above
Ski jumping was a major winter attraction during the mid-1930s. National competitions were held at Becker's Hill near Ogden River before the construction of Pine View Reservoir. Courtesy, Ogden Chamber of Commerce

Opposite
The early morning angler can still creel a catch of "browns and natives" on the Ogden River. Courtesy, Ogden Chamber of Commerce

Above
Pauline Malan Waterfall, daughter of Bartholomew "Tim" Malan, original owner of the land, joined city and Chamber of Commerce officials and golf enthusiasts to see the first divot struck on the Mt. Ogden Golf course. Photo by Barbara Parsons Bernstein

Ogden supported Gunn McKay in his election to the U.S. House of Representatives. At a Democratic banquet, out-of-town support arrived in the person of Thomas P. "Tip" O'Neill, Speaker of the House. Photo by Barbara Parsons Bernstein

redevelopment projects brought a fresh look to shopping districts. Recreation, too, was enhanced with the development of golf courses such as Schneiter's Riverside Golf Course and Mount Ogden Golf Course and ski resorts at Snow Basin, Powder Mountain, and Nordic Valley.

Several Ogden citizens—born, raised, and educated here —have become national figures. There are others who have come to Ogden for a period of time, during which they influenced the community just as the community influenced them, as they moved along their course to significant accomplishments. In these instances life in Ogden was a "junction" in their careers. Ogdenites are achievers in a variety of national endeavors. Serving as members of the U.S. House of Representatives were Gunn McKay, Blaine Peterson, Lawrence Burton, and Henry Aldous Dixon, who had also been president of Weber State College and Utah State University. Cuthbert L. Olsen, a reporter for the Ogden *Standard* in the 1920s and 1930s, went on to become governor of California in 1940. Marriner Eccles, prominent Ogden businessman, served as advisor to President Franklin D. Roosevelt and as chairman of the Federal Reserve Board. Ogden lawyer Richard Richards was the national chairman of the Republican party from 1981 to 1983.

James Sundquist, who attended Weber College, became the

deputy under secretary of the Department of Agriculture and later director of governmental studies at the Brookings Institution. Mark Evans Austad, an Ogden native, pursued a career as a media executive before being appointed as ambassador to Finland and later as ambassador to Norway. Rodney Brady, assistant secretary of the Department of Health, Education and Welfare and then president of Weber State College, served as a member of the Executive Committee of the National Executive Board of the Boy Scouts of America. Superintendent of the Weber School District, T.H. Bell, became secretary of education in the Reagan administration.

Chelsey Peterson, an Ogden resident, rose to the rank of major general in the U.S. Air Force; his early career included service in the British Royal Air Force, in which he was squadron leader of the Eagles Squadron during the Battle of Britain in 1940. A graduate of Ogden High School and member of a longtime Ogden business family, Lieutenant General Brent Scowcroft served as a military advisor to the Nixon, Ford, and Reagan administrations and as a member of the National Security Council.

In private business and church affairs several Ogden people

In this gathering of distinguished Ogdenites are Congressman Lawrence Burton, industrialist Willard Marriott, educator and legislator Aldous Dixon, and diplomat Mark Austad. Courtesy, Weber State College

Rodney Brady was chosen to lead Weber State College into the 1980s. Brady recently resigned this position to become the president of Bonneville International, Inc. Courtesy, Weber State College

Educator Terrel H. Bell brought honor to his native Ogden when President Ronald Reagan asked him to serve as Secretary of the Department of Education. Bell resigned in 1985 to teach at the University of Utah. Courtesy, Weber State College

have been nationally recognized. Tracy Hall, an Ogden-born Brigham Young University (BYU) professor, invented the artificial diamond, which became important in industrial applications. Weber County native J. Willard Marriott founded the Marriott Corporation, parent company of the well-known hotel chain and various international enterprises. Robert H. Hinckley, Ogden automobile dealer, was a co-founder and vice-president of the American Broadcasting Corporation; he was appointed by President Franklin D. Roosevelt as under secretary of the Department of Commerce, chairman of the Civil Aeronautics Authority, and member of the War Contract Settlement Commission. Ogden native Ernest Wilkinson, as attorney for the Ute tribe, won the first Indian claims case against the United States government. Wilkinson later became the president of Brigham Young University. David O. McKay, a Weber County native, became president of the worldwide Church of Jesus Christ of Latter-day Saints.

In the entertainment business, actor Robert Walker hailed from Ogden, as did the musical George Osmond family, known best for singing stars Donny and Marie.

In sports several major leaguers played early in their careers for the Ogden farm team, including Steve Garvey, Johnny Temple, Bill Buckner, Tom Paciorek, Hall of Famer Frank Robinson, and manager Tommy Lasorda. Plain City's Elmer Singleton pitched for several major league teams, winding up his career with the Chicago Cubs. Ogden High star Ken Hunt pitched for the Cincinnati Reds in 1961 and played in the All-Star game that year. Glenn Hubbard, Ben Lomond High School's "Most Valuable Player," went on to the Atlanta Braves and played in the All-Star game in 1983.

Ogden has also produced some notable football players, including Glen Redd, an Ogden High School graduate who played at BYU and later with the New Orleans Saints, and Jim McMahon, who played quarterback for Roy High School, BYU, and then the Chicago Bears. Two former Weber State College basketball coaches moved up to the National Basketball Association: Phil Johnson of the Kansas City Kings and Dick Motta, who guided the Washington Bullets to the championship in 1978. The Weber State College basketball team, coached by Neil McCarthy, made the National Collegiate Athletic Association (NCAA) regional semifinals on three different occasions: in 1968, 1978, and 1983.

Some Ogden runners have gained national recognition. Wade Bell went from Ben Lomond High School to the University of Oregon, where in 1967 he became the NCAA national champion in the 800-meter run; in 1968 he was the Track Athletic Congress champion in the 800-meter race and ran in the Olympics. Weber State College runner Farley Gerber won the NCAA 3,000 meter steeplechase championship in 1984. Both these runners, the only Utah runners to break the four-minute mile, were coached by Ogden's Chick Hislop. Ed Eyestone set state records at Bonneville High; at BYU he won the NCAA championship in the 10,000-meter cross-country race and in 1980 placed third in the World Cross-Country competition.

In medical achievements Ben Lomond High School graduate Dr. William DeVries performed the first artificial heart implant operation on Barney Clark in 1982. Dr. John Dixon, Ogden native, gained national acclaim for his work with lasers in gastroenterology.

Bernard De Voto—novelist, critic, and historian—was born and raised in Ogden. He is best known for his historical trilogy comprising *The Course of Empire, Across the Wide Missouri,* and *The Year of Decision: 1846. The Crooked Mile* is a De Voto novel set in Ogden. Biographer Fawn McKay Brodie, who was raised in Huntsville and attended Weber College, attained prominence with *No Man Knows My History* (a biography of Joseph Smith, Jr.) and *Thomas Jefferson, An Intimate History.* Other Ogden writers of note include Richard Scowcroft, whose *Children of Covenant* is set in Ogden. Distinguished in other fine arts are Metropolitan Opera baritone Gean Greenwell, representational artist Farrell Collett, and sculptor Solon Hannibal Borglum.

Ogden, as depicted in this history, has in many ways been the Junction City: the geographical junction of the Ogden and Weber rivers, the meeting place of Indians and pioneer settlers, the railroad junction of the transcontinental line, and an arena of confrontation of Mormon and Gentile societies. One might conjecture philosophically that historical Ogden now stands at a junction with the hopes and dreams of the Ogden City of the future.

Opposite page
Utah's most famous woman of letters, the noted historian Fawn Brodie, made her last Ogden appearance shortly before her death in 1981. She spoke at Union Station about her biography of Richard M. Nixon. Photo by Barbara Parsons Bernstein

Previous page
For three-quarters of a century, Ogden hosted professional baseball, from the old Federal Farm League to the Pacific Coast League. Now the setting sun no longer glares in batters' eyes at John Affleck Park. Photo by Barbara Parsons Bernstein

Above
Ogden's Welcome Arch, situated in the center of the city at Washington Boulevard and 17th Street, offers greetings to visitors. Photo by Grove Pashley

Opposite
A breathtaking view of Ogden rewards the hiker who climbs to the top of Waterfall Canyon. Beyond the Great Salt Lake, Pilot Peak marks the Nevada border. Photo by Grove Pashley. All color photographs by Grove Pashley unless otherwise indicated

Above
Ogden Canyon, the major route connecting Ogden City to Ogden Valley, serves as the distribution point for culinary and irrigation water supplied by Pine View Reservoir.

Right
Ben Lomond Peak is seen framed by Ogden's major thoroughfare. Washington Boulevard cuts through a canyon of banks, businesses, and service centers, highlighted by the Ogden Mall at 24th Street.

Above
Wall Avenue flanks the Ogden railway
yards. Across from Union Station stands
the former Toone Hotel, which provided
rest and refreshment for a multitude of
travelers. Renovated in 1980, it is now the
New Brigham Hotel and contains a private
club and luxury apartment units.

Above
In the summer months Snow Basin ski resort is a popular jumping-off spot for hikers, picnickers, and fishing buffs.

Right
Snow Basin, fifteen miles from the city, is one of a triad of ski resorts in the Ogden area. (Nordic Valley and Powder Mountain resorts also offer deep powder and short lines at the ski lifts.) The "Basin" opened operations in 1946, after years of anticipation and planning. The deep-powder bowls at Snow Basin and Powder Mountain have attracted skiers from across the country. *Courtesy, Golden Spike Empire*

Left
Water slides have been making a big splash in Ogden, although they are but one way to beat the heat of summer. Most Ogdenites enjoy nearby lakes, streams, and cool mountain retreats.

Below
Pine View Reservoir, five miles from Ogden, is a popular recreational area for sailing, water skiing, fishing, and swimming. During the winter months ice fishing draws a large number of enthusiasts.

Above
In addition to this children's playground, Mt. Ogden Park, on Ogden's east bench, offers an eighteen-hole municipal golf course, tennis courts, a soccer field, baseball diamonds, hiking trails, and picnic areas.

Left
Beus Pond, a major water source in the early days of Ogden, is being transformed into a city park, a serene setting high on the east bench.

Below and right
Formerly a junior college, Weber State College became a four-year institution of higher education in 1959. The college is now a large undergraduate center, serving some 11,000 day and evening students.

Left
Ogden High School was designed by architect Leslie S. Hodgson—who also designed the Municipal Building—and built by the Works Progress Administration. The building of Utah's first million-dollar high school brought an influx of capital and jobs that helped Ogden recover from the Depression.

Above
In 1903 the Carnegie Free Library opened its doors on Washington Boulevard and 26th Street. It was the first building in the state to be used solely as a library. The new Weber County Public Library, on Jefferson Avenue and 24th Street, opened in 1968.

Opposite page, top
The Ogden LDS Temple, on Washington Boulevard, is located almost in the center of Ogden. The carefully manicured grounds shelter not only the Temple but the LDS Tabernacle, a Daughters of the Pioneers Museum, and the Miles Goodyear Cabin.

Opposite
Beginning as the Intermountain Business School in 1891, Stevens Henager College has been established in downtown Ogden since 1958 as an accredited two-year junior college of business.

The Municipal Building, towering over the city, houses both municipal and county offices and a new jail annex. Carefully maintained gardens surround the structure, and each year a Christmas village highlights the holiday season.

Ogden's 25th Street began with respectable businesses and hotels but eventually declined into notoriety as a "two-bit street." During World War II it had to be placed off-limits to service personnel. Restoration after decades of blight has made 25th Street once again a source of civic pride.

Above and right
Historic 25th Street, being restored as a center for retail and commercial activity, links Union Station with downtown Ogden. Period-style lighting, courtyards, and restoration of historic facades are among the improvements being put into effect.

Above
Standing on "hotel corner" at 25th Street and Washington Boulevard, the Ben Lomond Hotel served travelers for over half a century. The site was occupied by the White House hotel from 1868 to 1890 and by the majestic Reed Hotel, considered one of the West's finest, from 1891 to 1927. The Ben Lomond has reopened as the Radisson Tower.

Above, above right, and opposite page, top left
The Ben Lomond restoration is shown under way. The grand old building features delicate architectural ornaments.

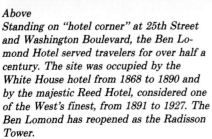

Ogden, the Junction City, still serves as a major transferring point for several Western railroads. The Ogden switching yards encompass some four square miles and eighty-five miles of track. Prior to World War II the Ogden yards were the biggest west of Chicago and Kansas City. Above, photo by Grove Pashley. Left, photo by Richard C. Roberts

Above
The Episcopal Church of the Good Shepherd, the oldest building in continuous use in Ogden, was built in 1874. It was the gift of the Hammersely family of New York, in memory of their daughter.

Left
A favorite stop three miles up Ogden Canyon, Graycliff Lodge stands near the former site of the famed Heritage Hotel, once the playground of presidents William Howard Taft and Theodore Roosevelt.

Opposite
The Bertha Eccles Community Art Center, built in 1893 for Ogden businessman James C. Armstrong, was acquired in 1896 by industrialist David Eccles for his wife Bertha.

Above
The Egyptian Theatre on Washington Boulevard, built in 1924, is noted for its rococo statuary and is listed on the National Register of Historic Places.

Right
Prior to 1912 the Elks building, located on Grant Avenue between 25th and 26th streets, was Central School, Ogden's major public school for thirty years.

Opposite page
Pine View Dam backs up the waters of the Ogden River to provide water storage, flood control, and recreational opportunities for northern Utah. The dam was raised to its present height in 1957.

Right
The Ogden Mall symbol beckons to downtown shoppers. Photo by Barbara Parsons Bernstein

Opposite page
At night Ogden's 25th Street is set aglow with neon magic.

Below
Ogden's Municipal Airport started operations in 1942, when it was a basic training base for navy pilots.

Right
Every summer antique-car enthusiasts gather at Liberty Park in Ogden to exhibit their carefully restored automobiles and trucks.

Below
Union Station serves as a cultural and community station for the Ogden area. The station's Browning-Kimball Automobile Museum houses a gleaming antique-car collection.

Since 1856 Ogden has celebrated the founding of Utah. Pioneer Days, featuring a lively parade and a rodeo, was popularized by Ogden's "Cowboy Mayor" Harmon W. Peery. Pictured is the 1984 Pioneer Days parade.

Right
The entertainment during Pioneer Days includes school bands, bluegrass and rock music groups, clowns, rodeo queens, dancers, rides, exhibits, and a chili-cooking contest.

Below
During the Pioneer Days festivities Washington Boulevard is cordoned off as hordes of visitors and locals enjoy the fun.

Above
Ogden's Pioneer Days rodeo, held at Lorin Farr Park, attracts riders from throughout the Intermountain West.

Above right
Hooper Tomato Days attracts visitors from all over Weber County. Photo by Barbara Parsons Bernstein

Right
Ogdenites turned out to cheer the progress of the Olympic torch toward the 1984 Summer Olympiad in Los Angeles.

CHAPTER SIX
PARTNERS IN PROGRESS

The Ogden area has always had a lot going for it—especially its geography and its people.

Early nomadic Indians frequently gathered at the confluence of the Ogden and Weber rivers to exchange gossip and goods. Artifacts from their primitive camps show that food—fish in the rivers, waterfowl in the ponds, and game in the Wasatch Mountains' foothills—was abundant.

When mountain men and fur trappers came, they followed the same pattern. Many "wintered over" near where the rivers joined. A popular rendezvous site was at Mountain Green, a few miles inside the north of Weber Canyon.

Miles Goodyear built Fort Buenaventura on the banks of the Weber, a scant mile from today's Ogden City-Weber County Municipal Building. He knew this was a key location, handy to the routes of pioneer travelers and providing ample foodstuffs.

Mormon leaders recognized the area's virtues, too. Soon after their arrival in the Valley of the Great Salt Lake in 1847, they dispatched James Brown to buy Goodyear's fort and others to establish farms in what they called Ogden.

Trade flourished especially when the nation's first transcontinental railroad came through Ogden in 1869 on the way to the golden wedding of the rails at nearby Promontory. Shortly after the last spike was driven, the junction of the Union Pacific and Southern Pacific was permanently established in Ogden. The depot and switchyards were located adjacent to the original location of Goodyear's fort.

Ogden prospered as "Junction City" with the construction of rail lines northward to Montana, northwestward to Oregon and Washington, and southwestward to Southern California.

Railroad builders realized—and so have the later-year architects of highway systems and airways—that Ogden is, within a score of miles, equidistant from Los Angeles, San Francisco, and Portland. Calgary and Phoenix are also about the same distance away, and Denver is even closer.

This provident geographical location is due to the little recognized curvature of the Pacific Coast. For example, Reno is actually west of Los Angeles!

During the defense buildups and wars of the twentieth century, the Ogden area became a favored site for military warehouses, distribution depots, munitions works, and the giant Hill Air Force Base.

However, geography wasn't everything. As business after business was established with Ogden as home base, the area's people proved their willingness to do a day's work for a day's pay. They are loyal, well-educated, sturdy folk, and most would rather live in or around Ogden than anyplace else in the world.

The organizations whose stories are detailed on the following pages have chosen to support this important literary and civic project. They illustrate the variety of ways in which individuals and their businesses have contributed to the city's growth and development. The civic involvement of Ogden's businesses, institutions of learning, and local government, in cooperation with its citizens, has made the community an excellent place in which to live and work.

Enthusiastic Pioneer Days paraders march for the entertainment of a prosperous, growing community.

OGDEN AREA CHAMBER OF COMMERCE

The jagged skyline of the Wasatch Mountains is reflected in the windows of the Ogden Area Chamber of Commerce offices at 2307 Washington Boulevard.

The Ogden Area Chamber of Commerce has shown farsighted, effective community leadership since its establishment in 1887, and its directors and officers have been the coaches and its executives the ballcarriers in winning scores of vital contests.

Hill Air Force Base is a prime example. Before World War II the government authorized an Air Corps supply center "somewhere" in the Mountain West. The chamber took the initiative, bought a site in Davis County with its own funds, and, when that site was selected as the base, turned the land over to the Air Corps at cost. As a result, Hill Air Force Base is now Utah's largest employer.

Another example is Weber State College. The Utah Legislature and governor had threatened to return it to private church ownership. The chamber mounted a statewide campaign, and Utahns overwhelmingly voted to retain it as a public institution.

President John F. Kennedy attempted to move the infant IRS Center to San Francisco to pay a political debt, but the chamber and the Weber Industrial Bureau made sure that it stayed in Ogden and expanded.

President Richard Nixon later threatened to close the Ogden regional office of the Forest Service, with the same outcome. President Jimmy Carter tried to shut down the Defense Depot Ogden; the chamber saved it. The chamber stoutly backed downtown redevelopment that brought the Ogden City Mall, Hilton, Radisson, and state office building to the area.

It has been this way since the predecessor chamber was organized in April 1887, the first in the state, with David H. Peery as president and J.H. Knauss as secretary. There were several name changes, including a close affiliation with the Weber Club, until 1933 when it became a completely independent organization. Its offices were in several Ogden buildings until the present Ogden City Mall quarters, where Twenty-third Street meets Washington Boulevard, were occupied a few years ago.

When the 1887 articles of incorporation were adopted, the chamber pledged itself to "advance the general prosperity of the varied interests of the Territory of Utah (statehood didn't come until 1896) and especially of the City of Ogden and vicinity and to promote efficient, honest, and economical government." That pledge has been met, all the way.

At the end of 1984 the Ogden Area Chamber of Commerce had 1,113 individual members, representing 753 businesses. Chamber president Steve Lawson and communications director Adele Smith express their expectations for the future in one word: "Exciting!"

"As we approach our own chamber's centennial and near the end of the twentieth century, we are certain that the Ogden area will prove to be one of the most dynamic regions in America," says Lawson.

THE KIER CORPORATION

If all the residents of northern Utah dwellings built by The Kier Corporation were to assemble for a convention, they would more than fill the 12,000-seat Dee Events Center at Weber State College. Jim and Norma Kier and a growing team of talented associates have been designing, constructing, and decorating houses, apartments, and commercial properties in Ogden and other Intermountain communities since moving to Utah from their native Canada in 1957.

The couple formed Kier Construction Company in 1961, with offices in their home, and concentrated on residential construction in Ogden, North Ogden, Pleasant View, Kaysville, and Washington Terrace. Scores of homes were built by the firm in Brigham City, including a series of apartment structures that were included in a government low-cost housing program. Kier apartment complexes also dotted Ogden—two of which were named Kara Manor and Kimi Lane for the Kier twins, youngest of the couple's five children.

Continued expansion led to the splitting of the construction firm into a pair of closely related firms—The Kier Corporation, as the development and construction arm, and Kier Management Corporation, to operate rental properties.

The National Remodelers Council gave The Kier Corporation a special award for the restoration of the elegant LeRoy Eccles Mansion on Ogden's East Twenty-fifth Street in the Eccles Historic District. The prestigious Weber Club retained quarters in the lower level. The dilapidated Creston Hotel in the heart of the Ogden business district was thoroughly remodeled into the Creston Plaza office complex. The former

Norma and Jim Kier stand in front of the offices of The Kier Corporation, which are located at 3710 Quincy Avenue.

Gorder branch post office in southeastern Ogden was tastefully refurbished as headquarters for the Kier enterprises.

Jim Kier concentrated on design and construction. Norma A. Kier was the decorating genius. Son Steve, starting as a laborer, rose to head of construction management. Son Scott, also beginning at the bottom, soon became a top estimator. Daughter Bonnie Jean works for the firm during Weber State College vacations.

Ogden native and former Army major Burrell Davis joined the Kiers in 1980, and in November 1983 became president of Kier Management Corporation, overseeing the rental of more than 1,300 dwelling units. All properties had high occupancy rates and, be-

cause of their desirability, created long lists of families waiting to move in.

"We try to create an atmosphere that makes people feel comfortable and happy in quality well-built units. We take pride in constructing far better buildings than expected for their price range. It's not always easy, but it can be done. And usually neighbors become inspired to match their improved surroundings," says Norma Kier. And that, she believes, is one key to the firm's success. Owners of Kier-built houses and apartments "live in a quality atmosphere to start their days with a smile. And that's what we like," she says.

Norma and Jim Kier were particularly pleased the morning of September 4, 1984, when they had breakfast with President Ronald Reagan, and shook his hand, during a campaign stop in Utah.

JETWAY DIVISION OF ABEX CORPORATION

More than two billion airline passengers all over the world have entered or left their jets on plane-to-terminal boarding bridges built in Ogden. These ingenious, tunnel-like structures are the major product of the Jetway Division of Abex Corporation, an IC Industries Company, at the firm's big plant on Pennsylvania Avenue in southwestern Ogden, near the

Production of Jetway-brand passenger loading bridges began in 1960 at this Pacific Iron and Steel Company plant at 3100 Pennsylvania Avenue in Ogden.

Welders begin fastening corrugated steel sides to floor girders as they build an early model of the Jetway passenger loading bridge.

municipal airport.

More than 3,000 loading bridges have been manufactured by the Ogden-based concern since the dawn of the jet age in the late 1950s. Seventy-five percent of the passenger loading devices at U.S. airports are the Jetway brand. Hundreds are in daily use overseas, including a gold-trimmed pair at Riyadh, Saudi Arabia, for the exclusive use of the royal family.

The Jetway story began in Southern California in the early 1930s when Howard Schmidt formed Pacific Iron and Steel Company to fabricate beams, plates, and girders for the booming Los Angeles-area market. Carl Lodjic and several associates

purchased the concern in 1953, and four years later sold it to J.W. Gillen and his Standard Railway Equipment Company, best known as Stanray.

Rapid industrial growth in the Intermountain States prompted the company to build a branch plant on a nineteen-acre site in Ogden. Ground was broken in January 1957, and production began within two months. With Robert Campbell as manager, the facility fabricated steel for scores of structures in Utah and neighboring states, including the Utah

State Office Building, adjacent to the capitol in Salt Lake City.

American-built, jet-powered airliners began commercial service in 1957, drastically shrinking global travel times. The Atlantic Ocean became only seven hours "wide," and the Pacific only ten hours. The continental United States became only five hours wide and two hours deep.

As air travel gained in popularity, it quickly became apparent that the existing terminals did not have adequate equipment to service the new jet airplanes and their passengers rapidly.

As Russ Williams, veteran Jetway Division executive, puts it, "Aircraft do not make money sitting on the ground. Traffic has to be expedited. Passengers have to be protected from the weather between the planes and terminals. And those old steep, dangerous outside stairways had to be eliminated."

Stanray recognized the problem. Chief engineer Hans Kjerulf, project engineer Robert Lichti, and their team—aided by United Airlines' vice-president for facilities, John Kukar—wasted little time in developing the first commercially successful passenger transfer bridge. They called it the Jetway, a copyrighted name.

The first unit was installed for United Airlines at New York City's La Guardia terminal. After building six in a rented Los Angeles facility, Stanray decided that the Jetway program could best be handled in Utah, and since 1960 all of the passenger loading bridges have been made in Ogden.

Inauguration of service of Boe-

Two United Airlines' planes are serviced by four Jetway passenger loading bridges at a mid-1960s "finger" terminal at San Francisco International Airport.

ing's huge 747 in the late 1960s, quickly followed by the McDonnell Douglas DC-10 and Lockheed's L-1011, with capacities of more than 400 passengers, led to the development of new, larger bridges until there are now many variations of the device in constant use.

Most popular has been the "apron drive" model. Its rotunda mates with the exterior of the terminal wall. Tunnel sections (usually three) are hinged so the entire bridge can be parked parallel to the waiting room exterior yet telescoped outward and securely mated to an airliner door within sixty seconds.

A pair of aircraft-type wheels provides mobility on the apron. An operator in a cab at the forward end controls direct current electricity flowing to motors that drive the wheel, extend or retract the tunnels, and adjust the level of the entrance. Once in place, the height is automatically controlled to compensate for changes in the aircraft's weight as passengers deplane or board. Floodlights facilitate night operation.

"Jetpower" units, produced in a recently built electronics laboratory at the Ogden plant, can be hung from below the cab to provide power to operate air con-

ditioners and other essential equipment when the airliner's own engines have been turned off. Some models of Jetway passenger loading bridges are fastened to pedestals at both ends. Cabs rotate to meet doorways of planes, and the ball and screw mechanisms inside pairs of supporting columns maintain the essential level entrance.

The Ogden employees, described by Williams as the "finest work force in the world," begin each unit with thick steel plates that are cut to size and corrugated for strength before being welded to heavy girders. After the rotunda, tunnels, and cabs have been shaped and polished, they are painted with weatherproof enamel, wall and ceiling panels are added, and carpeting, lights, and controls are installed. Trucks and trailers haul completed bridges to their destinations, or to ports for ocean shipment overseas. Jetway Division experts supervise installation at the airports.

Enthusiastic acceptance of the loading bridges led to the formation of Jetway Equipment Corporation in 1968 as a Stanray subsidiary. Jay Middlestead was the first president. He was succeeded by Russ Williams who served most of the years until

1976, when C.W. "Bill" Massie, a private pilot and former Tenneco executive, became president. In 1977 Stanray was purchased by IC Industries, and the new subsidiary, the Jetway Division of Abex Corporation, was formed.

The Ogden work force peaked in prerecession 1982 at 465, with a $7.8-million annual payroll. At that same time sales topped $33 million. Economic pains of the airline industry were reflected in a slight drop during the recession, but demand remains steady, and in mid-1984 there were 380 employees.

The list of Jetway passenger loading bridges is an honor roll of airports, both large and small, domestic and foreign. There are, for example, 185 in Atlanta, 110 in Dallas-Fort Worth, 141 at New York City's JFK Airport, 149 at Los Angeles International Airport, 37 at Salt Lake International, 33 in Honolulu, 30 at London's Heathrow Airport, 38 in Rio de Janeiro, and 56 in Riyadh (Saudi Arabia)— including those two with gold trim for royal use.

Mated with a terminal building, the Jetway passenger loading bridge can be extended, elevated, and turned, propelled by powered wheels, to mate securely to aircraft doors.

McKAY-DEE HOSPITAL CENTER

Thomas Duncombe Dee, the Ogden businessman for whom the Thomas D. Dee Memorial Hospital was named, posed for this portrait around the turn of the century.

This portrait, painted in the early 1900s, is of Annie Taylor Dee, founder of the Thomas D. Dee Memorial Hospital.

The McKay-Dee Hospital Center in Ogden observed its diamond anniversary in 1985, commemorating seventy-five years of caring and service. Annie Taylor Dee and her family, who founded the predecessor Thomas D. Dee Memorial Hospital in 1910, would be proud of the ultramodern facility that exists today.

Their pride would be shared by David O. McKay, the much-beloved president of the Church of Jesus Christ of Latter-day Saints for whom the health-care complex is also named. He insisted that good health should be a primary objective of his faith's millions of members.

Thomas Duncombe Dee, a native of South Wales, was sixteen years old when his parents immigrated to the United States as LDS converts and made their way by railroad and ox team in 1860 to the Utah Territory. That same year eight-year-old Annie Taylor, born in England, was in another

born there. After the family moved to a larger "country" residence on Washington Boulevard at Eighth Street, four more children, Edith, Florence, Rosabelle, and Lawrence, arrived. Thomas D. Dee had learned carpentry in Wales, and his skills and enterprise served him well in his new homeland. He combined industry with a keen interest in civic and church affairs. His business prospered and he eventually joined with

The Thomas D. Dee Memorial Hospital, at Twenty-fourth Street and Harrison Boulevard, as it appeared in the mid-1960s. It was demolished after the McKay-Dee Hospital Center was completed, fifteen blocks south on the same boulevard.

pioneer party that made the difficult journey to the Mormons' "New Zion."

The Dee and Taylor families were distant relatives and visited frequently. The friendship of Thomas and Annie bloomed and they were married on April 10, 1871, in Salt Lake City. The newlyweds set up housekeeping in a two-room adobe structure on Twenty-second Street, near Wall Avenue, in Ogden.

A son, Thomas Reese Dee, and three daughters, Maude, Elizabeth, and Margaret, were

other Weber County entrepreneurs in forming several concerns of great scope that included what are now Anderson Lumber Company, Amalgamated Sugar Company, First Security Corporation, and Utah International.

He was a member of the Ogden

School Board for thirty-five years and was president of Ogden's first library. He also served as an assessor, tax collector, city councilman, police court judge, state tax commissioner, and as a member of the State Board of Equalization.

Annie Taylor Dee's lifelong interest in health care was intensified by two tragedies, the deaths of a son and her husband.

Thomas Reese Dee was only twenty-one in 1894 when he became ill with "inflammation of the bowel." Ogden's first appendectomy was performed on the family dining table. However, the appendix had ruptured and he died.

In July 1905 Thomas D. Dee and several companions went to the south fork of the Ogden River, seeking to augment supplies for the Ogden Water Works which they had acquired when it went into receivership. The 61-year-old businessman slipped into the icy stream. He was thoroughly chilled and pneumonia developed. He died on July 9.

Mrs. Dee was convinced that both her older son and her husband might have lived had better medical facilities been available. The family consulted railroad physician Robert S. Joyce to study an endowment of a new hospital.

This resulted in the February 3, 1910, incorporation of the Thomas D. Dee Memorial Hospital Association with Mrs. Dee as president and Maude Dee Porter as secretary. The family purchased three acres at Harrison Boulevard and Twenty-fourth Street and conveyed the site to the association.

Construction began soon, and the $75,000, four-story brick Thomas D. Dee Memorial Hospital opened on December 29, 1910, with wards for 100 patients.

An open field, east of Weber State College and Harrison Boulevard, was converted in 1968 into Utah's newest health-care facility.

McKay-Dee Hospital Center annually provides the latest in health care to more than 88,000 patients. McKay Hospital is in the center, the Dee Hospital is on the left, and the Lawrence T. Dee Medical Arts Building is on the right.

Care in a private room cost three dollars per day, two dollars in a ward. Maternity patients paid twenty-five dollars for a fourteen-day stay.

During its first year Dee Hospital had 895 patients, 481 operations, and 5 births. Mrs. Dee personally paid mothers' delivery charges to encourage hospital births. Nurses worked twelve hours per day with a half-day off weekly, if the patient load permitted.

Dee Hospital progressed rapidly but the financial burden on the Dee family became so great that directors voted to close the facility

on November 15, 1914, unless an adequate maintenance fund could be established.

However, Annie Dee wouldn't give up. She called upon her friend David O. McKay, a member of the Council of Twelve Apostles of the Church of Jesus Christ of Latter-day Saints. After study by church authorities, ownership of Dee Memorial Hospital was transferred to the three Weber County LDS stakes, effective March 30, 1915. The institution remained a unit of the LDS health-care system for more than sixty years.

There were many changes during those years. A nursing home and school were completed in 1917, and a south wing and laboratory were built two years later. A north wing was added in 1927, and a pediatrics division was opened in 1938. Eight years later a blood bank was established, and the first outpatient clinic was started in 1948.

In 1951 Kenneth E. Knapp, a former airline salesman, was recruited and trained as an administrator by Dee Hospital's trustees. He found the hospital in precarious financial condition and showing its physical age. He would prove to be the spark plug for amazing growth during the next twenty-one years.

Knapp consolidated departments and began a floor-by-floor modernization program. A psychiatry ward, the first in a Utah general hospital, was established. A physical therapy department and emergency room were opened, and during the 1951 epidemic a polio ward was added.

The 42-year-old Dee School of Nursing was phased out in 1955 after graduating more than 700 nurses. A survey showed nurses could be better educated in colleges and universities with hospitals providing clinical experience.

Despite improvements in the physical plant, it became apparent to Knapp and his governing board that an entirely new institution was needed. A 27-acre site was acquired at 3900 Harrison Boulevard, fifteen blocks south of Dee Memorial and across from Weber College's new southeastern Ogden campus.

Architect Keith Wilcox drew plans for a modern complex to cost an estimated eight million dollars. A community committee, headed by former mayor and legislator W. Rulon White, raised nearly one million dollars, and the LDS Church provided the remainder.

Hospital officials decided to name the first unit at the new site after David O. McKay, who was elevated to the church presidency in 1951 at the age of seventy-seven. Board member Lawrence T. Dee, the sole surviving son of Thomas and Annie Dee, agreed

that the action was "fitting and proper" because of president McKay's long service to the community and his endeavors in 1914 that brought Dee Memorial into the church system.

McKay detonated the initial charge of dynamite to break ground on April 23, 1966. When McKay Hospital opened on July 9, 1969, administrator Knapp gave the keys to the frail church president, explaining that "these doors will never be locked again."

Work on a new Dee Hospital began early in 1970 with construction funds augmented by gifts from the ever-generous Dee family. It opened on November 10, 1971, the 127th anniversary of Thomas D. Dee's birth. The office building just north of McKay Hospital was named the Lawrence T. Dee Medical Arts Building following his death in 1977 at the age of eighty-six.

In 1972 Kenneth Knapp was named associate commissioner for the Health Services Corporation of the LDS Church and was succeeded at McKay-Dee Hospital Center by Kenneth C. Johnson, previously administrator of Primary Children's Hospital in Salt Lake City.

The LDS Church made headlines in September 1974 by giving its fifteen hospitals, then valued at more than sixty million dollars, to the communities they served. Management was delegated to the newly formed, not-for-profit Intermountain Health Care, Inc. Scott S. Parker became president and Thomas D. Dee II, an Ogden banker and Lawrence and Janet Dee's only child, became treasurer. Day-to-day control of McKay-Dee remained with the local governing board.

The never-ending process of keeping up with changes and improvements in health-care

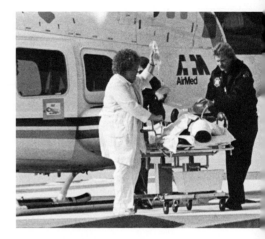

A trauma center nurse meets a patient who has been airlifted from an accident scene to McKay-Dee Helistop, located just outside the hospital's emergency room.

techniques continued. A three-year family practice residency program was inaugurated, and a helistop opened near the modernized emergency room. Open heart surgery was begun at the facility, and an auditorium and learning center was opened. A physical medicine and rehabilitation program was started, and a costly computerized axial tomography device (CAT scanner) was installed. X-ray machines were upgraded, and the psychiatry ward was expanded. There were 177,552 patients admitted and 36,384 babies born during the initial ten years of the center's operation.

A new element was added on September 25, 1979, when the McKay-Dee Medical Clinic opened at 2400 North Washington Boulevard. Physician services were provided from 5 to 10 p.m. on weekdays and from noon until midnight on weekends, the hours when doctors' offices are closed.

A second outreach clinic, the Fairfield, was developed later in Layton as an alternative-care facility for patient convenience. Together with the older Porter

Family Practice Clinic, these primary care facilities annually accommodate more than 30,000 patients.

The first annex to the new Dee Hospital was the Stewart Rehabilitation Center, which opened on November 15, 1980, and was named for benefactors Donnell B. and Elizabeth S. Stewart. Mrs. Stewart is a granddaughter of Thomas and Annie Dee. The goal of the center is to help physically disabled persons reach maximum physical, emotional, social, and vocational independence. On the staff are specially trained physicians, nurses, physical therapists, occupational therapists, speech

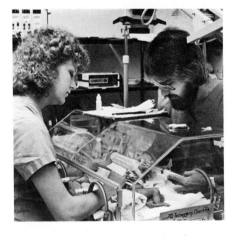

Even the tiniest premature infant has an excellent chance for survival in the McKay-Dee Hospital Center's neonatal intensive care unit.

pathologists, clinical psychologists, social workers, orthotists, prosthetists, and vocational counselors.

Kenneth Johnson was promoted by IHC in 1980 and was succeeded as McKay-Dee's administrator by H. Gary Pehrson, an experienced executive who was on the Ogden administrative staff from 1972 to 1977. Pehrson has maintained the center's growth. A $6-million program included remodeling multiple-bed wards until more than 95 percent of patients

enjoyed private rooms. By mid-1984 the McKay and Dee hospitals had 380 beds and 40 nursery bassinettes.

New emphasis was placed on outpatients. Not many years earlier less than 10 percent of surgical care was administered on an outpatient basis. By late 1984 more than 45 percent of surgical patients did not remain hospitalized overnight, and the percentage was rapidly increasing.

As Gary Pehrson explains, hospitals previously had emphasized "nearly total institutional care, but now we're back to an era of patients taking more care of themselves so we are able to provide even better care for more serious patients."

This trend was reflected in improvements throughout the center. New space was added on the west face of the McKay Hospital so intensive care, coronary care, newborn intensive care, and stroke units could be expanded and the latest electronic monitors installed.

An innovative "total fitness" program attracted scores of individuals and members of groups, including police and fire agencies. A three-phase course includes assessment and testing of an individual's general health and any physical deterioration; education in exercise, nutrition, and mental well-being; and motivation to increase personal determination to stay fit.

The residency training of new physicians increased at McKay-Dee, working closely with the University of Utah. Clinical experience is provided in nursing in cooperation with both the University of Utah and Weber State College, and in inhalation therapy with WSC.

An expanded McKay-Dee Hospital Women's Center includes a

"short-stay" program for mothers who deliver babies under careful supervision and return home less than twenty-four hours later.

Utah's first hospital-sponsored, home-care program, begun at the "Old Dee" Hospital, provides more than 20,000 home visits a year by nurses, physical therapists, nurse's aides, speech therapists, and dietitians. Over the years the staff has traveled more than one million miles.

McKay-Dee Hospital Center is the largest private employer in the city of Ogden, with more than 1,400 people receiving salaries and benefits exceeding twenty-two million dollars a year. That was a major portion of the facility's 1984 budget of fifty-five million dollars. There were 18,500 admissions in 1984, and more than 40,000 outpatients and 26,000 persons requiring emergency room care were treated. There were 3,500 babies born, an average of nearly 10 per day.

McKay-Dee Hospital Center is a major health-care facility for northern Utah, southeastern Idaho, and southwestern Wyoming. It has exceeded, in its outstanding success, the fondest dreams of Annie Taylor Dee and David O. McKay.

State-of-the-art laser equipment is used to perform microsurgery.

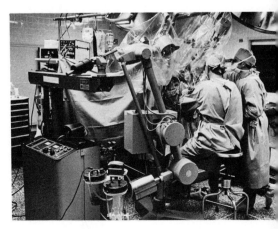

BROWNING COMPANY

Ogden inventor John M. Browning holds the Browning Automatic five-shot shotgun that he invented. It is still being manufactured and highly popular after eighty-four years.

Ogden native John Moses Browning is universally acclaimed as the greatest firearms inventor the world has ever known. At least fifty million sports and military weapons, based on the 128 patents he obtained over his forty-seven active years, have been manufactured.

The Browning Company that he and his brothers founded has been a major factor in northern Utah's economy for more than a century. And the many civic contributions made by this generous family have made the Ogden area a better place in which to live.

The family traces its American history back to Captain John Browning, who sailed across the Atlantic from England in 1622 and settled in the Virginia Colony.

One of the captain's many descendants was Jonathan Browning, born in Tennessee just after the turn of the nineteenth century. As a youth he was a blacksmith's apprentice, then turned his talents to the repair of black powder guns that were so essential to our nation's frontiersmen.

Jonathan Browning opened his own shop at Brushy Fork, Tennessee, in 1824 but soon joined the westward movement. While a blacksmith and gunsmith in Quincy, Illinois, he became a convert to the new Church of Jesus Christ of Latter-day Saints.

This prompted him to join LDS president Joseph Smith and his followers in Nauvoo, Illinois, a few miles up the Mississippi River from Quincy. When the Mormon faith's founder was assassinated, Browning joined the new church leader, Brigham Young, in fleeing to the banks of the Missouri River near what is today Omaha, Nebraska.

When Young led the Mormons to their "New Zion" on the western flanks of the Rocky Mountains in 1847, Browning remained at the Kanesville base camp to manufacture weapons, including two repeating rifles he had invented.

Arriving in what is now Utah in 1852, Browning established his home and general repair shop in Ogden. In keeping with Mormon doctrine of those days, he married three women and fathered twenty-two children before he died at the age of seventy-four.

Among those children were John Moses and Matthew Sandifer, sons of Elizabeth Clark Browning, and Jonathan Edmond, Thomas Samuel, William Wallace, and George Emmett, sons of Sarah Emmett Browning. These brothers and half-brothers were close friends in their youth and business associates as adults.

John Browning began tinkering in his father's primitive shop as a young child and in his teens became exceptionally adept at the repair of guns. He soon decided the old weapons could stand considerable improvement, and when he was only twenty-three years old he invented a single-shot rifle of unique design. His first patent was granted on October 7, 1879.

The brothers built a new shop in 1880 and began the manufacture of that first Browning rifle. They made 600 of the guns before the patent was purchased in 1883 by the Winchester Arms Company, and this famed New England firm took over their production.

John Browning sold forty-four of his patents to Winchester over the next nineteen years, including a wide variety of repeating-type rifles and shotguns. Meanwhile, the Browning brothers' sporting goods store relocated to Ogden's Main Street and prospered as one of the best-stocked establishments

A picture of John M. Browning's first invention, a single-shot rifle, hangs over the Ogden shop built by the Browning brothers in 1880. Left to right are Sam, George, John M., Matthew S., and Ed Browning and their British-born gunsmith, Frank Rushton.

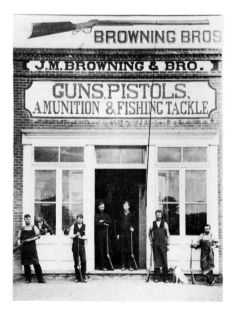

of its kind in the West.

Winchester produced only a few of the Browning-invented guns, withholding the others from the market to avoid obsolescence problems within its own product line. Between 1883 and 1902 all of Winchester's new products were based on Browning's genius.

John Browning noted reeds bending in front of his muzzle while hunting in marshlands near Ogden and decided gas developed by the exploding powder could be harnessed to make a truly automatic gun. Recoil, he figured, could also be productively utilized.

These theories led to the first successful machine gun, initially adopted by the U.S. Navy in 1895 as the Colt Peacemaker, and used by Marines to defend the American legation in Peking during the Boxer Rebellion.

Heavier caliber improved machine guns followed, including the famed Browning Automatic Rifle, so vital to infantrymen. During World War I, World War II, and the Korean War, all automatic weapons fired by U.S. field forces, including those in airplanes, tanks, and naval vessels, were of Browning design.

The Browning brothers parted company with Winchester at the end of the nineteenth century when the firm declined to produce their now-famous automatic shotgun. John Browning then crossed the Atlantic to Liege, Belgium, and licensed production of the unique sporting firearm to Fabrique Nationale d'Armes de Guerre.

The Belgian firm's manufacture of the Browning Automatic-5 began in 1902 and has continued to this day. Before he died while at the FN plant in 1926, John Browning made sixty-one trips across the Atlantic.

He was succeeded as company president by his son, Val, also a successful firearms inventor. John Val Browning, Val's son, became president in 1962, serving until 1976 when Harmon G. Williams took over; Don Gobel became president in 1980. Fabrique Nationale purchased the Browning Company in 1977 after the close association that had existed between these two businesses for seventy-nine years. Manufacture of the firm's sporting firearms continues in Belgium, Portugal, Italy, Japan, and Salt Lake City.

The Browning Company diversified its line of products over the years and moved its headquarters to a peaceful valley at Mountain Green, in Weber Canyon. Catalogs now list a wide variety of sporting rifles, shotguns, pistols, knives, fishing rods and reels, outdoor clothing, and golf equipment.

Many of the inventor's models are now on display at the Browning Museum in Ogden's historic Union Station. Adjacent to the museum are the Matthew Browning Theater and the Browning-Kimball vintage auto display.

The Center for Performing Arts at Weber State College and a radiation therapy department at St. Benedict's Hospital proudly

The world headquarters of the Browning Company is now in this park-like setting in Mountain Green just sixteen miles from Ogden.

carry the name of Val A. Browning as a testimony to his generosity.

The Browning Company is now recognized as one of the leading sporting goods manufacturers and distributors in the world. Its long-standing reputation for high-quality, reliable sporting goods products has been its hallmark throughout its 106-year history.

The firm is still best known for its hunting and sport shooting equipment, marketing a complete line of shotguns, rifles, pistols, archery equipment, outdoor knives, boots, and other rugged outdoor wear. In more recent years it has gained a strong position in the fishing tackle market with an extensive line of rods and reels.

In 1970 the company entered the golf pull cart business and became a leader in this field with its well-known "Bag Boy" and "Play Day" lines. Golf clubs, bags, and other accessories followed in 1976. The Ektelon Company, widely recognized as the leader in high-performance racquetball equipment, was acquired in 1980.

The Browning Company now employs 210 people at its Utah headquarters, which also includes its research facilities. Many more are employed at its distribution center in St. Louis, Missouri, and in factories overseas. Sales volume exceeds one hundred million annually in North America. Distribution in other countries is handled by Fabrique Nationale of Belgium.

The Browning brothers built their second sporting goods store near the center of Ogden in 1910. The offices were upstairs, and inventor John M. Browning's shop was in the back.

WEBER STATE COLLEGE

The Latter-day Saints (Mormon) Tabernacle at Twenty-second Street and Washington Boulevard at one time served as quarters for Weber Stake Academy, now Weber State College.

"I realize that I can only lay a foundation for a true education in the minds of young people, but with this they will progress eternally and none can stop them."
—Louis F. Moench

Those were the words of Louis F. Moench, principal, when he addressed the initial class of the Weber Stake Academy on January 7, 1889, in the old LDS Second Ward meetinghouse at Twenty-sixth Street and Grant Avenue in Ogden. The academy had two faculty members and ninety-eight students.

From this modest beginning nearly a century ago has grown one of Utah's most progressive institutions of higher learning—Weber State College, with an enrollment of more than 10,000 students and a faculty and staff of more than 1,000.

Rodney H. Brady, president since 1978, has elaborated on Moench's philosophy by setting out three "very ambitious but achievable goals" for the college. These goals are to cause Weber State College to continue on its course toward becoming the finest undergraduate college in America;

to cause Weber State to become widely known as a college at which every member of the faculty is clearly recognized as being a master teacher or is in the process of becoming a master teacher; and, finally, to cause Weber to become widely known as an institution where the student is clearly regarded and recognized as the most important person on campus.

The college, Brady believes, is "well on its way" toward accomplishing these objectives and will continue to concentrate "our attention and resources on providing a quality undergraduate education to every one of our students."

More than 100,000 men and women have been graduated from Weber State College and its predecessors. Many have gone on to become national and world leaders in government, business, technology, law, education, medicine, communications, the humanities, arts, and sciences.

That was what founders of the institution hoped would happen in 1889 when Lewis W. Shurtliff, president of the local Latter-day Saints Church Board of Education, appointed Moench as principal of the new Weber Stake Academy.

Within a few years permanent quarters were erected north of Twenty-fifth Street, between Adams and Jefferson. Several of the early trustees mortgaged their homes to provide funds for construction. The first structure was later called the Moench Building after the founding principal.

The school's name was changed to Weber Academy in 1908. Preparatory classes were dropped and only high school courses were offered beginning in 1912. Two years of college were added to the regular four-year high school

curriculum, and the first college class was graduated in 1917. Another name change, to Weber Normal College, was made in 1918. High school classes were discontinued in 1923 by the again renamed Weber College.

The Church of Jesus Christ of Latter-day Saints gave the college and its downtown campus to the State of Utah in 1933. It has since remained a tax-supported institution despite threats by an economy-minded legislature and governor in 1953 to return it to the church. That proposal was resoundingly defeated by a state-wide referendum.

Growth of the student body made authorities recognize that the crowded campus had to be abandoned, particularly because of accelerated enrollment after World War II. The state provided $50,000, and the community raised an equal amount for the purchase of 175 acres of farmland nestled against the Wasatch Mountains, east of Harrison Boulevard.

The Stewart Bell Tower, presented by Elizabeth and Donnell Stewart in 1971, is a memorial to Weber State College alumni, faculty, students, and staff. It stands 100 feet high, contains a 183-bell electronic carillon, and includes four cast bells.

The Weber State College campus covers more than 400 acres on the southeastern bench lands of Ogden.

Four functional new buildings were erected and occupied in 1954. Eventually thirty-three more major structures were added, and the campus expanded to more than 400 acres under a careful plan that recently earned Weber State College the superior award for campus development and beautification from the American Institute of Landscape Architects.

Millions of dollars were contributed by generous citizens to facilitate the improvements. These included the Val A. Browning Center for the Performing Arts, the Dee Events Center, the Ada Lindquist Plaza, the Stewart

The Ada Lindquist Plaza and Fountain, with the Val A. Browning Center for the Performing Arts in the background, provide a restful scene on the beautiful Weber State College campus.

Library and Bell Tower, the E.O. Wattis Business Building, the J. Willard Marriott Health Sciences Building, and the Willard L. Eccles Chair for Business Administration.

Academic progress has continued, especially after the institution became a four-year college. The first seniors were graduated in 1964—one year before the state legislature formally changed the name to Weber State College.

The institution is divided into seven schools—arts and humanities, natural science, social sciences, education, technology, business and economics, and allied health sciences. More than seventy different areas of study are available in a wide range of subjects. Postgraduate courses leading to master's degrees in education and accounting were recently authorized.

Weber State College's economic impact upon Ogden and the surrounding communities exceeds

$150 million a year, making it one of the most important contributors to the growing prosperity of northern Utah.

And don't forget the Weber Wildcats! Men and women wearing uniforms of purple and white compete in nine major sports. Weber's tremendous basketball teams have long dominated the Big Sky Conference and have gone on to compete in NCAA and NIT post-season tournaments.

Weber State College had a humble beginning a century ago but, as Louis Moench said of its young people, "None can stop them."

Weber State's basketball teams have consistently reached into the top U.S. collegiate rankings. Here Bruce Collins (22) goes against North Carolina during the Far West Classic in 1976.

213

ST. BENEDICT'S HOSPITAL

St. Benedict's Hospital occupied this facility at the head of Thirtieth Street from its opening in 1946 until 1977.

St. Benedict's Hospital combines an age-old philosophy and the very latest techniques in providing health care for residents of the Ogden area. The original facility that opened in southeastern Ogden in 1946 and the ultra-modern hospital in Washington Terrace that replaced it in 1977 were founded on the fundamental principles of the Sisters of the Order of St. Benedict.

St. Benedict, born more than 1,500 years ago, established a doctrine that stressed the need "to give glory to God through service to man." The Rule of St. Benedict centers around the statement that "before all things and above all things, care must be taken of the sick, so that they will be served as if they were Christ in person, for He Himself said, 'I was sick and you visited me' and 'what you did for one of these least ones, you did for me.'" The key phrase of that philosophy is etched on the face of a 32-foot

pillar in front of St. Benedict's Hospital as a constant reminder of the institution's principles.

Establishment of the hospital in Ogden was a direct outgrowth of World War II. Hill Field, Clearfield Naval Supply Depot, and the Utah General Depot joined the older Ogden Arsenal early in the 1940s as military authorities recognized Ogden's key strategic location. Consequently, the population of the area sky-rocketed.

Within a week after the December 7, 1941, bombing of Pearl Harbor, local and federal leaders recognized the need to provide health-care facilities beyond those already available. Monsignor W.J. Giroux, the pastor of Ogden's St. Joseph Catholic Church, aided by Drs. Max Seidner, E.R. Dumke, and George Fister, led the movement.

After a few false starts, Monsignor Giroux turned to the Sisters of the Order of St. Benedict and went to the motherhouse in St. Joseph, Minnesota, to contact the prioress, the Reverend Mother Rosamond Pratschner. His per-

suasion was effective, and the Ogden challenge was accepted on May 10, 1943.

A barren site of nearly ten acres was selected at the head of Thirtieth Street, east of Harrison Boulevard. Architect John K. Monroe drew plans for a four-story, 150-bed hospital. A $1.2-million contract was awarded, and ground was broken on October 3, 1944. Wartime shortages delayed construction, but the hospital's doors were finally opened on September 18, 1946. Benedictine nuns arrived months before the dedication and sewed drapes and bottled fruit while waiting to serve the sick.

The hospital was hailed as one of the most modern in the West. Its unique isolation ward was put to a severe test during the 1947-1948 polio outbreak, caring for almost 150 patients. Utah's first complete blood exchange of an infant because of Rh factor problems was performed at St. Benedict's Hospital on March 27, 1949. A 24-hour emergency room service was offered in 1969, and an innovative unit for the care of alcohol and chemically dependent patients was established in the early 1970s.

There were constant improvements made in the physical plant and equipment, keeping up with the parade of postwar advances in medical science. Departments of Pastoral Care and Social Services were organized. The St. Benedict's School of Nursing flourished from 1947 until 1967 when it was discontinued, and a cooperative educational program was established with Weber State College.

Financial problems led to the formation in 1971 of a lay governing board, the hospital's first, that included local business leaders and physicians as well as sisters. Robert K. Eisleben became the first permanent lay administrator on May 1, 1975.

After a quarter of a century of operation, it became apparent that entirely new facilities were needed. Twenty-five acres in Washington Terrace were secured. A 133-bed hospital was planned by architect John L. Piers, and ground was broken on October 30, 1974.

The old site was sold to the state, and a fund drive was conducted to help meet the fifteen million dollar cost. Patients moved into "New St. Ben's" on March 6, 1977. Within a few years a privately owned professional office building and convalescent center were opened, and a new alcohol and chemical dependency treatment wing was added to the hospital to round out the full-care campus.

The Val A. Browning Radiation Therapy Center, the first in northern Utah, opened in July 1977, and the Willard L. Eccles Eye Center began service the following year. By mid-1984 there were 201 beds in St. Benedict's Hospital, including 31 in the busy Alcohol and Chemical Dependency Treatment Center, and an updated nursery had 24 bassinets.

The Utah Priory of Benedictine Sisters, a dependent priory of the Minnesota motherhouse, was established in 1980 with Sister Francis Forster as regional superior.

A significant broadening of endeavors came in 1982 with the creation of St. Benedict's Health System, a not-for-profit corporation sponsored by the Sisters of the Order of St. Benedict and the Catholic Diocese of Salt Lake City.

Robert Eisleben was named system president, and P. Denny Oreb succeeded him as St. Benedict's Hospital president/chief exec-

utive officer. In addition to operating the Utah facility, system subsidiaries specialize in fund raising, real estate operations and management, and financial and computer services.

The system, located on the Ogden site of the old "St. Ben's," directs a variety of joint ventures. St. Benedict's ACT Corporation operates substance abuse and psychiatric programs in six states. Behavioral Health Systems Corporation is a joint venture with Arizona and Wisconsin sources in extending similar substance abuse and psychiatric programs to other states and abroad.

The new system was formed, president Eisleben explains, to strengthen the hospital after inflation elevated operating costs, and shorter patient stays and changes in governmental reimbursement systems decreased basic revenue.

By August 1, 1984, St. Benedict's Hospital had 860 full- and part-time hospital employees and a payroll of thirteen million dollars. In addition the System, with other subsidiaries, had 250 employees and a payroll of four million dollars.

Throughout the growth and expansion of St. Benedict's Hospital and Health System, the Rule of St. Benedict has been emphasized. As Robert Eisleben says, "Quality of care at St. Ben's is *not* negotiable."

The 1,500-year-old Rule of St. Benedict is etched on a pillar that dominates the entrance to St. Benedict's Hospital in Washington Terrace.

Ground was broken on October 3, 1944, for the original St. Benedict's Hospital on the city's East Bench. Present (left to right) were Bishop Lennox Federal of the Catholic Diocese of Salt Lake City; Bernie Diamond, executive secretary, Ogden Area Chamber of Commerce; Sister Estelle Nordick, hospital administrator; and Monsignor Joseph Kennedy, pastor of Ogden's St. Joseph Parish.

ROBERT H. HINCKLEY, INC.

Robert H. Hinckley, Inc., of Ogden has been selling Dodge cars and trucks longer than any other dealership in the United States.

In 1915 Robert Hinckley and his brother-in-law, Leonard Seely, opened their dealership in Mt. Pleasant, Sanpete County, in central Utah. Each partner put up $168. They purchased Dodge Serial No. 270 from the one-year-old Dodge Brothers manufacturing plant. That vehicle sold quickly, and the pair purchased more cars until volume had increased sufficiently for Hinckley and Seely to retain an automobile for personal and family use.

But, as Hinckley put it, "You can't sell cars to jack rabbits." The partners found there simply were not enough potential purchasers in the sparsely settled Mt. Pleasant area to assure long-range success. The partnership was terminated. Hinckley moved to Ogden in 1927 and rented a showroom at 2566 Washington Boulevard, across the city's main street from the municipal building. In 1928 a permanent home for Robert H. Hinckley, Inc., was built, three blocks to the south at 2810 Washington. The firm has operated at that site ever since.

Born in Fillmore, Robert Hinckley was the son of Edwin Smith Hinckley, a native of historic Cove Fort, Utah. The elder Hinckley was a counselor to the president of Brigham Young University and a superintendent of the Utah State Industrial School in Ogden.

Robert Hinckley was a schoolteacher before he went into the automobile business. So was his wife, the former Abrelia Clarissa Seely, whose father, John Seely, was noted for pioneering the raising of the famous Rambouillet breed of sheep.

A lifelong Democrat, Hinckley served a term as mayor in heavily

The principals of Robert H. Hinckley, Inc., are (left to right) Robert H. Hinckley, Jr., James S. Hinckley, and John S. Hinckley.

Republican Mt. Pleasant before moving to Ogden. Throughout his long and active career, he maintained a keen interest in politics. Eventually, he founded the Hinckley Institute of Politics at the University of Utah.

Abrelia Hinckley became, in effect, the nation's first female automobile dealer in 1932 when her husband became western regional director of the Depression-born Works Progress Administration (WPA).

Hinckley's tremendous record in this assignment led to his appointment as a member and eventually chairman of the Civil Aeronautics Authority (CAA) in Washington, D.C. He also was vice-president of the Sperry Corporation, the director of The War Contracts Settlement Board, and, until his retirement in the early 1970s, a vice-president of the American Broadcasting Company (ABC).

Initially, Dean Brimhall was associated with Hinckley in the Ogden automobile sales enterprise. The two were also partners in ownership of Utah-Pacific Airways, based at the old Ogden Airport in South Ogden.

When the Depression deepened in the mid-1930s, Hinckley took over full proprietorship of the Dodge agency and Brimhall retained the aircraft service, training pilots, selling planes, and offering aerial charters.

Robert and Abrelia Hinckley had four children—sons Robert

Robert H. Hinckley, Sr., and his wife, Abrelia, stand between a 1969 Dodge and the 1915 Dodge they drove to Yellowstone Park for their honeymoon.

Robert H. Hinckley opened his original Dodge dealership at 2566 Washington Boulevard in Ogden in 1927.

Jr., John, and Paul and daughter Elizabeth, who became Mrs. Preston Nibley. Robert Jr. and Paul were graduates of the U.S. Military Academy at West Point and spent many years in the service. John graduated from New Mexico Military Institute and the University of Utah. John also went into the U.S. Army during World War II and emerged, as a captain in the Infantry, in 1948 to take over operation of the Ogden dealership and begin his own career as a leader in the American automobile industry. Robert, upon his early military retirement, opened a Hinckley Dodge dealership in Salt Lake City at 2309 South State Street in 1955.

A third generation of the Hinckley family has also entered the automobile business. James S. Hinckley, son of Robert Jr., became active in the Salt Lake City operation and, eventually, its manager.

The family also became involved in a number of other enterprises— real estate, vending and food services, and cattle and horse raising. Welsh ponies, Arabian horses, and Swiss-originated Simmental cattle became the pride of the Garden of Eden, the Hinckley ranch near Eden in Ogden Valley, where Robert Hinckley spent his later years.

John Hinckley was president of the National Automobile Dealers Association in 1973 when the full impact of the worldwide fuel crises, including the OPEC oil embargo, and competition from foreign manufacturers nearly devastated the U.S. industry.

He recalled in a 1984 interview that American-made cars had become "bigger and bigger," weighing up to 6,000 pounds and getting only eight to ten miles to the gallon of gasoline. Foreign producers, he said, began on a foundation of American technology and know-how and produced lighter, cheaper vehicles that made great inroads on the U.S. market.

"Competition is the name of the game, however," John Hinckley added, "and the American industry has come back strongly, particularly Chrysler under the heroic leadership of chairman Lee Iacocca. Our cars now weigh 1,800 to 2,500 pounds, and many get forty to fifty miles per gallon."

He admitted the ten years from the mid-1970s to the mid-1980s were "tougher than the Depression and I wouldn't want to go through them again." Today's U.S.-made vehicles, he insisted, are tops in the world in economy and steadily improving in quality. As a result, American production is again increasing, despite high interest rates. "I agree with Lee Iacocca when he said 'We don't want to be the biggest, just the best, automobile manufacturer,'" Hinckley concluded.

Membership in the National Automobile Association Dealers declined from 25,000 to 19,000 during the decade-long crises. John Hinckley attributed much of this to improved highways that permitted purchasers to range farther to look over larger inventories available in bigger cities. Improved quality, he explains, has lessened the need for local service facilities.

Robert H. Hinckley, Inc., emerged from the disruptive changes stronger than ever, with more than 150 employees in the Ogden and Salt Lake City dealerships and the company-owned, prosperous Kwik Vending Service. And, according to John Hinckley, "America has not lost its love affair with the automobile."

The Hinckley Dodge dealership as it appears today.

BURTON-WALKER LUMBER COMPANY

This was the Burton-Walker Lumber Company yard, located at 2427 Lincoln Avenue, shortly after it was founded in 1920.

The Burton-Walker Lumber Company, founded in 1920, is a family-owned and -operated retail lumber and hardware dealer.

When Elmer L. Burton and Thomas E. Walker established their lumberyard it was one of eleven in the city, which then had about 38,000 residents. Over the years the population of Ogden has doubled, and that of Weber County has tripled, while seven of the lumber firms have foundered on economic shoals and three others have become units of chain operations.

Burton-Walker's history has not been without its problems. Rapid expansion during the prosperity of the late 1970s was followed in the early 1980s by recession and a deep depression in the lumber-consuming building industry. This forced an unwelcomed contraction that prompted E.A. "Ed" Burton, principal owner and company president, to comment, "We're

lucky to have made it through the recession. Times in the lumber business are still tough. And they will remain difficult until and unless interest rates come down permanently."

However, Burton-Walker Lumber Company has operated at the same 2427 Lincoln Avenue location in downtown Ogden, through good times and bad, since its formal incorporation on February 1, 1920. Elmer L. Burton, a Missouri native, and Thomas E. Walker, an enterprising Idahoan, arrived in Ogden on February 1 and opened the yard that same day.

At the outset, Walker was general manager and Burton secretary/treasurer. The president and majority stockholder was Roland S. Eccles, a member of a noted family with widespread business interests that included the development of Oregon's Blue Mountain Timber Tract. He was a son of William H. Eccles and a nephew of David E. Eccles.

Walker left the lumberyard in 1926 to run a new business in Davis County and was never again

involved in the firm. Burton was then named president, treasurer, and general manager.

Stock transfers brought a close alliance that lasted for the next thirty-four years with the Anderson Lumber Company, another Eccles family-based concern. The connection was financial only. Total management control was vested in the Burtons and has remained that way.

During the Great Depression Burton purchased several Ogden lots and homes were built on them during the winters to provide steady employment for skilled carpenters. These craftsmen included two sets of brothers—Ed, Gus, and Blaine Stromberg and Leonard, Leo, and Winslow Hurst. According to a corporate history prepared by Carl E. Thompson, veteran Ogden-area lumberman and onetime Burton-Walker manager, the firm also built many homes in Ogden's Sullivan Hollow district, in Roy, and in Burton Park in southeast Ogden.

Elmer Burton and Sylvia Salmon were married on March 17, 1916, in Burley, Idaho, and lived there for nearly four years before taking up permanent residence in Ogden. They had four children—Jay, Max, Betty, and Edward. Jay was active in the family lumber enterprise briefly after World War II, then went into custom cabinet and millwork. Max, an interior designer, and Betty, a physical therapist, moved to California.

Ed Burton, born July 31, 1931, spent much of his youth in the lumberyard, particularly during the war when he helped his father and the Burton-Walker crew assemble pallets, shipping boxes, and bundles of survey stakes. Ed married Bonnie Burnett in December 1949. They have four

The Burton-Walker Lumber Company, still at its original location.

children—David, Susan, Ronette, and Sandra. After a hitch in the U.S. Navy, the founder's youngest son began his own career as a lumber merchant in 1954 by taking over the vital order desk.

Elmer Burton, one of the earliest presidents of the Rocky Mountain Lumber Dealers Association, turned seventy years old in 1960 and gradually gave complete operation of the corporation to his son. He died on February 1, 1979, fifty-nine years to the day after co-founding the Burton-Walker Lumber Company.

Ed Burton realized that the days of a lumberyard based almost entirely on sales to contractors were numbered. He established a wholesale division, a pre-hung door plant, and opened a second retail yard in the booming, mid-Davis County city of Layton. Property surrounding the U-shaped Ogden plant was acquired, the old offices and store demolished, and a new two-story brick

structure built.

The larger, more efficient facility permitted the firm to continue its sales to contractors and at the same time sell an ever-broadening line of building supplies to individual home owners. Retail sales, formerly only 5 percent of the business, had reached 30 percent and were growing steadily.

In 1982 Burton-Walker had 125 employees and recorded sales for the year of more than twelve million dollars. Then came the recession, and construction of homes throughout the country came to a near standstill.

The Layton store and yard were sold and so was the wholesale division. In 1983 sales barely topped five million dollars. This saddened Ed Burton, whose own family had acquired control of all of the firm's stock by late 1975. But the Burton-Walker president tightened his belt and was determined to adjust to the changing conditions by placing near-equal

emphasis on four operational divisions—carload, wholesale, contractor, and consumer sales.

He was joined by members of his close-knit, hardworking family. Son Dave became retail manager, and son-in-law Michael McMickel managed sales to contractors. Daughter Sandra Myers helped with an expanded retail advertising program. Daughter Ronette Davis became adept at operating computers in the central office.

"I didn't believe dad when he said, during the boom, that things were not going to go on like that forever," Ed Burton says. "But I found out how right he was! It's going to be tough sledding, until interest rates come down, but we're determined to make it."

The Burton family record proves they most likely will.

COMMERCIAL SECURITY BANK

Harold E. Hemingway, 1887-1949.

The Ogden-based Commercial Security Bank has roots that extend back more than a century to a small general store in a rough-and-tough railroad town in northern Utah. From that tiny beginning has emerged a strong financial institution with twenty-six offices and assets of over $700 million. The tremendous growth for the past half-century is a tribute to the Hemingways, one of Utah's most noted banking families, and their loyal associates.

Commercial Security Bank's ancestry is traced directly to the store that John William Guthrie opened early in 1869 in Corinne. The town was known locally as the "Burg on the Bear," because of its site on the meandering Bear River, a few miles upstream from the Great Salt Lake and twenty-five miles northwest of Ogden.

Guthrie arrived in Corinne as Union Pacific construction gangs were racing their rivals from Central Pacific to complete America's first transcontinental railroad. The last spike—of pure gold—was driven on May 10, 1869, at Promontory Summit, twenty-three miles west of Corinne.

After the Golden Spike was put in place, it was several years before auxiliary rail lines were laid northward to the booming mining camps of Idaho and Montana. The main shipping point for their supplies, hauled in huge wagons, was Corinne.

Guthrie, mayor of Corinne, enlarged his store until it became the largest structure in town. Signs in front proclaimed the availability of flour and grain, crockery and glassware, groceries and provisions. In 1875 he added another word: Banker.

No preliminary applications had to be filed in those days to start a bank. All that was required was a strong safe to hold the cash and currency and an entrepreneur with a reputation for honesty and fair dealing. Guthrie had those qualities.

Corinne suffered a severe blow, however, when Ogden was officially designated as the junction between the Central Pacific and the Union Pacific. Guthrie recognized that Corinne would soon decline, and in 1877 he moved to Ogden to open the J.W. Guthrie Co. Bank at 325 Fourth (now Twenty-fourth) Street. After a year Guthrie opened an investment company and sold the bank to Harkness & Co.

The name was changed to Commercial National Bank when a national charter was secured on March 8, 1884. New offices were opened on the northeast corner of Twenty-fourth and Washington Boulevard. When that structure burned in 1911, the bank moved to 369 Twenty-fourth Street.

Meanwhile, T.D. Ryan opened the Security Trust and Savings Bank on the east side of Washington Boulevard, near Twenty-fifth Street, on August 29, 1910. Three years later the renamed Security State Bank moved to the southwest corner of Hudson (now Kiesel) Avenue and Twenty-fourth Street.

The Commercial Security Bank was formed on July 30, 1925, through the merger of Ryan's Security State Bank and Commercial National Bank, then headed by Patrick Healy. Its headquarters were in Commercial National's offices.

Another strong ingredient was added on June 10, 1930, with the acquisition of the National Bank of Commerce, opened in 1904 by pioneer Ogden banker James Pingree as the Pingree National Bank, and eventually housed at 2453 Washington Boulevard. The architect of the 1930 merger was Harold Edgar Hemingway, who had moved to Ogden in 1929 to assume leadership of the Commercial Security Bank—the institution still principally owned by his family.

Hemingway was born in Ontario, Canada, in 1887, and was graduated from Victoria College of the University of Toronto. He sold

Robert G. Hemingway, 1915-1966.

Richard K. Hemingway, chairman of Commercial Security Bank.

Robert H. Bischoff, president of Commercial Security Bank.

bonds, insurance, and real estate for a few years, then moved to Bryant, South Dakota, a farming hamlet near Watertown, and opened the first Hemingway bank. He was joined by his bride, the former Isabel Whitlam. Their first son, Robert, was born shortly after the family settled in the United States.

By 1922 the Hemingways had moved three more times, buying then selling increasingly larger banks in Yerington, Nevada, and Bingham Canyon, Utah, before settling in Burley, Idaho. Harold Hemingway acquired the Burley National Bank, the beginning venture that continues today, still under Hemingway ownership, as the Idaho Bank & Trust Co.

Tragedy struck in 1927 when Mrs. Hemingway was fatally injured in a traffic accident while Christmas shopping with her sons, Robert and Richard, who was born while the family was in Bingham. Two years later the elder Hemingway moved to Ogden to assume control of Commercial Security Bank.

A severe challenge came as the Great Depression threatened the survival of all financial institutions. The most strenuous test for Commercial Security Bank came on August 31, 1931, two days after the Ogden State Bank became the latest Utah financial institution to fold. Worried depositors formed long lines in front of the bank before it opened. Hemingway anticipated this and had cash piled on the counters. When the doors opened, all withdrawal orders were honored. Hemingway even provided sandwiches for staff members and customers. By nightfall the lines had disappeared, and there was still cash available.

No depositor of Commercial Security Bank has ever lost a penny because of CSB's failure to meet its obligations. Harold Hemingway was proud of that record, and so are the bank officers who have followed him.

Harold Hemingway's distinguished career ended in 1949 when he died at the age of sixty-two, victim of a rare form of brain cancer. He was succeeded as Commercial Security Bank president by his elder son, Robert, who had trained for this eventual responsibility with New York City bond firms and as an executive of Idaho Bank and Trust Co. The younger son, Richard Keith Hemingway, became vice-president.

Three suburban offices were soon opened at 3775 Wall Avenue, at 124 West 4600 South in Washington Terrace, and at Harrison Boulevard and Thirty-sixth Street, near the Weber State College campus. The venerable but deteriorated Broom Hotel, once Ogden's finest, at Twenty-fifth and Washington, was purchased, razed, and replaced by a modern, two-story structure. Opened on May 8, 1960, this facility remains the home office of Commercial Security.

Quiet, soft-spoken Bob Hemingway was a civic leader like his father. He became president of the Ogden Area Chamber of Commerce, an adviser to St. Benedict's Hospital, and a charter trustee of Weber State College. Then he, too, was struck down, suffering a fatal heart attack on January 22, 1966, at the age of fifty.

Richard Hemingway assumed the presidency of the bank and continued the Hemingway tradition of community leadership. He has served as president of the chamber, the Weber Industrial Development Agency, and the Ogden Industrial Development Corporation. As a member of the Utah State Building Board, he was influential in furthering legislation that led to construction of buildings vital to the growth of what became Weber State College.

When Richard Hemingway became chief executive officer of Commercial Security Bank early in 1966, it was exclusively an Ogden area institution, with four

The CSB Tower, at 50 South Main Street in Salt Lake City, was completed in 1980. At 251 feet it is the tallest bank building in Utah.

when Commercial Security Bank acquired Beehive State Bank, headquartered in Salt Lake City, with branches in Tooele and Grantsville. In 1971 the Granite National Bank in the Sugar House area of Salt Lake City was acquired, followed two years later by the Murray State Bank, with offices in Murray and Midvale. Both the Orem State Bank and the Bank of Salt Lake were acquired in 1974, giving Commercial Security Bank new offices in Orem, South Salt Lake, and near the University of Utah in Salt Lake City. In 1978 the Helper State Bank was acquired, providing new offices in Helper, Price, and Green River, Utah. The most recent acquisition was the 1981 purchase of the Bear River State Bank in Tremonton.

The management team developed by chairman Hemingway to operate and expand the impressive banking network includes seven key individuals: Robert H. Bischoff, president and chief operating officer; Ross E. Kendell, executive vice-president; Roy M. Adreon, senior vice-president and manager of the mortgage loan department; David E. Bronson, senior vice-president and manager of the branch administration division; L. Brent Milne, senior vice-president and manager of the administration and operations division; Richard L. Nelson, senior vice-president and manager of the credit administration division; and Eugene Overfelt, senior vice-president and manager of the marketing division.

President Bischoff spoke for his colleagues in paying tribute to the farsighted leadership of Richard Hemingway:

"He has been the driving force behind the expansion of Commercial Security Bank. He was absolutely determined that CSB

offices in the city and its suburbs. Total assets of the bank at the end of 1965 were $71.4 million, and total stockholders' equity amounted to $4.9 million.

With these corporate resources as a base, Hemingway put together a management team, which formed the Commercial Security Bancorporation in 1972 as a major Utah regional banking system that now owns the state's fourth-largest bank.

By the end of 1984, some nineteen years later, Hemingway, his management team, and a dedicated staff had increased total assets to over $700 million. During this same period the total number of banking offices increased from

four to twenty-six. This includes offices in Logan and Tremonton on the north, Price, Helper, and Green River on the south, and as far west as Wendover.

During those eighteen years total assets of Commercial Security Bank (now Commercial Security Bancorporation), grew at the remarkable annual rate of 13.4 percent. An amazing aspect of the growth and expansion of Commercial Security Bank is that it was achieved without dilution of the stockholders' equity. The entire program was financed from profits created through efficient operations and effective management.

The growth of the bank during the Richard Hemingway administration has been through acquisition and merger, as well as conventional branching. The first of many mergers came in 1968

should become a statewide institution as a banking system of major importance. He also made certain that all acquisitions should be paid for in cash, without diluting stockholders' equity. In acquiring new banking offices, we have also acquired many fine people, and it is the people who make the banks go, not the brick and mortar of the buildings where they work."

Bischoff also describes Hemingway as a "great delegator" who assigns responsibilities to members of the senior management team that has been developed by Commercial Security Bank.

The tallest achievement, literally, of the bank's expansion was the completion of the CSB Tower in the Crossroads Plaza Shopping Center on Salt Lake City's Main Street. A new CSB branch was opened there on August 1, 1980, with administrative offices on the nineteenth and twentieth floors.

Aiding the 650 employees in the twenty-six banking offices is a

"J.W. Guthrie, Banker." The addition of "banker" on the Guthrie store in historic Corinne, Utah, in 1875, marked the first advertisement of the banking organization known today as the Commercial Security Bank. Courtesy, Utah State Historical Society

growing network of "InstaBankers," CSB's Automatic-teller machines (ATMs) in key locations allowing around-the-clock access. Commercial Security was the first bank in Utah to provide a discount brokerage service to facilitate the purchase of stocks. A new operations center was opened in

1984 in Salt Lake City, where the latest in sophisticated devices have been installed.

Commercial Security Bank, its officers, and staff have met all challenges for well over a century. They expect to continue in the decades to come.

The Broom Hotel, at the corner of Twenty-fifth Street and Washington Boulevard, was Ogden's showplace hostelry in 1889. A "donkey engine" pulled two trolley cars on tracks along the dirt street. This corner is now occupied by the home office of Commercial Security Bank. Courtesy, Utah State Historical Society

The bank's first computer-based data center was opened in Roy, Utah, in 1972 by (left to right) CSB vice-president John F. Howard, Utah Governor Calvin L. Rampton, and CSB chairman Richard K. Hemingway.

AMERICAN NUTRITION, INC.

Jack Behnken, president,
founded the company in 1972.

American Nutrition's major production facility is a
100,000-square-foot building located at Twenty-ninth Street and
Reeves Avenue.

Mel Carey, plant manager,
was the firm's first employee.

The most enthusiastic supporters of American Nutrition, Inc., are thousands of well-fed dogs and cats throughout thirteen western states. The Ogden-based firm annually produces more than 90,000 tons of pet foods and snacks, as well as feed for mink raised for their valuable fur. It is an unusual industry, and important to the economy, as well. Sales in 1984 exceeded thirty million dollars.

Jack Behnken, a Pennsylvania native who had worked for the Kellogg Company, founded the Ogden concern in 1972 as Animal Nutrition, Inc. Kellogg had been selling mink feed but decided to drop this particular line. Fur breeders of the region persuaded Behnken to acquire production equipment and formulas from the Kellogg Company and start a plant in the former Carnation Company building between Wall Avenue and the railroad tracks, just north of Twenty-ninth Street.

Mel Carey came from Michigan to join the new enterprise, the only non-Utahn among the firm's Ogden employees. He was the original plant manager, overseeing not only production and packaging, but supervising the quality-control laboratory that ensures cleanliness and proper formulation of the products.

Operations were expanded in 1977 when the Reeves Warehouse, also known as the Western Auto Warehouse, directly west across Reeves Avenue from the original plant, was purchased.

The company name, Animal Nutrition, Inc., was changed in 1977 to American Nutrition, Inc. The stockholders felt this name better expressed the firm's broadened markets.

The original plant is now operated as a subsidiary, called Rocky Mountain Milling Company. Producing mink feed and private-label pet foods, it accounts for about 25 percent of overall production. Another 25 percent is produced by the wholly owned Southwest Pet Products, Inc., in Phoenix, where dry dog and cat foods are made.

The remainder of the production is in the main plant, where the corporate headquarters is also located. This includes the

Co-Founders	
Jack Youngs	Jim Corell
Doren Boyce	Bill McDavid
Don Lloyd	John Webster
Jim Allen	Lloyd Harmon
Nancy Behnken	Don Frahm
Ennis Rushton	Ryan Judson
Russ Shupe	Art Werre
Mike Nelson	Bruce Clark
Jon Perry	Dave Doxey

contract manufacturing of pet foods as well as the formulation, preparation, packaging, and shipping of American Nutrition's own brands.

Its food for pets is sold under the company's "Atta Boy" label and includes various package sizes of dry dog food, snacks, and large and small dog biscuits called "Vita-Bones." They are shipped on plastic-wrapped pallets by rail or truck, in boxes and bags containing from eighteen ounces to fifty pounds. "Tri Pro," another American Nutrition line, includes dog, puppy, and cat foods packaged in a variety of sizes.

Special formulas have been devised for different pet customers, and special preparations are made up by request for distributors who have their own specific requirements.

American Nutrition, Inc., has 100 employees, most of them in Ogden, with others in the Southwest Pet Products plant in Phoenix and in sales offices maintained in California and Washington. The corporate staff is dedicated to high quality and customer satisfaction. They are Mel Carey, product development manager; Ennis Rushton, customer service; Ryan Judson, quality control; Maurine Wilson, accounting; and Scott Matthews, marketing.

CASE, LOWE AND HART, INC.

Case, Lowe and Hart, Inc., is the only Ogden firm that provides its industrial and commercial clients with architectural and engineering services from the same suite of offices. President Edward T. Case is a mechanical engineer, vice-president Richard D. Lowe is an architect, and secretary/treasurer Robert J. Hart is an electrical engineer. Their combined professional experience totals more than ninety years.

Individually, and as a team, they and their skilled staff have designed more than 1,000 projects throughout the Intermountain West with construction costs well over $100 million. Main offices are in Suite 500 of the Kiesel Building in downtown Ogden, with a branch office in the Judge Building in Salt Lake City.

They take pride in all of their jobs, but the partners are especially proud of the engine house at the Golden Spike National Historic Site at Promontory, fifty-five miles northwest of Ogden. That is where America's first transcontinental railroad was completed in 1869. The CLH-designed engine house not only shelters replicas of Engine No. 119 and *Jupiter,* but provides steam to keep the boilers warm and ready to operate when the locomotives are not on display.

Other unique projects include hydraulic operators for sixty-ton doors of a jet engine-testing facility at Hill Air Force Base, a geothermal heating system for the Utah State Prison, steam-generation units to capture waste heat from incinerators, a heat-recovery system for a cheese plant whey evaporator at a large dairy, and a bank's data system building that is warmed by excess heat from computers.

The firm also designed the large buildings near the Ogden Mu-

The three top executives of Case, Lowe and Hart, Inc., examine blueprints at the Ogden office. From left to right are Richard D. Lowe, vice-president; Edward T. Case, president; and Robert J. Hart, secretary/treasurer.

nicipal Airport where Williams International makes turbine engines to power America's cruise missiles. A service center designed by the firm for Brigham City won special awards from the Consulting Engineers Council of Utah and the Utah Society of the American Institute of Architects.

The firm's wide range of clients includes the federal, state, and local governments, school systems, individuals, and various industries.

Ed Case graduated from Oregon State College in 1949 as a mechanical engineer and is now registered in five western states. He is a past president of the Consulting Engineers Council of Utah and of the Northern Utah Chapter of the Utah Society of Professional Engineers. He practiced privately from 1963 until 1975 when Case, Lowe and Hart, Inc., was formed.

Dick Lowe received degrees in architecture and engineering from Kansas State University in 1951 and 1952. He had his own architect's office in Ogden from 1960 until the 1975 merger. He is a past president of the Northern Utah Chapter of the American Institute of Architects.

Bob Hart, a 1963 electrical engineering graduate of Brigham Young University, began working with Case in Ogden in 1968 and became an officer of the firm when the present company was organized. He is a past president of the Utah Society of Professional Engineers.

At present, Case, Lowe and Hart, Inc., has a staff of twenty-one men and women, including three licensed architects, four mechanical engineers, two electrical engineers, six draftsmen, one interior designer, a specification writer, and four administrative personnel, including computer operators.

The engine house that shelters replicas of historic locomotives Jupiter *and Engine No. 119 at the Golden Spike National Historic Site is one of the most visible of the more than 1,000 projects designed by Case, Lowe and Hart, Inc.*

UTAH POWER AND LIGHT COMPANY

Ogden's early hydroelectric generating plants, situated in Ogden Canyon, were frequent victims of spring floods.

When the primitive generators of the Ogden City Electric Light Co. began turning in 1881, they produced enough electricity for forty-five small light globes. By today's standards that's not even enough power to warm one modern electric frying pan!

The firm's successor, Utah Power and Light Company, today has a system-wide capacity of more than 3.2 million kilowatts. That's more than sufficient to meet the myriad of domestic and industrial needs for about 500,000 customers over a 90,000-square-mile service area in Utah, southwestern Wyoming, and southeastern Idaho.

Ogden City Electric Light's first-year revenue was only a few hundred dollars, barely meeting its two-man payroll. UP&L now has operating revenues approaching one billion dollars annually, with 4,500 employees, assets of $2.8 billion, and thousands of stockholders all over the nation.

Utah Power and Light's Ogden-based northern Utah division has 386 employees, with a yearly payroll exceeding nine million dollars. It serves, through 1,800 miles of lines, nearly 100,000 customers in Weber, Davis, Box Elder, Morgan, Cache, and Rich counties.

That first Ogden power plant was subsidized by the town's residents. In 1983 UP&L paid $1.5 million in property taxes in the six northern counties, including $1.2 million for the support of schools. In Weber County alone, the investor-owned utility paid $753,465 in property taxes, in-cluding $386,275 for schools.

The 1881 Ogden facility, at Twenty-fourth Street and Adams Avenue, housed one small, eighty-horsepower boiler and two carbon arc generating devices. Their direct current went only a few blocks to the thirty-six private thirty-candlepower (less than twenty watts) lights and nine municipal streetlights that were only slightly brighter. Power was generated during a few evening hours—dusk until not later than 10 p.m. On nights when the moonlight was bright, the system didn't operate in order to save coal.

UP&L now obtains its electricity from a variety of sources, including hydroelectric plants, particularly on the Bear River in Utah and Idaho; massive steam plants, whose equipment includes generators of 400,000-kilowatt capacity; connections with West-wide energy networks; and even natural thermal hot water and steam.

The state of Utah was among the American pioneers in generating, distributing, and using electricity. Thomas Edison invented the world's first incandescent light globe in 1879 to inaugurate the era of electric light and power. Within two years Salt Lake City became the fifth city—after New York City, London, San Francisco, and Cleveland—to have its own utility with the formation of the Salt Lake Power, Light and Heating Co.

Ogden City Electric Light Co. was incorporated on May 10, 1881, only a few weeks after the Salt Lake City firm was started. This was only twelve years to the day after the Golden Spike was driven at Promontory, fifty miles northwest of Ogden, to unite tracks of America's first transcontinental railway.

Edison's novel incandescent lights were still in the experimental stage in mid-1881 when Ogden gained nationwide publicity with its "Rube Goldberg-like" attempt to light the entire downtown area from a single tower. The steel structure, 100 feet tall, was erected adjacent to the generating station, located where Larkin's Mortuary is now. Four big carbon-arc light fixtures were placed at the ends of 25-foot arms.

As dusk fell the municipal band stopped playing. A switch was thrown in the plant. The lights arced brightly and the crowd, which had dispersed to see if, as advertised, a newspaper could be read a block away, cheered. The cheers turned to groans when the lights flickered, then went out, after only a few minutes. The light tower was a failure.

The Ogden City Electric Light Co. tried to sell the tower to the mayor and commission, contending that it could be used to house the fire bell "since iron does not absorb sound like a wooden tower." There would be no sale, and the structure was demolished.

There were also problems with Ogden's first hydroelectric generating station, built in Ogden Canyon near Lewis Canyon. It was constructed, below a small dam, in May 1883, but was washed out by spring floods in early 1884. Another small plant was built farther up the canyon but was plagued by floods and ice. Canyon winds frequently disrupted lines to the city.

Sponsors of the Ogden company plugged away. Peebles Drug Store and Mark Goldsmith Clothing were connected to the system after they pioneered the installation of electric lights in their establishments.

Rates were far more expensive

When the Pioneer power plant was built in 1896 near the mouth of Ogden Canyon, its owners boasted it would be "second only to Niagara in capacity."

than they are today. The bill for power to a single arc light from dusk until 10 p.m. was $17.50 per month. If the light burned all night it cost $24 for electricity.

Contributions to the community's welfare included lighting for the July 24, 1881, Pioneer Days celebration. The *Ogden Daily Herald* reported:

"The night was given up to the enjoyment of all folks who took an unstinted part in the terpsichiosean [sic] sports with accompaniment of Fowler's string band, and under the effulgent raise [sic] of two electric lamps generously placed there and operated by the Electric Light Co. who have thanks of the commit-

tee and of the whole public for liberality."

Incandescent lamps began replacing the unreliable, smoky carbon arc devices in the mid-1880s, and Ogden's electric company switched from direct current to alternating current, proven easier to transmit longer distances by experiments in Colorado and Utah.

The brighter lights drew praise from the *Ogden Daily Herald,* which described them as "ornamental, safe, make no dust, give out no heat, and are absolutely harmless so far as fire is concerned." The newspaper went too far, however, in suggesting that "electric current necessary to run them is also so small that the ends of the wire may be taken in the finger and placed against the tongue with perfect safety."

The new lamps proved so pop-

Power lines, including those for trolleys, were conspicuous along Washington Boulevard in the early 1900s.

ular that several were installed in the Ogden LDS Tabernacle on February 21, 1883. By 1887 there were 2,220 lights in Ogden!

The increased load and unreliability of the canyon hydro plants led Ogden City Electric to build a second steam-powered plant in 1890 at Twenty-first Street and Wall Avenue.

There were no government regulations in those days, and utilities frequently competed vigorously for the same contracts. Citizen's Electric Co., backed by municipal officials, won the street lighting franchise and built its own generating station at Grant and Twentieth Street. It began production in January 1891, and soon its lines powered 1,200 incandescent lights. Then the Ogden Gas, Light and Fuel Co. was organized, and in December 1891 it took over the customers of both City Electric and Citizen's

Electric.

Electric cars replaced mule-drawn "jitneys" in Salt Lake City in 1890, and this more efficient style of street transportation soon was expanded to Ogden.

Ogden made electrical industry headlines again early in 1893 when the Pioneer Electric Power Co., capitalized at one million dollars, was formed with George Q. Cannon as president, Fred J. Kiesel as vice-president, C.K. Bannister as secretary/treasurer, and Frank Cannon, former editor of the *Ogden Standard,* as general manager. Its goal was to construct a water-powered hydroelectric generating station "second only to Niagara in capacity."

Planned were a dam at the upper mouth of Ogden Canyon (where Pine View Dam is now), six miles of pipe, and a ten-generator plant just west of the canyon's lower end. "Ogden is going to be THE manufacturing town of the West," the *Standard* editorialized. "Nothing can stop it . . . Ogden will be a city of fac-

tories, but there will be no smoking chimneys."

However, costs were above estimates, and only five of the generating units were installed, with a total capacity of 3,730 kilowatts. The plant, with the words Pioneer Electric Power Co. above its big doors, is operating today. A pair of 2,500-kilowatt generators in 1912-1913 replaced those installed in 1896.

Pioneer Station went on line in May 1897. Two months later its ownership was taken over by the new Union Light and Power Co. Pioneer employees did retain a novel "sickness insurance" plan inaugurated to provide free hospital care and medicine when off the job because of sickness or injury. Each worker paid fifty cents a month, and the company picked up other costs.

Another new hydroelectric plant in the area was built in 1910 by the Utah Light and Railway Co. to provide power for its growing network, especially the Ogden and Salt Lake City street railways.

This station was built in Weber Canyon, near Devil's Gate, and is also still operating today. Its capacity, when the water is high and the gates wide open, is 3,500 kilowatts.

The Davis and Weber Counties Canal Co., formed in 1884, developed its own generating station, providing power for irrigation pumps, in 1912. Located at the end of a seven-mile-long canal, the 3,750-kilowatt plant operated until 1971. It is still a major switching terminal for Utah Power and Light Company.

Five other companies, in turn, were formed to deliver electricity to Ogden and vicinity. They were the Salt Lake and Ogden Gas and Electric Co., February 14, 1893, to November 4, 1897; Union Light and Power Co., August 9, 1897, to December 30, 1899; Utah Light and Power Co., December 30, 1899, to January 2, 1904; Utah Light and Railway Co., January 2, 1904, to September 18, 1914; and Merchants Light and Power Co., February 20, 1911, to July 7, 1913.

At times, poles and lines of two competing power firms, plus those of various telegraph and telephone concerns, crowded Ogden's streets and alleys, causing critics to complain about the mess of wires and obstructions to traffic. Finally, Utah Power and Light Co. was organized in 1912 and began to consolidate the various electric services, taking over four major power companies and, eventually, more than 130 smaller suppliers. UP&L began operations in the Ogden area on July 7, 1913. The firm was controlled originally by Electric Bond and Share Co. but became independent in 1946.

The Bear River was developed with a series of dams, reservoirs, and plants that provide 125,000 kilowatts of generating capacity. In the modern times of high fossil fuel costs, this comparatively inexpensive water power is a blessing to the company and its ratepayers, especially in recent "wet" years when stream flow has been high.

Distribution systems have been greatly expanded, with tremendous growth during world wars I and II as the Weber-Davis area was selected for several large military installations, including the old Ogden Arsenal and Clearfield Naval Supply Depot and the still-expanding Defense Depot Ogden and Hill Air Force Base.

Growth of industries in the area

Utah's first hydroelectric facility was built in the spring of 1883 by Ogden City Electric Company, a Utah Power and Light Company predecessor. The plant, in Ogden Canyon near Lewis Camp, operated for only a year before it was destroyed by high water.

has also prompted the installation of new, heavier transmission lines and intricate switching centers, such as the Ben Lomond substation near Willard Bay. A small gas-turbine generator was placed near Little Mountain in the mid-1960s to generate electricity for the adjacent Great Salt Lake Minerals and Chemicals Company refinery.

The three-state territory served by Utah Power and Light Company represents one of the largest areas in the world covered by a single investor-owned utility. Company officials are proud of the firm's record for reliability, modernization, and efficiency. From its formation in 1912 until inflation's inroads hit in 1962, the company never raised rates; instead, they were frequently lowered. And today the amount of electricity Utah Power and Light Company can provide would heat about 3.2 million electric frying pans.

COCA-COLA BOTTLING COMPANY OF OGDEN

A popular form of advertising in the 1940s, this sign proclaims the merits of Coca-Cola from the wall of Fred Timmerman's market.

Coke is "the real thing" for the Day family. So it's only natural that they own and operate the Coca-Cola Bottling Company of Ogden. Their ultramodern plant, located at 2860 Pennsylvania Avenue, serves thirsty consumers throughout Weber, North Davis, and Box Elder counties.

A.M. Day is president and general manager. Ben H. Day is vice-president, manager, and the driving force of the firm. Joe Day is vice-president and treasurer.

It is a major operation with nearly 100 employees, many of them driving the thirty-four route trucks and sixteen other vehicles that carry Coke and associated beverages to stores, cafes, lunch-rooms, and other establishments.

The Day family of Douglas, in the southern part of Georgia, has long been associated with the parent Coca-Cola Company of Atlanta.

Coca-Cola, the world's most

popular soft drink, was formulated in 1886 by a Dr. Pendleton, an Atlanta druggist. The company's president for scores of years has been R.W. Woodruff, born in 1890 and, at this writing, still active as the firm's chief executive.

The precise formula for the beverage is still one of the nation's most closely guarded trade secrets, known only to Woodruff and a few key company executives.

Woodruff's hobby is hunting game birds. That's what brought him to the fields near Douglas and initiated a personal acquaintance with the Day family of seven brothers and two sisters. Six of the brothers went to work for Coca-Cola as young men and made the soft drink industry their lifelong careers in a variety of capacities.

One of them, R.V. Day, came to Utah in 1934 and became sales supervisor in the Ogden district for the Salt Lake City plant of the Coca-Cola Company. He helped open a warehouse on Twenty-fourth Street in 1936 and directed a move in 1941-1942 to the intersection of Riverdale Road

and Grant Avenue. A bottling plant was built there in 1942. The parent company decided to divest itself of many of the regional operations and in 1949 sold the Ogden facility to brothers A.M. and R.V. Day and the Salt Lake City plant to another group.

One of the brothers' first merchandising efforts in Ogden involved the formation of a task force, headed by Jack Hardman, that went through the three-county territory, leaving a six-pack (then a new-style package), of 6.5-ounce bottles of Coke at every home. Sales skyrocketed as a result.

Another brother, Hoyt Day, sent his son, Ben H., to Ogden in 1954 to join his uncles in the rapidly growing company. He later was joined by a cousin, Joe R. Day, son of S. Joe Day.

During Ben Day's thirty-plus years in the Ogden beverage business, operations have become increasingly complex. Initially, Coca-Cola only came in its distinctive, hourglass-shaped green bottles. Then came larger bottles, of glass and eventually plastic. Twelve-ounce cans were added. So were five-gallon metal containers of both premixed beverages and of syrup that was mixed at the dispenser outlet.

Simple refrigerated boxes for display at point-of-sales outlets became big devices, retailing assorted cans and bottles or drinks in paper or plastic cups. Route trucks had to be increased in size accordingly.

Sprite became a member of the Coca-Cola family in 1958. Again, samples were distributed door to door by the Days in the Ogden territory. Then came Tab, Hi-C, Fanta, Fresca, Ramblin' Root Beer, and Diet Coke.

The Riverdale plant couldn't handle all this, and a new beverage bottling and distribution center was built on Pennsylvania Avenue. It was completed on September 30, 1973.

Dispensers of Coke and the other popular drinks became commonplace at most community functions in Ogden and surrounding cities.

Ben Day became one of the principal supporters of the Ogden Pioneer Days Rodeo and Parade. In 1984 every can of Coke sold in the region carried a special label, its silver and gold letters blending into the familiar red of the container, that promoted the big celebration's fiftieth anniversary. The label noted that Ogden was the "Heart of the Golden Spike Empire."

This all-out participation prompted Weber County Commissioner Roger Rawson to write a letter to the editor of the *Ogden Standard-Examiner* praising Coca-Cola of Ogden in these words:

"Ben Day and the entire staff at Coca-Cola are to be commended for their fine gesture of community service for presenting to each and every parade participant a cool, refreshing soft drink at the end of the Ogden Pioneer Days Parade." At Weber State College's Wildcat Stadium, fans know the score and other vital statistics of games in progress through a $50,000 donation for an electronic scoreboard by Coca-Cola of Ogden.

Five to eight thousand elementary school students in Weber, Box Elder, and North Davis counties are more safety conscious every year because of the Ramblin' Route Bear. A trained safety expert dons a shaggy brown bear costume to appear before dozens of classes. He gives tips to the youngsters on safety practices they should use while walking, biking, playing, or making Hal-

Coca-Cola Bottling Company employees John T. Newberry and Lee Chapman posed in front of Defense Depot Ogden's administration building while making deliveries in 1947.

loween trick-or-treat rounds.

Bottling of the beverages has become an exacting operation. Syrup comes from the Coca-Cola Company in 5,000-gallon containers. The sweetener added at the Ogden plant makes the firm one of the area's largest purchasers of sugar. Nonsugar sweeteners are also used.

Culinary water goes through filters that, as Joe Day puts it, "take out everything the city puts in and make sure it is absolutely pure." Bottles and other con-

tainers are inspected manually and then by special devices after they are washed a number of times.

"Our philosophy is different," Day explains. "We have attempted to position Coke in the community and state as something special. That's why we spend more dollars promoting Ogden and the other cities than we do advertising in the media." This formula of operation works, and the success of the Coca-Cola Bottling Company of Ogden proves it.

The Day family assumed ownership of the Ogden bottling plant of the Coca-Cola Company, at Riverdale Road and Grant Avenue, in 1949.

LIVING SCRIPTURES

The Living Scriptures organization of Ogden began in 1974 when two ambitious young men shared a dream. Within ten years that dream had become a reality, and Jared Brown and Seldon Young headed a unique firm that annually ships more than one million cassette tapes to appreciative customers nationwide.

Their six major productions are sold by a field force of 60 full-time and 300 part-time sales representatives, with 150 to 200 college students added during summer months. Annual revenues are $5.5 to $6 million.

Three of the sets of tapes are based on the doctrine of the Church of Jesus Christ of Latter-day Saints. These are "The Dramatized LDS Church History," "The Golden Plates," and "Great Mormon Women." The other three sets of tapes are more general in nature and include "The Dramatized Bible," "Dramatized New Testament," and "American Heritage Dramatized." In each set there are twenty-four to thirty-six cassettes, all handsomely presented in custom binders suitable for placement in a fine library.

A native of Price, Utah, Jared Brown enrolled in Brigham Young University to study medicine. Working his way through school as a salesman prompted him to change his mind and to go into commerce instead. He brought his wife to Ogden while working for an already-established company that produced illustrated Bible stories.

Brown decided to branch out on his own and, at age twenty-seven, established Living Scriptures and became its president and general manager. As a partner he selected Seldon Young, age twenty, of Layton, who had been selling products door to door since early childhood.

Living Scriptures produced its first dramatized tapes in 1974 in an old duplex at 3608 Orchard Street.

They began the firm in a battered duplex in Ogden but in 1979 moved into the newly established commercial plaza at the southeast corner of Ogden Municipal Airport. Since then their facility, at 4357 South Airport Plaza, has been the scene of constant expansion.

It takes three years to bring a single production to market. Scripts are usually written by Orson Scott Card, a former Utahn now living in North Carolina. Actual production is done in Salt Lake City under contract with Gary Jackson's Recording Arts Studio, with production costs averaging $10,000 an hour.

Living Scriptures officers are delighted with the letters of appreciation they constantly receive. Brown says many "thank us for what the tapes have done, not only for themselves but for their children and grandchildren." Other letters praise the inspirational dramatic tapes "because of their positive influence that offsets the negative and evil influences in the world."

Another testimonial points out that "the home is the major influence in a child's early, formative years ... and what habits, values, traits, and principles are established last the child's entire life ... so we are grateful to have a product that helps parents do their primary responsibility to provide a spiritual foundation for their children and build a strong moral character."

Jared Brown and Seldon Young are appreciative of Living Scriptures' commercial success but believe their greatest reward is in providing a means of strengthening the nation's moral and spiritual backbone.

NICE Corporation and Living Scriptures occupy this newly enlarged building at 4357 South Airport Plaza.

NICE CORPORATION

Few northern Utah residents realize that one of the Ogden area's largest employers is the firm with the unusual name of NICE, housed in a newly enlarged building at 4357 South Airport Plaza. NICE is the corporate acronym for National Instant Consumer Exchange. It handles, through specialized computer equipment, 25,000 to 80,000 telephone calls a day, depending on the season, and has 1,200 employees—800 full time and 400 part time.

Its billings of twelve to fourteen million dollars a year earn the firm ranking as one of the top two telemarketing specialists in the country. President Seldon Young and vice-president Jared Brown estimate that overall sales generated through calls handled by NICE account for one billion dollars annually in economic turnover.

The organization is little known in its home territory of Ogden because most of the calls come from other states, a characteristic of Wide Area Toll Service, or WATS, telephone lines.

NICE had only three lines when it was established in 1977 in an old duplex at 3608 Orchard Avenue in southeastern Ogden. The operation moved to its Airport Plaza location in 1979. When the latest expansion was completed, there were 150 to 175 lines for incoming calls and 30 to 60 lines for outgoing sales messages.

The key to the concern's rapid expansion—an average of 100 percent growth each year—is the unique computer software that Young and Brown developed from the start. "NICE was the nation's first telemarketing company to design a system specific to this brand-new industry," Brown explains. "Competitors who simply tried to adapt existing systems to

Employees of NICE (National Instant Consumer Exchange) work on telephones and computer consoles that have made the firm one of America's leading telemarketing concerns.

this unique business couldn't keep up."

Among the firm's clients are more than 300 companies offering in excess of 600 products. In most cases the "800" toll-free number is flashed on the television screen following a message designed to prompt a call. Other calls to NICE, acting for those engaging its services, are the results of radio, newspaper, magazine, or direct-mail campaigns.

Each call is taken by an employee of the firm, most often a young woman wearing a special headset, who enters the information directly by keyboard onto a computer screen. The com-

pany's special software program guides the operator in asking the essential questions. Names, addresses, and other information are then relayed to the client.

Outgoing calls are growing in importance as NICE contracts to deliver a sales message to individuals on a selected list of prospects. Random calls by impersonal tape messages, so annoying to most recipients, are not part of the company's technique. Custom equipment to handle the heavy telephone and computer load has cost the firm more than six million dollars to design, build, and install.

Young and Brown expect NICE Corporation to have at least 1,500 employees by the end of 1985 and to keep on growing as this form of telemarketing becomes an even more important ingredient in the American marketplace.

FIRST SECURITY CORPORATION

The First Security Corporation, formed in Ogden in 1928, is the oldest multistate bank holding company in the United States. First Security's 165 banks have assets of about five billion dollars. They serve nearly three million residents of Utah, Idaho, and Wyoming in a territory that is 600 miles wide and 1,250 miles long.

Ogden-born Spencer F. Eccles, a member of the family that has been most closely associated with the corporation's leadership since its inception, is chairman, president, and chief executive officer. Robert S. Heiner, also from Ogden, has the same positions with First Security Bank of Utah, National Association, the corporation's largest subsidiary. James Phelps heads First Security Bank of Idaho, N.A.

Other subsidiaries include First Security Bank of Rock Springs, Wyoming, First Security State Bank of Salt Lake City, First Security Realty Services, First Security Leasing, First Security Financial, three insurance companies, and a variety of support services.

First Security is known nationally to bankers and investors. The corporation has 7,000 owners of common stock and 2,400 holders of preferred stock living in all fifty states, the District of Columbia, and several foreign countries.

This widespread financial base was not achieved by accident. It originated, in part, in the philosophy of David Eccles, a leading northern Utah financier and civic leader at the turn of the century, who told his family, "... You should always work for the success of the business, and if you will keep your mind and attention on the business, you'll never go wrong and money will come."

Marriner, Spencer, George, and Willard Eccles, the four sons of

The twelve-story First Security Building in Ogden, completed in 1927 and still the city's tallest structure, has been the corporate home office of First Security Corporation since its inception.

David and Ellen Stoddard Eccles, followed their father's recommendations. And today Spencer F. Eccles is adhering to his grandfather's policy of diligence in business.

Among his many enterprises, David Eccles acquired control of the Thatcher Brothers Bank in Logan, Utah, as well as state banks in the nearby Cache Valley communities of Hyrum and Richmond. He also had banking interests in Blackfoot and Preston, Idaho. Headquarters of the Eccles Investment Co. were established in Ogden in 1920 when he bought controlling interests in the First National Bank of Ogden and the Ogden Savings Bank.

Marriner Eccles, eldest of the sons, took over direction of the banks when he was only thirty years old and began assembling a cadre of executive associates. Spencer Eccles, second in the line, served primarily as a consultant and concentrated his talents on other family businesses, including Amalgamated Sugar, Utah Construction, and Sego Milk.

George Eccles, after graduating from the University of California and Columbia University, apprenticed with the Irving Trust Co. in New York City and joined the Utah banks in 1922. Willard Eccles began his banking career in 1933 upon graduation from Babson College.

Banking in the early 1920s was a challenge. Books were posted with pen and ink. Manual typewriters and mechanical adding machines were just coming into common usage. It was a precarious business, too; 1,711 U.S. banks failed early in that decade.

In 1922 Matthew Browning, brother and close associate of firearms inventor John M. Browning, proposed to Marriner Eccles that the Browning-controlled Utah National Bank be merged with the Eccles' banks. George Eccles worked out details that resulted in formation of the First National Bank of Ogden and the First Savings Bank of Ogden. When Browning died in mid-1923, his son, Marriner A. Browning, replaced his father as a key executive of the combined facilities and worked closely with the Eccles brothers for the rest of his life.

A bank was purchased in Rock Springs in 1925, and another was founded in Montpelier, Idaho. When the Anderson Brothers Bank in Idaho Falls was acquired, Elbert G. Bennett joined the Eccles organization and became one of its most important executives.

The continued expansion made it apparent that some form of operational supervision was needed to increase efficiency. Branch banking, as such, at that time was against federal and state regulations. The Eccles' answer was unveiled on June 9, 1928, in Ogden. It was the First Security Corporation, established to serve as a holding company although it did not directly operate the individual banks, which retained their own officers and directors.

An official statement on the corporation's formation emphasized that First Security, controlling seventeen banks in three states, would be "beneficial alike to the depositors and the banks." The new organization, it was added, would afford "a diversification of bank loans and investments as wide as the varied resources of the Intermountain country."

The four Eccles brothers (from left to right), Spencer S., Willard L., Marriner S., and George S., founders of First Security Corporation and its banks.

The innovative step was formalized on June 15, 1928, when First Security Corporation was incorporated under Delaware laws. The charter president was Marriner Eccles, with Marriner Browning serving as vice-president, E.G. Bennett as vice-president and general manager, and George Eccles as secretary/treasurer. Other Ogdenites among the sixteen directors were Spencer Eccles, W.H. Harris, John Browning, Joseph Scowcroft, R.B. Porter, and W.H. Wattis.

Two men who were to play important roles in the new corporation joined the firm's ranks with acquisitions during this critical period. Ralph J. Comstock was with a Nampa bank and J. Lynn Driscoll was with one in Boise. Both eventually served as presidents of the First Security Bank of Idaho, N.A.

The financial statement at the end of 1928 showed system-wide assets were steadily increasing despite the national financial panic that began in the fall of that year. From 1921 through 1929 there were 5,711 U.S. bank failures, costing depositors $564 million. From 1930 through 1933 failures skyrocketed to 9,096 and

losses to $1.3 billion.

The First Security banks all remained open and sound. Safety and security for those trusting their money to the banks was stressed. A policy was adopted that approved loans for investors but refused loans to speculators.

In mid-1931 the Ogden State Bank failed on a Saturday. First Security Bank opened the following Monday with a generous supply of readily visible cash on hand. Employees were warned to avoid the appearance of panic, and they were asked to take as much time as possible in handling transactions. Banking hours were increased both mornings and afternoons for the convenience of customers. As a result, the threatened run on the Eccles-Browning banks was avoided.

In early 1932 Marriner Eccles was told that the Deseret Savings Bank in Salt Lake City was nearly insolvent, imperiling the Deseret National Bank—Utah's oldest, founded by LDS president Brigham Young—with which it shared quarters.

First Security Corporation rescued the pioneer commercial bank, consolidating it with the National Copper Bank which it had acquired earlier, and forming First National Bank of Salt Lake City. Offices eventually were moved to the First South and Main building where the corpora-

First Security Corporation's board of directors in 1929. Front row, from left: Spencer S. Eccles, Marriner A. Browning, Marriner S. Eccles, G.G. "Bib" Wright, and E.G. Bennett. Back row, from left: W.H. Wattis, Roy Bullen, John Thomas, Louis S. Cates, W.H. Harris, R.B. Porter, A.C. Ellis, Jr., Dr. D.C. Budge, Joseph Scowcroft, and Edgar S. Hills. Directors not pictured: John Browning, John Hood, and George S. Eccles.

tion now maintains its executive offices. As a direct aftermath of the nation's many bank failures, two First Security officers were virtually drafted for service in Washington.

Marriner S. Eccles became a special assistant for monetary and credit policies to Secretary of the Treasury Henry Morgenthau early in 1934. He agreed to serve only sixteen months, but remained seventeen years, most of the time as chairman of the Federal Reserve Board. E.G. Bennett was one of the organizers of the Federal Deposit Insurance Corporation, which has proved so successful in protecting the solvency of America's banks.

When it became obvious that Marriner Eccles was in Washington for a long stay, Bennett, returning to Utah, became First Security Corporation president. George Eccles was named president of First Security Bank of Utah, and Willard Eccles was promoted to assistant manager in Ogden.

The family was careful to avoid any tinge of conflict of interest between its executives' federal posts and the Intermountain banks. There was some criticism, even widespread controversy, upon at least one occasion, but all attacks were successfully defended.

An important banking industry change came in 1933 when Utah, Idaho, and the federal government legalized branch operations. First Security Corporation in 1935 acquired the Central Trust Co., merging it with Bankers Trust Co., and establishing First Security Trust Co. Payroll and check-cashing facilities were opened at nine defense installations in Utah and Idaho, leading

to branch offices now established at Hill Air Force Base and Defense Depot Ogden, among others. Banks in Rexburg, St. Anthony, and Park City and two in Brigham City were added to the system between July and November 1942.

E.G. Bennett retired at the end of 1944 and was succeeded as First Security Corporation president by George Eccles.

Early in the days of First Security, a rule had been established that no banks were to be acquired that were "more than an overnight train ride from Ogden." But as transportation and communications improved after World War II, this policy was modified and the corporation expanded swiftly into northern Idaho and southern Utah. By 1952 there were twenty-eight offices in Idaho, seventeen in Utah, six at military bases, and the one at Rock Springs, Wyoming. In 1953 there were a half-dozen more acquisitions in Utah, with many being located in the Moab area where mining and processing of uranium was booming. Others were in communities where tourism was the major industry.

This pattern continued for the next thirty years—acquiring or opening branches in strategic urban and suburban locations throughout Utah and Idaho. Drive-ins were later added to accommodate the new mobility of First Security customers.

By mid-1984 the Ogden-based Northern Division of the First Security Bank of Utah, N.A., had more than 500 employees in its twenty-two branches. There were ten in Weber County: Ogden Main, Roy, Main Point, South Ogden, Harrison Boulevard, Washington Terrace, Old Post Office Place, Twelfth Street, North Ogden, and Defense Depot Ogden.

Others in the division were Kaysville, Layton, Layton Hills Mall, two at Hill Air Force Base, Brigham City, Tremonton, Hyrum, Logan, Cache Valley Mall, Smithfield, and Richmond.

An ultramodern data center was built at the International Center, west of Salt Lake International Airport, and equipped with the latest in computers and electronic-banking devices. This center was essential to the introduction of "Handi-Banks," which were integrated into a nationwide network, that permit customers to make machine deposits or withdrawals twenty-four hours a day, seven days a week, with the aid of their bank cards.

First Security joined the "plastic revolution" in 1966 with cards originated by BankAmerica. Later the credit card system was renamed "VISA" to better indicate its wide scope.

There were many other changes as government regulation of the banking and financial industries changed and competition became keener. Floating rates were introduced for some loans, and negotiable certificates of deposit were made available. Trust departments were strengthened, and financing of leased equipment, ranging from aircraft to tankers, became more common.

Spencer F. Eccles, son of Spencer S. and nephew of Marriner, George, and Willard Eccles, worked for New York's First National Bank for two years after graduating from the University of Utah and Columbia University with degrees in banking and finance. He joined the First Security organization in 1960 and, after stints in Utah and Idaho branches, moved into the administrative headquarters. He assumed more and more responsibilities, particularly after the deaths of

WEEK

The Eccles—Marriner (left) and George: "As a team, oh brother!" (page 40)

The cover of Business Week *of August 7, 1954, featured the team of Marriner and George Eccles.*

Marriner and George, until he became chairman of the board, president, and chief executive officer of First Security Corporation early in 1982.

In 1983 Spencer Eccles and his veteran team of associates announced a complete corporate restructuring after making a lengthy study of all operations. An official announcement described the many changes as "primarily focused on determining those management decisions, organizational changes, and marketing actions necessary to strategically reposition the First Security organization for its effective transition into the increasingly competitive, deregulated banking environment of the 1980s."

"First Security welcomes deregulation," president Eccles says. "To resist change is to stagnate. Managing change is fundamental to maintaining a viable organization, to anticipating our customers' new needs, to providing the services they desire, and to sustaining the long-term, profitable growth of the corporation." He adds that "we are in a new era, with new competition, demands, risks, problems, and opportunities."

Officers of the First Security Corporation and its banks have always spoken the language of change. Formation of the basic holding company in 1928 met the changes of those days. The 1983 reorganization "to provide a better, faster, more consistent level of service to our customers" was an answer to the need for change. Other changes are certain to come in the future.

Spencer F. Eccles tells his staff that "we intend to take bold, aggressive measures and to be the force to be reckoned with in all our markets." David Eccles might have used those same words at the turn of the century.

THE AMALGAMATED SUGAR COMPANY

The Ogden-based Amalgamated Sugar Company is one of America's largest producers of beet sugar. Its four Idaho and Oregon factories turned out more than one billion pounds of sugar during the 1983-1984 processing campaign. Annual sales exceed $300 million.

The 1983-1984 crop was harvested by 2,500 growers on 155,000 acres. Amalgamated has nearly 1,400 full-time employees, and its factories have the capacity to slice 27,000 tons of beets daily.

These figures represent a tremendous increase from the 2.6 million pounds of sugar processed by the Ogden Sugar Co., Amalgamated's corporate ancestor, during its initial 1898-1899 campaign. In that season 839 farmers in Utah's Weber, Davis, Cache, Box Elder, and Morgan counties grew only 15,205 tons of beets on 1,994 acres.

The Ogden Sugar Co. was formed December 6, 1897, when a group of Weber County civic leaders, brought together by financier David Eccles, met at the Weber Club. Ten days later articles of incorporation were filed with the Utah secretary of state naming Eccles as president, Thomas D. Dee as vice-president, Henry H. Rolapp as secretary, and James Pingree as treasurer. Other directors were Hiram H. Spencer, Joseph Clark, George Q. Cannon, John R. Winder, John Scowcroft, Fred J. Kiesel, and Ephraim P. Ellison.

Ground for the Ogden factory was broken on Wilson Lane within six weeks, and the plant was completed in October 1898. About the same time a similar factory was constructed at LaGrande, Oregon, and in 1901 the corporation formed the Logan Sugar Co. Utah operations were consolidated with the Oregon firm in July 1902

Sugar beets must be transported by rail or truck to the factory for processing. Here a modern truck hoist unloads twenty-five tons of sugar beets at an Amalgamated factory.

as Amalgamated Sugar Company. A factory was built in 1905 at Lewiston, Utah, and when it merged with the others in 1914, the word "The" was added to the legal corporate name. Thus began The Amalgamated Sugar Company.

"The Story of The Amalgamated Sugar Company," written in 1962 by veteran executive J.R. Bachman, details the growth and contraction, successes and failures of the firm's early years. Leafhoppers brought curly-top disease

to beet plants, a problem the company solved by breeding disease-resistant plants. Development of a single-segment seed produced well-spaced beets, and hand labor gave way to mechanical planting, thinning, and harvesting.

David Eccles died in 1912, and Rolapp succeeded him as president. During the next seventeen years they were in turn succeeded by Anthon H. Lund, M.S. Browning, and A.W. Ivins.

The Denver-based American Sugar Company obtained control of Amalgamated briefly, and from

This wagon load of sugar beets took six horsepower to haul to a factory of Amalgamated Sugar Company in 1909.

January 30, 1930, until June 15, 1931, the Ogden offices were closed and affairs conducted from Colorado. Other stockholders, led by Marriner S. Eccles, regained control after a struggle, and, with Eccles as president, the Ogden headquarters reopened.

Marriner S. Eccles had first been elected to the board of directors in 1916. Until his death sixty-one years later, he served the firm as a director and an officer, including the chairmanship from 1941 to 1976.

The driving force of The Amalgamated Sugar Company for a half-century were the Bennings, father and son. H.A. Benning, an experienced sugar man, joined the firm in 1920. When control was regained by Utahns, he was general manager and determined "to make Amalgamated the best sugar company in the business."

He did, aided by a staff of experienced beet sugar specialists who ran the plants, contracted for growing acreage, invented new seeds and machines, improved financial records, opened sales branches and distribution centers in Portland and Seattle, and handled delicate negotiations with the government on the ever-changing Sugar Acts.

A.E. Benning, who began with the company as a mechanic's helper in the Ogden plant in 1933, succeeded his father as president in 1962. Under his leadership the factories were nearly doubled in size and the firm developed operating techniques that increased sugar production. A.E. Benning became chairman in 1976, and two years later Allan M. Lipman, Jr., who had been executive vice-president, legal counsel, and secretary, became president.

Over the years factories were built or acquired at Lewiston, Ogden, Smithfield, Logan, and

This is the way the Nyssa, Oregon, factory of The Amalgamated Sugar Company appeared in 1970. It has been constantly modernized and now is one of the most efficient sugar beet factories in the nation.

Brigham City, Utah; Burley, Twin Falls, Paul, Whitney, and Nampa, Idaho; Missoula and Whitehall, Montana; LaGrande and Nyssa, Oregon; and Clarksburg, California.

The Ogden factory was closed September 13, 1941, when expanding defense installations in northern Utah took over much of the best growing acreage. Its stack still standing proudly, it remains to this day a sugar storage warehouse and liquid sugar-making plant. Others were closed or traded until the Nyssa, Oregon, factory and the Idaho factories at Nampa, Twin Falls, and Paul were all that remained. These have been extensively modernized and their capacities increased.

When Amalgamated Sugar began in the early 1900s, virtually all production was in granulated white sugar shipped in 100-pound bags. There were some sales of brown and powdered sugars. That, too, has changed drastically. Consumer packages of all sizes, bearing the "White Satin" trademark evolved in 1954, are now marketed. Consumers of large quantities buy their Amalgamated sugar in bulk, granulated or liquid, and receive the product from huge rail cars and tanker

truck trailers.

The corporation was listed on the New York Stock Exchange until November 1982, when a majority of stock was purchased by organizations controlled by financier Harold C. Simmons. Following the stock purchase Simmons became board chairman and Allan M. Lipman, Jr., was retained as president.

The Amalgamated Sugar Company has, except for the brief span in the 1930s, maintained its headquarters in Ogden since its inception in 1897, even though the harvest of sugar beets in Utah ended in 1980. The headquarters offices have entertained visitors from every significant sugar beet-producing country in the world. From those offices have originated technical articles and papers that appear in sugar beet journals throughout the world. Today the firm is not only one of America's largest producers of beet sugar but is recognized by its customers as the "premier" sugar company in the United States, having received the prestigious "Supplier of the Year Award" from the Pillsbury Company in 1984.

Ogden has always been proud of The Amalgamated Sugar Company, and civic and community leaders have especially appreciated the loyalty of the firm and its officials who have remained in their Ogden birthplace, even though Utah beet production has ended.

MOUNTAIN BELL

Mountain Bell and its predecessor companies have been making telephone history in Ogden for more than a century.

Inventor Alexander Graham Bell gave the initial public demonstration of his revolutionary method of voice communication on March 10, 1876. Less than three years later, in early 1879, merchant George A. Lowe installed telephones in his Ogden warehouse and store, connected by a strand of wire.

Lowe was so satisfied that he helped form the Ogden Telephone Exchange Co. on March 1, 1880, the first in Utah and the Intermountain states. A.J. Pattison (spelled Patterson in some accounts), was the local Western Union manager and provided quarters for the exchange.

By the fall of 1880 Pattison and president J.N. Keller had strung twenty-five miles of iron wire on 150 poles and had installed a switchboard with twenty-four lines to serve Ogden's population of 6,000. Their investment was $7,000.

First calls were made on October 9, 1880. Within three weeks the Ogden exchange had fifty-six subscribers. The *Ogden Junction* published glowing accounts and told subscribers how to turn cranks on their combination transmitter-receiver to contact the operator. Names, not numbers, were used.

The first interstate telephone call west of the Allegheny Mountains was made from Ogden to Evanston on November 19, 1880, utilizing telegraph wires strung along the Union Pacific tracks. The *Junction* reported the "animated conversation ... worked to a charm" and that "voices were heard at each point with great distinction."

Pattison organized the Utah

Handling the Ogden telephone exchange in 1889 were, left to right, messenger George Snively, operators Emma Leaman Anderson and Christina N. Willis, chief operator Nettie Caldwell, and manager W.W. Crossman.

Telephone Co., taking over the Ogden Exchange Co. system, and built an exchange in Salt Lake City where acceptance of telephone service had been slow. The first Ogden-Salt Lake City call, again using telegraph circuits, was made on April 26, 1883. A regular line—only one wire was needed, with the earth providing a needed "ground"—was installed in 1884.

Pattison expanded his operation on February 26, 1883, by forming the Rocky Mountain Bell Telephone Co., licensed by the American Bell Telephone Co. The new firm absorbed the Utah concern and began planning service through-

out Utah, Montana, Idaho, and Wyoming. By 1887 there were circuits from Logan to Park City.

All long-distance calls had to be made from the central office. Operators timed them with stop watches and frequently had to repeat the conversations, especially if more than sixty miles separated the callers.

The Ogden exchange started in the Dooley Building at 2414 Washington Boulevard. Its second home was in the Peery Building at 2439 Washington. It moved to 2444 Washington in 1898 when the technically important "common battery" system, the first in the Intermountain West, was installed and two-piece instruments became common, allowing

The Ogden exchange in 1909 featured this long switchboard. Chief operator Janet "Nettie" Hunter Nelson is standing at the back.

The mid-1950s saw the installation of microwave towers atop Mountain Bell's Ogden exchange, which has been located at 431 Twenty-sixth Street since 1941.

callers to initiate a conversation without turning a crank.

Initial rates were five dollars per month for businesses and four dollars for homes, payable three months in advance on a one-year contract. A five-minute Ogden-Salt Lake City call cost fifty cents. At the turn of the century there were 325 Ogden subscribers.

Improvements came rapidly. Mountain States Telephone and Telegraph Co. was organized on July 20, 1911, and the Denver-based utility bought Rocky Mountain Bell. The first transcontinental telephone call was made soon after circuits were spliced together at Wendover, on the Utah-Nevada border. Alexander Graham Bell, in New York City, told Thomas Watson, his longtime assistant, "Mr. Watson, come here. I want you." This time Watson was in San Francisco and replied "Sorry, Mr. Bell, I can't. I'm too far away."

Ogden subscribers made their first calls to New York City in 1914 and by 1927 could telephone overseas. Utah's second private switchboard (PBX) was installed in the Ogden Union Railroad and Depot Co. office on June 29, 1929.

The Ogden Exchange found a permanent home on May 24, 1941, when a million-dollar office and plant were completed at 431 Twenty-sixth Street, and dial telephones were "cut in" to expedite service. Other exchanges were eventually added in North Ogden

Telephone operators serving the Ogden area in the 1950s.

and in western Weber County.

There were about 10,000 subscribers in 1940. After the World War II buildup in the greater Ogden area and postwar industrial expansion, the list increased to 25,000 in 1949.

Direct-distance dialing was inaugurated in 1963. Touch-tone calling came to North Ogden in 1967 and to the remainder of the Ogden area three years later. Central office equipment became computer-based and microwave links expedited long-distance service.

A government-decreed divestiture order became effective on January 1, 1984, and Mountain Bell and its parent holding company, U.S. West, became independent of the American Telephone and Telegraph Company. Mountain Bell continues to provide basic local service and handles intrastate calls.

Phil Selander, Ogden district manager of distribution services including engineering, construction, installation, and maintenance, believes the change has many positive aspects. "In the old environment, one Bell system provided the greatest telephone system the world has ever known," he says, "but one nationwide plan didn't necessarily fit all areas. We can now tailor our services to best suit our own territories."

Selander says that competition on equipment and long-distance calling offers users more options. This, he explains, is important, because circuits installed for basic telephone service are also used for transmission of many other varieties of information, including computers "talking" to other computers.

A new digital electronic switching office will be installed in Ogden to handle the main exchange calls in November 1986. By the end of 1984 the Ogden district's 330 employees worked with 132,000 "access lines," with each line representing an individual telephone number. Mountain Bell's capital investment, averaging $1,235 for each line, totaled more than $163 million in the district.

Older, wrist-size cables containing up to 900 pairs of copper wires are on the drawing boards to be replaced, where necessary, with fiber optic cables the size of a little finger. The first system to be turned up in 1986 will run from Ogden south to Salt Lake City and from Ogden north to Brigham City. Each cable of 144 fiber optic strands, actuated by a tiny laser that blinks forty-four million times a second, can simultaneously handle 450,000 voice conversations.

Ogden telephone pioneer A.J. Pattison wouldn't recognize today's telephone-information network. But, then again, neither would Alexander Graham Bell.

OVERLAND WEST, INC.

Ogden-based Overland West, Inc., with offices at fifteen locations in five Intermountain states, covers more square miles than any other Hertz system car rental agency in the United States. The vehicles Overland West rented in 1984 were driven 2,087,639 miles—equal to more than eighty-five times around the world at the equator!

President Jerry H. Petersen is proud of his firm's four-decade record of growth and service and expects the busy corporation to continue to expand in future years. He and his associates are also proud of their new headquarters building at 2805 Washington Boulevard with its copper-clad roof and tastefully decorated administrative offices. The firm moved there in May 1984 from its longtime location at 451 Twenty-

Jerry Petersen, president.

fifth Street, a move delayed several months because an arsonist torched the structure when the remodeling of the former automobile sales agency was nearly complete.

Wilford Gwilliam acquired the Hertz franchise for Ogden in 1941, purchased a used Dodge truck, and promptly rented it to the

Union Pacific Railroad. Petersen feels the identity of the initial customer was significant since Ogden, the "Junction City," was the hub of the nation's western railroad network.

Gwilliam purchased other cars and trucks, despite the World War II shortages, and rented them to companies and residents flocking to northern Utah to facilitate operations of the new defense establishments.

In the early 1940s Devere J. Sparrow came to work for Gwilliam and soon became like a son to the Gwilliams, who had no family of their own. He quickly became the moving force behind the early growth of the company.

By 1950 W. Gwilliam, Inc., had added Hertz franchises in Idaho Falls and Pocatello, Idaho; Jackson, Wyoming; Bozeman and West Yellowstone, Montana; Flagstaff, Arizona; and Las Vegas, Nevada. The firm opened the Las Vegas agency in 1950 with five cars and sold it to the Hertz Corporation in 1956, when its owner retired from operations.

D.J. Sparrow purchased the organization in 1964 and directed its activities until January 1976, when he sold it to his son-in-law, Jerry Petersen.

A native of Logan, a graduate of Weber High School, and a former student at Weber State College, Petersen had joined the organization in 1962 as a car salesman. He moved into the rental end of the business as assistant general manager in 1966, becoming president and general manager ten years later.

One of Petersen's first actions as owner was to change the name of the company to Overland West. He explains that many possibilities were considered, but "We liked the sound of Overland West because it pretty well describes

The executive committee of Overland West, Inc., Ogden-based Hertz system member, is composed of (left to right) Claudia Allred, corporate secretary; Doug Hurst, controller and corporate treasurer; Jerry Petersen, president and general manager; and F. Lynn Petersen, fleet and sales administrator.

our business and the territory it serves."

As energy exploration boomed throughout the Intermountain West and tourism increased dramatically, additional Hertz agencies were acquired or opened. During the ten years from 1973 to 1983 Overland West began operating in Casper, Rock Springs, Gillette, and Evanston, Wyoming; Billings and Great Falls, Montana; and Boise and Sun Valley-Hailey, Idaho.

Other franchises the firm owned at one time but later sold or closed included Williams, Kingman, Grand Canyon, and Winslow, Arizona; Soda Springs, Montpelier, and Victor, Idaho; Brigham City, Utah; and Pinedale and Kemmerer, Wyoming.

By mid-1984 Overland West, Inc., was operating a fleet of about 1,500 vehicles during summers and about 800 during winter months, reflecting seasonal changes in oil exploration activity and tourist travel. Scores of Petersen's rental units are light-duty trucks and four-wheel-drive vehicles, particularly popular with the petroleum firms and their crews that travel the rugged,

mountainous country of the oil- and gas-rich Overthrust Belt east of Ogden.

Ogden rentals account for only one or 2 percent of the corporation's revenues, but Petersen has insisted on maintaining headquarters in Weber County because "it's home" as well as being one of the strongest and more stable used-car markets in the West. To facilitate regional travel the firm owns one aircraft and has partial ownership of a second. Petersen is a pilot and is frequently at the controls on visits to the other fourteen agencies.

Each location acts independently, yet is interdependent on the Overland West network of cities, Petersen explains, adding that "the outstanding personnel and strong company identity along with a tightly monitored communications network are significant factors in the success of the operation."

Overland West has about 120 employees in the system, including those in the Ogden headquarters. Kathy Petersen, wife of the president and general manager, is corporate vice-president; Douglas Hurst is controller and corporate

An oak-trimmed lobby welcomes customers to Overland West's new Ogden-based headquarters.

treasurer; F. Lynn Petersen, Jerry's younger brother, is fleet and sales administrator; and Claudia Allred is administrative assistant to the president and corporate secretary.

Innovation is a key word, both in vehicle rentals and in Overland's used-car sales operations, which are located in Ogden, Idaho Falls, Billings, Great Falls, and Boise. An example is the unique computer software package—the first of its kind in the entire car rental industry—that goes far beyond the customary accounting functions.

With its completely computerized preventive maintenance program, Overland West has state-of-the-art control of vehicle servicing and repairs.

Times have changed dramatically since Wilford Gwilliam rented his first truck to the railroad. But the spirit of the organization that now flourishes in five states as Overland West, Inc., remains the same—providing essential transportation services at a reasonable cost and doing it with pride.

LEAVITT'S CHAPEL OF FLOWERS MORTUARY, INC.
AULTOREST MEMORIAL PARK CORPORATION

Leavitt's Chapel of Flowers Mortuary and Aultorest Memorial Park have a unique distinction. The Ogden facilities were the first in the nation, possibly in the world, to combine a mortuary and a memorial park on the same grounds. It began serving bereaved families of the Ogden area several months before the famed Forest Lawn Memorial Park, burial place of many Hollywood stars, was opened more than a half-century ago.

President/manager Thomas T. Leavitt points out that the eighty acres occupied by his establishment represent the largest single land area within the city of Ogden under one ownership. Offices, chapels, and the crematorium are all located at 836 Thirty-sixth Street. "Less than 50 percent of our property is now utilized," he adds. "We believe that, following modern practices, we have space enough to bury everyone in Ogden who will die during the next 100 years or more."

The previously unpracticed idea of combining a mortuary and a memorial park was conceived in 1927 by James M. Harbertson when he purchased forty-six acres of farmland in the southeastern section of the city. It took many months to prepare the ground properly for its new role; roads were created, sprinkler systems installed, and burial plots surveyed.

Harbertson opened the gates of Mount Ogden Memorial Park on March 5, 1929. One of his first objectives was to educate residents of the area about the difference between traditional cemeteries, with their raised and sometimes massive headstones, and a memorial park where all grave markers are ground level and of a uniform, nonpretentious design.

Public acceptance of the newer

Offices and chapel of the Mount Ogden Memorial Park and Mausoleum as they appeared in the mid-1930s. With many additions they are now the central facilities of Leavitt's Chapel of Flowers and Aultorest Memorial Park.

concept was enough that the Mount Ogden Mortuary was added in July 1933, the Mount Ogden Mausoleum was added in 1935, and a crematory, the first in Ogden and possibly the first in Utah, was constructed in 1937. Harbertson changed the name from Mount Ogden to Aultorest— a coined word combining "all," "to," and "rest"—Memorial Park and Mortuary on February 3, 1938.

The size of the facility was nearly doubled on December 1, 1946, when the 34-acre, century-old but nearly abandoned, Mountain View Cemetery was purchased from John Guthrie Haywood. More than $100,000 was spent refurbishing and rehabilitating the old burial ground, adjacent to Aultorest on the north. Old gravestones and memorials were, of course, retained but all burials from then on followed the memorial park concept.

Thomas T. Leavitt became a member of the organization in 1947, following three years of U.S.

Army service and a brief career as a semipro baseball pitcher. A native of Ogden and a graduate of Ogden High School, Leavitt had earned the Bronze Star and two Purple Heart medals during his two years in the South Pacific during World War II.

He was a laborer in Aultorest Memorial Park while finishing his studies at Weber State College. Leavitt then became an apprentice mortician, and in 1950 was graduated from the California College of Mortuary Science and received licenses as an embalmer and funeral director. In March 1948 he married Lynnette Harbertson, daughter of the Aultorest founder, and in 1950, upon returning to Ogden from California, became manager of the memorial park and mortuary.

Leavitt purchased the property in 1958 and changed its name to its present designation, Leavitt's Chapel of Flowers Mortuary, Inc., and Aultorest Memorial Park Corporation. He made the change because he felt that Aultorest "by itself took too much explaining as to what it did. We have always had a profusion of flowers on the property and have long had our own greenhouse, so we felt that 'Chapel of Flowers' would be simpler, more descriptive, and easier to understand."

Patronage has more than quadrupled since Tom Leavitt became president in 1958, and three of his sons have joined him in the business. Thomas Jr. and Scott are involved in the ski profession during the winter but work on the grounds crew when not on the slopes. Son Mike has become an apprentice mortician and will become an integral part of the business.

The main chapels have been enlarged and refurbished until now more than 500 people can be accommodated at a single funeral service. There are thirty-five employees, including sixteen counselors in the recently established "pre-need" sales department. More than a dozen vehicles are required for services and ground maintenance.

Thomas Leavitt has been active in community life, including the Ogden Area Chamber of Commerce, the United Fund, and St. Benedict's Hospital Foundation. His memorial park has been a strong supporter of anti-drug abuse programs and the Hospice and Heart program.

He began singing in the seventh grade, and over the past four decades his voice has been added in song to more than 5,000 funerals in his own chapel and at others in the Ogden area. "I enjoy singing songs that are meaningful," he told an interviewer a few years ago. Most popular selections for services are "Oh, What a Day," "Sing Me to Sleep," and "The Lord's Prayer."

Asked what made his Chapel of Flowers so successful, Leavitt replied that he believed it was "the dignity of the quiet surroundings" in the park-like setting near the base of the Wasatch Mountains. Of equal importance

Thomas T. Leavitt has been owner, president, and general manager of Leavitt's Chapel of Flowers and Aultorest Memorial Park since 1958.

Leavitt's Chapel of Flowers Mortuary was remodeled early in 1985.

was the availability of all options for funerals—mortuary, memorial park, cemetery, mausoleum, and crematory—at the one location.

Leavitt recognized the need for bereaved families to be associated at the time of their loss with individuals who are not only professionals in mortuary sciences but are sincere. "This is a time when we must not only be compassionate, with a deep sense of sympathetic understanding, but we must be sincere in every detail," he said.

Leavitt has found that one appreciated way to provide sympathetic guidance and understanding is to offer family members references from the Holy Scriptures for spiritual comfort, guidance, and consolation. Suggested Bible readings are printed and distributed to the bereaved in a special folder as part of the Chapel of Flowers service.

WEBER COUNTY SCHOOL DISTRICT

This old rock school in Riverdale was built in 1865. Courtesy, Lucille C. Judkins

The Weber County School District, organized in 1905, has long been noted as one of America's most progressive, innovative educational systems. The district's philosophy was summarized by superintendent Jay B. Taggart when he said, "We simply won't allow negative attitudes in our district.

"We feel strongly that the answer to excellence is in attitude," Taggart adds. "We are in the people business. Kids are the common denominator. As administrators, teachers, the school board, and parents work together, we should all have the interest of the kids at heart. If the kids feel good about their schools and themselves, they will stay in the classes and seek excellence, too."

Richard H. Thornley, president of the school board, quoted this statement by author Norman

Cousins in the district's annual report for 1982-1983: "Education fails unless the Three R's at one end of the school spectrum lead ultimately to the Four P's at the other—Preparation for Earning, Preparation for Living, Preparation for Understanding, [and] Preparation for Participation in the problems involved in the

Weber High School is nestled at the foot of Ben Lomond Peak in Pleasant View.

making of a better world."

Thornley also points out that "we live in an age of dynamic social change and a virtual knowledge explosion. Assisting students in acquiring this knowledge, in developing the wisdom to properly use the knowledge acquired, and then to function in society at their highest individual potential, is a challenge second to none in importance."

Attainment of an education has always been the goal of most residents of Utah. The state has long led the nation in the percentage of its youths who graduate from high school and go on to college or university. When Mormon pioneers arrived in Weber County in the middle of the nineteenth century, they usually built a combination church-school, however primitive, before completing their personal dwellings.

School programs were well established in several Weber County communities by 1852. Support came from church tithings until independent, local school districts were formed to levy taxes and build better facilities. Early in the twentieth century the Utah Legislature enacted laws permitting larger cities to establish their own districts and independent districts to consolidate.

The City of Ogden set up its

own district, and in June 1905 farsighted community leaders combined the independent schools outside Ogden into one of Utah's first consolidated districts.

Growth since then has been steady. By the 1984-1985 school year Weber County School District was operating twenty-six elementary schools, seven junior high schools, three comprehensive high schools, one adult high school, and a school for the severely handicapped. Buildings, including administrative and maintenance facilities, boasted of 2.7 million square feet of floor space and 315 acres of grounds.

The more than 23,000 enrolled students made Weber the sixth largest school district in the state. There were 1,600 men and women on the district's payroll, including 1,028 teachers. A fleet of sixty-four buses brought students to classrooms in rural areas, and the district's operating budget for the year exceeded fifty million dollars.

Basic policy is established by a five-member, elected school board representing all sections of Weber County, outside of Ogden. Superintendent Taggart points out that an elected board is one of the keys to the district's success.

"It makes the district a democratic organization to have a board that is elected by the people," he explains. "This is one of the last bastions of direct public involvement and provides an important interplay between the public and the schools."

The Weber County School District was one of the first districts in the state to establish a merit pay program to determine teachers' salaries. It was also a pioneer in "team" teaching, permitting students to share the talents of exceptional educators.

Dr. Terrell H. "Ted" Bell, superintendent from 1958 until

Bates Elementary School is located in North Ogden.

1963, introduced the concept of teaching by television in the district. The district had its own TV station for a few years but later shifted to the use of video cassette players as they became standard equipment in each classroom. Dr. Bell's experiences with the district were applied on a nationwide scale when the former Ogdenite was named U.S. Secretary of Education in 1981 by President Ronald Reagan.

Dr. Leland Burningham, also a former superintendent who became state superintendent of education, selected the Weber District for pilot studies in productivity. The objective of the program is to help schools create incentives for teachers and to increase student achievement scores.

Weber County School District was the first in the state to establish a foundation to provide enrichment programs for students beyond what the tax dollar supports. The foundation is a separate entity from the Weber Board of Education and works in close harmony with district objectives.

Another innovation calling for public involvement has been the Free Enterprise Fair, held annually to display studies in practical economics conducted by students. Several thousand dollars are awarded as prizes for outstanding exhibits.

An unusual teaching tool is the Swanson Environmental Learning Center, located in North Fork in the upper Ogden Valley. Up to eighty students at a time can be accommodated in dormitories and classrooms during summers and throughout the school year. An abundance of wildlife and vegetation, plus unusual geological phenomenon, make the center ideal for the appreciation of nature's bounties.

The Farr West Elementary School, opened in the fall of 1984, is the newest facility in the Weber County School District.

TRW INC.

A company called TRW is a major contributor to the defense and life-style of the United States—and to the economy of northern Utah. This diversified, $5-billion-a-year corporation has about 100,000 employees worldwide. About 300 are on staff of the Ogden Engineering Operations of the Ballistic Missiles Division of TRW's Defense Systems Group.

About one-third of the Utah staff is made up of administrative personnel and softwear technicians, working in offices at 550 Twenty-fourth Street, just east of St. Joseph's Catholic Church. The others are mostly engineers and technical experts, with quarters in former warehouses in the West Area of Hill Air Force Base. The operation's primary assignment is to provide systems engineering and technical assistance (SE/TA) to the Air Force in support of the nation's missile force, especially the Minuteman ICBM.

TRW Inc. became the corporation's name in 1965. It was a simplification of the longer Thompson-Ramo-Wooldridge

designation that came from the 1958 merger of Thompson Products Corporation and Ramo-Wooldridge, Inc.

Charles E. Thompson, for whom Thompson Products Corporation was later named, built the Cleveland Cap Screw Company into one of America's largest manufacturers and suppliers of automobile and aircraft parts and subassemblies.

Si Ramo, who grew up in Utah and was graduated from West High in Salt Lake City, and Dean Wooldridge were classmates at California Institute of Technology. In 1953 the pair formed their own company, specializing in the new concept of systems engineering—assuring that all parts of a complex system work together harmoniously. Both Ramo and Wooldridge played a significant role in development and deployment of the Thor, Atlas, Titan, and Minuteman missile systems.

Since the Ogden Air Logistics Command has worldwide management responsibility for all U.S. Air Force missile systems, an operations office was opened locally in 1977. As operations manager Bill Schilling explains, since it is the nature of the Air Force that officers directing various phases of missile activities are transferred every few years, it is important that continuity be

A Cleveland machinist, working in an old Thompson Products plant, prepares valves for installation in early-day automobiles. Thompson was a predecessor of today's TRW Inc.

maintained through civilian contractors and personnel.

Working closely with their military counterparts, TRW experts help devise criteria for maintenance, improvement, and operation of the 1,000 Minuteman silos and their launch control centers in Montana, North and South Dakota, Wyoming, and Missouri.

TRW engineers are also on hand for test firings on the range west of Great Salt Lake and at Vandenberg Air Force Base in California. Specifications are prepared for competitive procurement contracts and data is accumulated for presentation to Congress at appropriation time.

The system works. Guidance systems in many Minuteman warheads have operated nonstop for three years and more. It was originally believed motors would have to be replaced at no more than five year intervals. In practice, they have lasted two to three times longer. Accuracy, reliability, and survivability have also been enhanced.

TRW Inc. operates in the car and truck industry, in industrial and energy pursuits, and in electronics and space systems. It is space systems—the Air Force missiles—that occupy the talents of the personnel of the Ogden Engineering Operations.

Two TRW Inc. engineers examine a schematic drawing of a missile motor of the type that powers the Minuteman missile. William H. Schilling, manager of Ogden Engineering Operations, appears on the right; Leonard C. Flocken, a technical staff member appears on the left.

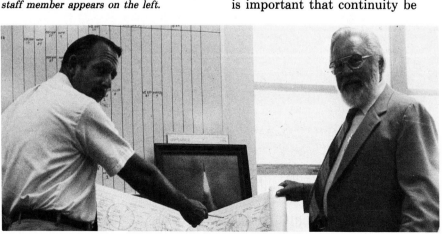

AMERICAN FENCE COMPANY

Members of the McCafferty family study fencing plans in front of their American Fence Company office and shops. From left to right, Arnold McCafferty, operations manager; David McCafferty, president; and Terry McCafferty, sales manager.

If all of the chain link fence that David R. McCafferty has installed since 1948 was placed in a straight line it would stretch from Ogden to San Francisco and beyond. He and his family are the proprietors of the American Fence Company, the only locally owned and operated fencing firm in the Ogden area.

David McCafferty is the president and general manager. His older son, Arnold, is operations manager, and his younger son, Terry, is sales manager. His wife, Geraldine, helps out occasionally in the office, and so did his daughter, Mitzi McCafferty Larsen, until she became a buyer at Hill Air Force Base.

American Fence Company has an average of thirty employees.

That figure ranges from thirty-six during the warm months, when fence installations reach their peak, to fourteen during the winter.

A farm boy from Central Utah's Ephraim-Mount Pleasant area, McCafferty spent four years in the U.S. Navy during World War II, serving with the Seventh Fleet in the Pacific. Discharged in 1948, he went to work for W.E. Stratton's American Fence Company in Salt Lake City as a laborer, but soon became a foreman and salesman.

The firm took over a defunct Ogden fencing installer in 1960, and McCafferty moved to Weber County as its manager. He turned it from a loser to a winner within a year and eventually purchased the facility and changed its name to American Fence Company.

The concern was originally located near the intersection of Washington Boulevard and River-

dale Road. In 1976 McCafferty and his sons relocated to the new modern plant, which they built at 2939 Pennsylvania Avenue. In the late 1970s satellite firms were established in Pocatello, Idaho, and Green River, Wyoming, but were later sold to their managers.

"I decided it was a full-time job running one large company, serving four states, out of Ogden," McCafferty explains. "Competition is tough, especially when bidding against out-of-state-owned fencers who use inferior materials that do not adhere to the Chain Link Fence Manufacturers Institute specifications." As an example, he cited a fence around an Ogden property that "began sagging along the top rail after only one winter." It failed because the pipe used was too thin in its walls.

American Fence Company uses an average of two 45,000-pound carloads of fencing material each month. That amounts to about 2.25 miles of residential and industrial fencing, or about 27 miles a year. All the material used is American-made and of top quality.

Included among the firm's most interesting projects have been the fencing of miles of interstate highway in northern Utah, relocating the boundary fence at Clearfield's Freeport Center, and building a fence around an oil company's field of operations in the rugged Wasatch Mountains.

David McCafferty is also active in community affairs, which include serving as a director of the Ogden Area Chamber of Commerce. He has also served as president of the Intermountain Chapter of the 1,000-member International Fence Industry Association. He also holds a "PHD" from the Texas-based "University of Experience." Appropriately, the initials stand for "Post Hole Digger."

WESTERN ZIRCONIUM

Western Zirconium, a division of Westinghouse Electric Corporation, has been producing zirconium and hafnium metals in this plant at Little Mountain west of Ogden since 1980.

Zirconium: A fairly soft, ductile, gray or black metallic chemical element . . . used in alloys, ceramics, and cladding for nuclear fuel in reactors, as a deoxidizer, etc. . . .
—Webster's New World Dictionary.

Western Zirconium is a comparative newcomer to northern Utah, but the products of its Ogden plant are of exceptional importance to the nuclear power industry in the United States and throughout the Free World. The firm, a division of Westinghouse Electric Corporation, has invested more than eighty million dollars in the plant, which is located on a 1,100-acre site on the eastern side of Little Mountain, twelve miles west of Ogden and near the shores of Great Salt Lake. Process buildings occupy fifty acres of the site and contain about 300,000 square feet of productive area.

Production began in the spring of 1980. Within five years Western Zirconium had about 500 employees with an annual payroll exceeding twelve million dollars and the capacity of three million pounds of product per year. The firm's general manager, S.A. "Les" Weber, and his colleagues anticipate steady growth in the years ahead, particularly as utilization of nuclear power increases in conventional-fuel-short nations of Western Europe, Africa, and Asia.

Zirconium, in tubular form, is used in power reactors to hold uranium fuel pellets. It is relatively transparent to neutrons produced by the uranium fuel source. As a result, more neutrons are available for energy production, thus minimizing the amount of fuel needed to generate power.

A companion metal also produced in commercial quantities at Little Mountain is hafnium, which—just the opposite of zirconium—absorbs the neutrons produced in the nuclear fission process. Consequently, hafnium rods are used to slow, control, or stop the fissioning of the uranium.

There is also increasing demand for zirconium because of its unique resistance to corrosion. The metal is widely used in the production of synthetic fibers such as rayon. Vats and pipes fabricated from zirconium have double or triple the ability of stainless steel to withstand highly caustic liquids without weakening. An unusual market for the metal is in pyrotechnics. Shredded into fibers, it becomes filaments in flashbulbs.

There are only three major producers of zirconium outside of the Soviet Union. One is in France; Western Zirconium is in Utah; and there is another American producer in the Pacific Northwest.

Western Zirconium was formed in 1976 by Dr. Steven Yih, a pioneer in zirconium production, and two associates, Dr. Young Kwon and Sam Worcester. Worcester and Kwon are still key executives with the firm, while Yih is a consultant.

The company proved the commercial value of its newly developed process at a small pilot operation near the Columbia River in Washington. After a lengthy search, Utah's Weber County was selected as the site for the full-scale plant. Factors in that decision included the availability of land in the new Little Mountain Industrial Park, access to western railroad and highway networks, an easily trained pool of labor, and a usually dry climate essential to the evaporation of waste process liquids.

Ohio-native Les Weber, a veteran of twenty years with Westinghouse Electric enterprises, became president and chief executive in 1978 and immediately moved to the Ogden suburb of Pleasant View to supervise construction and operation of the complex facility. At an Ogden Area Cham-

Zirconium tubes in this stack will eventually become containers for uranium fuel in America's civilian nuclear power plants.

ber of Commerce luncheon announcing the decision to locate in Utah, a Westinghouse vice-president jokingly told Weber, who pronounces his name in the more conventional "Web-er" style, that he should change to the local pronunciation of "Wee-ber." But he hasn't, and no one in the community seems to mind.

Western Zirconium officials emphasize that an important consideration in the design of the plant and its operation has been the attainment of product quality by closely monitoring materials during manufacturing. "The facility design, its personnel, and quality assurance procedures constitute the commitment Western Zirconium has made to provide its customers with products that meet their specifications," a

company spokesman said.

The basic raw material used by the facility is zircon sand from the beaches of northeastern Australia, which is washed and processed there, shipped by ocean freighter across the Pacific, and unloaded at a Columbia River port near Portland. The sand, containing about 1,000 pounds of zirconium per ton and an ample supply of hafnium, is then shipped by rail to Little Mountain.

The Australian sand is employed because of its high content of these comparatively rare metals. There is also zirconium in deposits near Delta, Utah, for example, but in such a dilute amount that it is more practical to import the sand.

The process of zirconium production consists of five major operations: chlorination, separations, reduction, melting, and fabrication.

Zirconium metal goes through an intricate process of refining and purification. In this photograph, zirconium "sponge" is removed from the magnesium chloride in a metal extraction process.

In the first step, the zircon sand is mixed with petroleum, coke, and chlorine at high temperatures. Waste gases given off at this stage are carefully cleansed by a multi-stage scrubbing system prior to release into the atmosphere.

Impurities and hafnium are separated at the next portion of the plant through solvent extraction, precipitation, filtration, and calcining. The reduction process reacts pure zirconium tetrachloride with magnesium metal in a retort and crucible, under high vacuum, to produce zirconium metal sponge, with valuable magnesium chloride as a by-product. The zirconium sponge (hafnium is handled through a parallel process) is melted in electric arc furnaces, also under vacuum, and ingots are poured.

The recovered metal then goes through forging and annealing processes before it is extruded or rolled into wire, strips, shapes, sheets, coils, or tubes that are shipped to commercial customers for further processing into final forms.

A sophisticated laboratory provides chemical and metallographic analyses used to support plant operations and to certify Western Zirconium products as meeting the high standards of the users. A small amount of potentially hazardous solid wastes that come from the processing of the zirconium-bearing sands is barreled and sent to a government-approved waste-disposal site.

Until a few years ago, not many Utahns had heard of either zirconium or hafnium. But now many have since Western Zirconium became a member of the Ogden area's growing industrial family, and economic benefits of this unusual firm's intricate operation have become so important to the community.

ST. JOSEPH'S CHURCH

This drawing shows the rectory of St. Joseph's Church as it appeared in the early 1900s. A new rectory was built in 1949, which serves as the pastor's residence.

St. Joseph's Church has been a vital element in the lives of thousands of Ogden-area Catholics for more than a century.

St. Joseph's parish has flourished since it came into being in 1875 with the purchase of a site for Ogden's first Catholic church. And the church, its pastors, and parishioners have been instrumental in establishing the six other Catholic parishes now thriving in northern Utah. St. Joseph's has also been the foundation upon which Catholic educational and health-care institutions in the region have been built.

Settlers of the Ogden area were all members of the Church of Jesus Christ of Latter-day Saints, sent northward from Salt Lake City shortly after the Mormons arrived in what is now Utah in 1847. When Union Pacific crews, racing toward Promontory and the historic meeting with the Central Pacific, arrived in Ogden in 1869, there were many Catholics among the Irish construction workers. Contemporary histories are vague and sometimes contradictory, but it is generally agreed that several priests visited Ogden and may have offered mass during the next few years following the completion of the transcontinental railroad.

The first authenticated record of Catholic services tells of the Reverend Patrick Walsh of Salt Lake City celebrating mass on January 5, 1872, in the home of Michael Maguire at Twenty-fifth Street and Lincoln Avenue. There were seventeen men and women present, and Frances Maguire received the first Catholic baptism in Ogden.

A great stride forward was taken on April 26, 1875, when the Reverend Lawrence Scanlan purchased a lot at 240 Twenty-fifth Street. Funds were raised through contributions and a fair. Construction on Ogden's first Catholic church began on May 1, 1876.

Named in honor of St. Joseph, the church opened for services on Easter Sunday of 1877 and was formally dedicated on October 5, 1879, by the Most Reverend J.S. Alemany, archbishop of San Francisco. The Reverend Scanlan, who later became the first bishop of Salt Lake City, conducted the solemn high mass. He was assisted by the Reverend Patrick M. Smith, who had been assigned to St. Joseph's as pastor.

The Reverend P.A. Foley was the next pastor, and in turn was succeeded by the Reverend Patrick M. Cushnahan, who remained at his Ogden post for the next forty-seven years.

A native of Ireland, the newly ordained Father Cushnahan took up residence in the sacristy of the church in September of 1881. At the time the parish had fewer than 150 members, but this did not daunt Cushnahan. Within a year he obtained another lot at Twenty-fifth and Lincoln and built a rectory, where he lived for six years. Attendance increased dramatically, and parishioners recognized that the small St. Joseph's Church would soon be outgrown.

A large lot at the northeast corner of Twenty-fourth and Adams, overlooking the city's downtown business district, was purchased. A new rectory was completed on the site by 1890 and so was the red sandstone basement, which measured 90 by 150 feet, for the cathedral.

However, the United States suffered a financial panic at that time, and, having sold their old church to pay for the larger property, Ogden Catholics had to meet in the partly furnished basement until construction could resume in 1899.

The new St. Joseph's was formally dedicated on December 14, 1902. Appropriately, Bishop Scanlon led the services with Father Cushnahan at his side. Both praised members of the parish for the many sacrifices they had made to assure the Catholics of the region an adequate, inspirational meeting place.

Built of gray sandstone, trimmed with red stone, St. Joseph's has a tall Gothic spire visible from throughout the city. Its heavy buttresses provide a feeling of strength. Within a few years an ornate, $5,000, thirty-foot-high altar was unveiled as the first of many additions and improvements to the sacred structure that have been made over the years.

In recognition of his services, Father Cushnahan was elevated by Pope Benedict XV on October 14, 1917, to the dignity of Domestic Prelate of his Holiness with the title of Right Reverend. He died on February 2, 1928, and was succeeded by one of his assistants, the Reverend Patrick F. Kennedy.

Father Kennedy served until November 1937, when he returned to the Cathedral of the Madeleine in Salt Lake City, where he had been ordained in 1917. St. Joseph's next pastor was the Reverend Wilfrid J. Giroux, who remained until his sudden death in 1947. At that time, Patrick Kennedy, now a monsignor and soon to be elevated to Protonotary Apostolic, came back to Ogden and remained until his retirement in 1972. He died in 1978.

The Reverend John A. LaBranche became pastor of St. Joseph's upon Monsignor Kennedy's retirement but died five years later. The Reverend Thomas J. Kaiser, who had served several varied assignments for the Diocese of Salt Lake City, was installed as St. Joseph's pastor in October 1977, and continues to serve the 1,300 families of the parish.

Father Cushnahan was recognized for many remarkable achievements during his long tenure. Not only was the new church built, but he directed the expansion of St. Joseph's School, first at Twenty-sixth and Washington and later at Twenty-eighth and Lincoln, as well as the construction of a new, larger Sacred Heart Academy on Twenty-fifth Street between Quincy and Jackson.

St. Joseph's School was relocated a few years ago into the former Quincy School. St. Joseph's High School was opened in 1954 at 1790 Lake Street and flourished. Sacred Heart Academy, closed in 1939, was razed to make room for a clinic in 1961.

Monsignor Giroux was the leader in a movement that led to the construction of St. Benedict's Hospital in Ogden, which opened in 1946. Father LaBranche was pastor during extensive remodeling of the church and its placement on the Utah Historical Society's roll of historic monuments in 1971. When St. Joseph's School moved to the East Bench, the old facility on Lincoln Avenue was converted, under Father Kaiser's direction, into the Kitchen of St. Anne's Center, serving meals to the indigent.

St. Joseph's parish has also helped in the establishment of six other parishes in northern Utah: St. Mary's in western Ogden, St. James in northern Ogden, Holy Family in South Ogden, St. Thomas Aquinas in Logan, St. Henry's in Brigham City, and St. Rose of Lima in Layton.

The Reverend Kaiser, pastor of St. Joseph's Church when it completed its first century of service,

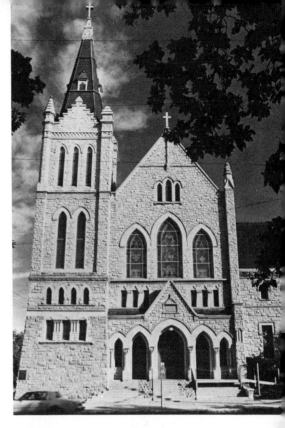

Construction began on St. Joseph's Church in 1889. Located on the northeast corner of Adams and Twenty-fourth streets, the structure was designed by Francis C. Woods and has been placed on the Utah Historical Society's roll of historical monuments. Courtesy, Clyde Mueller, Ogden Standard-Examiner

captured the spirit of the parish and its sandstone home when he wrote in a centennial letter, "On any day when I come home and St. Joseph's steeple comes into view, my heart is filled with joy, for it is the outward sign, a sacrament, of the faith-filled living stones that built it, the people."

The Reverend Thomas J. Kaiser, pastor of St. Joseph's Church since 1977, watches a bride and groom sign their wedding certificates.

W.R. WHITE COMPANY

W. Rulon White, founder, inspecting a project where pipe made by his Ogden firm was being installed in 1962.

When W. Rulon White went into business in Ogden more than a half-century ago, his largest piece of equipment was a wheelbarrow. The W.R. White Company now produces more than 100 miles of concrete pipe a year in its Ogden manufacturing facility, and the family-owned firm supplies pipes and fittings of a variety of materials to scores of Intermountain users.

The late Rulon White and his son, Bob, who succeeded his father as company president, stressed that the growth of their enterprise was due to a team effort and that a great deal of

credit for success should go to the firm's loyal employees. At last count there were more than 120 workers in the Ogden offices and plant and in distribution, warehouse, and sales branches in Murray, Helper, and Vernal. The company's sales figures and payroll are in the multimillion-dollar category.

Rulon White was born in Willard, where his ancestors had established a farm in 1850. After migrating to Chicago as a youth, he and his wife, Reva, settled briefly in Norton, Kansas, where he sold fruit and other produce. But neither liked the Kansas weather, especially after a tornado struck near their home, and they returned to Utah.

White found a coal yard for

sale, at Twentieth and Lincoln streets in downtown Ogden, and purchased it, using his wheelbarrow to move fuel around the premises. It became the Ogden Coal and Clay Pipe Co. when he realized that sale of coal was seasonal, at best, and that clay pipe was in demand in the summers. He also sold asphalt shingles. In 1939 White added concrete pipe to his line of merchandise and began manufacturing this product in a primitive plant on the corner of Wall Avenue and Rushton Street.

Increasing demand for concrete pipe for agricultural irrigation and highway drainage led to closure of the obsolete facility in 1946 and a move to 1625 Wall Avenue, where a big, flat, empty site proved ideal for the construction of a new plant. He bought out the interests of four partners in 1945 and 1946 and the W.R. White Company, with all stock owned by members of his family, was formally incorporated in 1947. First-year sales for the firm and its twelve employees were $186,000, a fraction of today's total.

Threats of secondary boycotts prompted White, during the 1950s, to invite unionization of his employees. Says Bob White, who joined his father in 1948 after working in the plant during high school and college vacation, "We've never had a strike, and we've never lost an hour's production because of a labor problem."

Improved casting machines manufactured larger pieces of concrete pipe that found ready acceptance in sewer lines, both in the sanitary systems and as storm water drains. Corrugated steel pipe was added to the White line in the late 1940s and is still fabricated in the Ogden plant, mostly as a convenience to customers, by forming flat sheets into pipe

Son of the founder, W. Robert White succeeded his father as president and chief executive officer.

Stacks of concrete pipes await shipment from the W.R. White Company plant in Ogden.

shapes and welding them together.

In the 1950s the Whites helped develop the concrete pipe industry's first "roll-on gasket," which enabled the firm to provide precision joints between pipe sections as they were installed. Bigger and better machines were also invented that enabled the casting of concrete pipes in eight-foot lengths, instead of the traditional four. Diameters were increased up to forty-eight inches.

Techniques were also improved in the forming and welding of the steel reinforcement that is an integral part of the pipe. Manholes and other fittings are manufactured at the White plant in a similar manner.

Skyrocketing population and industrial growth in Salt Lake County led the Whites to open a branch in 1960 in Murray, on a site formerly occupied by a smelter. The Helper branch was inaugurated in 1978 to serve the Carbon County coal industry, and the Vernal facility was established in 1981 during the oil, gas, tar

sands, and oil shale boom in eastern Utah and western Colorado.

The manufacture of plastic pipe also accelerated as better, stronger, and more versatile materials became available. The W.R. White Company followed the market trend and became a distributor for a full line of plastic pipes ranging from one-half inch to twenty-seven inches in diameter.

Brass and cast-iron fittings, including fire hydrants and their accessories, meters, and dozens of styles of valves, were also added until the Whites became confident they could meet all demands for pipes and associated hardware that might be made by waterworks customers. Within five years sales of plastic pipe, and, recently, strong plastic fabrics, represented half of the firm's volume.

In 1981 a new casting machine, with busy vibrators that assured maximum compaction, was installed in Ogden. It can make concrete pipe up to 120 inches in diameter. Square and oval shapes were added to the inventory of round piping.

Rulon White was active in community and civic affairs most

of his busy life. He was twice named speaker of the Utah House of Representatives, and was the last mayor elected in Ogden under the old commission form of government. He was also on the original board of directors of the Weber Basin Water Conservancy District and twice served as its president.

W. Robert White joined the Weber Basin board upon his father's death. He was one of the organizers and prime movers of the highly successful Weber County Industrial Development Corporation, serving a long term as president, and has also served as president of the Ogden Industrial Development Corporation.

The third generation of the White family is also involved in the business. Bob's son Rob serves as controller, and another son, Rulon A., is the Vernal warehouse manager. Son-in-law Rick Fairbanks serves as vice-president of new products and marketing.

The spirit of "We'll do anything," which is shown by the White family and their co-workers, is an important reason why the W.R. White Company of Ogden is one of the leaders in the pipe industry. The firm serves all of Utah, southern Idaho, western Wyoming, eastern Nevada, and western Colorado.

ANDERSON LUMBER COMPANY

The Ogden-based Anderson Lumber Company, nearly a century old, is the largest supplier of building materials in Utah, southeastern Idaho, and southwestern Wyoming. Sales at the firm's twenty-two retail, wholesale, and manufacturing centers exceeded eighty million dollars in 1984. An aggressive expansion and remodeling program should assure continued industry leadership in the region for many years to come.

James C. Beardall, president and chief executive officer since 1979, and his almost 600 co-workers are particularly proud of the three "Home Center of the Year" awards received by the firm in 1983 from *Home Center Magazine.*

This recognition from peers in the $50-billion-a-year home center industry was bestowed for the innovations displayed at the $2.2-million, 43,000-square-foot building materials center opened on July 16, 1983, in the Salt Lake County community of West Jordan.

Singled out by judges in the competition were unique features designed to assist do-it-yourself shoppers, and to tie into the company's slogan, "Come to Anderson for answers." An "Answer House," an 800-square-foot house within a store, illustrates procedures for hanging doors, installing wiring, and making many other improvements. An "Answer Center" is staffed by friendly, courteous, and knowledgeable "Answer Persons" ready to assist shoppers with their projects. An "Answer Clinic" offers further guidance to customers at free lectures. The West Jordan store is the model for the remodeling of other Anderson Lumber centers and for the construction of new centers.

Further recognition came when the Ogden City Council adopted a resolution honoring the firm for its long service to the community and gave Anderson Lumber its prestigious "Commitment to Ogden" award for its "high caliber of corporate citizenship."

Ogden has been Anderson Lumber's corporate home since mid-1927, when offices were moved from Logan where the enterprise was founded by Anthon Anderson in 1890. Anderson's family came to Utah from Norway as converts to the Church of Jesus Christ of Latter-day Saints in 1861 and settled in Weber County's Plain City.

Anthon moved to Cache Valley in 1867 as a carpenter's apprentice. Later he leased a waterpowered mill and then, with sons Edward and Robert, he organized his own lumberyard and mill.

He remained as head of the growing establishment until 1923, and was elected president in 1904 when Anderson and Sons Company was formally incorporated. He then started the series of expansions that has continued throughout the firm's life.

In 1909 Anderson arranged for lumber purchases from timber companies in Oregon owned by Utah financier David Eccles. This began a relationship with the Eccles family that has continued to be mutually beneficial to both families.

Anthon Anderson guided his company through the troubled times of World War I. He resigned shortly before his death in 1923 and was succeeded as president by Robert H. Anderson. One of the new president's first steps was the purchase of the Eccles Lumber Company in Ogden and the move of the firm's headquarters to the new First Security Building in Ogden.

When Robert Anderson died in 1930, Anthon Edward Anderson, the other founding son, became

E. LeRoy Anderson, chairman of the board.

president. He directed further expansion, particularly before and after World War II. During the war Anderson Lumber built 870 prefabricated houses as residences for Utah defense workers. Improvement of transportation systems, especially highways, led to the closing of some smaller yards in rural communities while others were opened or purchased in metropolitan areas, including Salt Lake City.

A.E. Anderson died in 1950 at the age of seventy-seven and Wesley W. Anderson, general manager since 1930, became president. One of his many achievements was the purchase of the Pioneer Wholesale Supply Company of Salt Lake City, which Anderson Lumber still operates.

George Ward served as president from 1959 until his death in 1961. E. LeRoy "Roy" Anderson, son of co-founder A. Edward Anderson, was elected president in early 1962. Roy started his long career with Anderson Lumber in 1925 as a laborer and eventually held just about every position

James C. Beardall, president and chief executive officer.

The West Jordan, Utah, center of Anderson Lumber received national awards as an outstanding customer-oriented home building center.

in the company. The firm prospered under Roy's capable leadership. Several new centers were opened during his tenure and in 1974 he led the company into the computer age with the purchase of Anderson Lumber's first computer. Roy spent fifty-five years actively involved in the firm's success, retiring in 1980. He remained as chairman of the board after James C. Beardall was named president and chief operating officer in 1979 and chief executive officer in 1980.

A Utah native, Brigham Young University graduate, and a certified public accountant, Beardall joined Anderson Lumber in 1966 as an accountant and was controller, secretary/treasurer, and vice-president before his elevation to the presidency.

One of Beardall's many ambitious goals is to appeal vigorously to the do-it-yourself market and to housewives, who do 60 percent of the shopping in home centers. Anderson's overall sales in recent years have been 70 percent wholesale and 30 percent retail to individuals.

Beardall and his managers and sales people intend to make the sales mix 50-50 by providing the "Answer" services, a comfortable place to shop, and quality merchandise at competitive prices.

The prize-winning West Jordan center is, he feels, "the finest home center of its kind anywhere." Beardall is determined to make sure others built on this model, including the proposed Wall Avenue center in Ogden, will be just as efficient and appealing.

Other new building material centers in recent years have been completed in Evanston, Wyoming, and St. George, Cedar City, and Layton, Utah. Those in Preston and Grace, Idaho, and Price, Bountiful, and Park City, Utah, have been extensively remodeled. Modernization is also scheduled or under way at Ketchum, Twin Falls, Rupert, and Rexburg, Idaho, and Tremonton, Utah. Sites have been purchased for centers in Rock Springs, Wyoming, and Vernal, Utah. Beardall has additional expansion plans along the Wasatch Front, and later will move south into the Sun Belt states.

Anderson Lumber Company has about 600 employees on its multimillion-dollar payroll, including 90 in Ogden. That's quite a growth from Anthon Anderson's original work force in Logan— himself and his two sons.

The architectural millwork division of Anderson Lumber has been located on Lincoln Avenue for many years. It was recently replaced by this modern facility.

WILLIAMS INTERNATIONAL

Williams International is the world's largest producer of small jet engines at its plants in Utah and Michigan. The firm's newest plant, its main building covering approximately 100,000 square feet, is at 3450 Sam Williams Drive, adjacent to the northern boundary of Ogden Municipal Airport. The facility employs more than 400 men and women. Its 46-acre site offers plenty of room for later expansion.

Headquarters of Williams International and its other production quarters are in the small township of Walled Lake, Michigan, about thirty-five miles north of Detroit. Since 1955 Dr. Sam Williams and his associates have developed more than thirty different small jet engines (defined as those producing less than 1,000 pounds of thrust), for a wide variety of governmental and civilian applications.

Designing and manufacturing these mini-jets is an intriguing business. Precision is vital. Tolerances are exceptionally fine, measured in one-thousandth of an inch.

Primary products of the Ogden plant are turbofan engines to power U.S. Air Force and Navy cruise missiles and turbojet engines for unmanned, remotely piloted reconnaissance aircraft and target drones. The missile engines are small enough to fit inside a tour-size golf bag. One foot in diameter and less than a yard long, they weigh only 145 pounds but produce 600 pounds of thrust. The pilotless aircraft engines are also a foot in diameter but only 18 inches long and weigh a mere 45 pounds. They produce 190 pounds of thrust.

Dr. Sam Williams, chairman, president, and chief executive officer, has always been fond of Utah, with his parents being

The Ogden plant of Williams International occupies the center of a 46-acre site on the northwest corner of Ogden Municipal Airport.

graduates of the University of Utah. E.L. "Gene" Klein, executive vice-president and chief operating officer, formerly lived in Ogden while with the Marquardt Company.

After an early career as an automotive mechanical engineer, Williams formed Williams Research Corporation on January 1, 1955, to begin development of an experimental marine gas-turbine engine. Other contracts for small engines led to the 1959 move to Walled Lake from the original small plant in Birmingham, Michigan. New experimental engines were built for industrial and automotive applications, to power jet "belts" and manned "flying platforms." Particularly successful were auxiliary power units for commercial and private aircraft.

The engine for the Air Force and Navy cruise missiles was developed in the mid-1970s. When it became apparent that additional facilities would be needed, a nationwide search for a second plant site was started. Ogden was selected because of its talented work force and convenient geographical location in relation to West Coast aircraft manufacturers.

A small plant was opened in rented quarters in the Weber County Industrial Park in 1974.

The initial unit of the permanent Ogden facility began operation in June 1978. A second segment, virtually doubling the size, went on line in March 1981.

Williams International was adopted as the corporate name in mid-1981. Its executives are optimistic about the future of the company, including the Ogden plant. New engines now being designed and developed could find wide utilization by makers of executive aircraft because of their tremendous efficiency and small size. New industrial applications of the mini-jets are also on the horizon.

One of the more than 400 employees of Williams International prepares parts of small jet engines for heat treatment.

JIM WHETTON BUICK

The Jim Whetton Buick dealership has been located at 3520 Wall Avenue in Ogden since January 1964.

Jim Whetton Buick has sold more than 14,000 new automobiles since it was established in Ogden more than a quarter-century ago. President-founder Jim Whetton is proud of this record, especially since the motor car business has, during that same period, undergone what he calls a "revolution."

"The vehicles we sold in 1960 were, to use aeronautical terms, 'propellor driven,' compared with the sophisticated 'jets' of today," he says. "And we haven't, by any means, reached the peak as electronic devices rapidly replace many of the old moving parts."

He forecast that television-like screens would report all essential functions to drivers, replacing less accurate old-style instruments. Some autos already have fourteen microcomputers in their operating systems, with more to come.

Whetton should know. He was the 1966-1967 and 1984-1985 chairman of the 3,000-member National Buick Dealers' Council and has frequently met with top officials of General Motors. Rubbing elbows with national luminaries is nothing new to the Utah dealer. He was administrative assistant to billionaire Howard Hughes from 1954 to 1958 and general manager of the Hughes-owned Desert Inn and Country Club in Las Vegas from 1973 to 1978, dividing his time between Utah and Nevada.

An Ogden native, Whetton attended Weber College until he was appointed to the U.S. Naval Academy in July 1941. Upon graduation from Annapolis in 1944, he was assigned as a division gunnery officer on the USS *Montpelier,* a heavy cruiser. He saw World War II service in Saipan and Okinawa waters. He left the Navy in 1947 but was recalled in 1951 for the Korean War and became an aide to the admiral commanding battleships and cruisers in the western Pacific.

Whetton began his frequently interrupted career in automobile sales in 1938, washing vehicles for Ogden Buick at Twenty-sixth and Washington. He became general manager there after his naval duty. Whetton purchased the Ogden Buick agency from banker-dealer Frank Browning on November 1, 1960. The renamed Jim Whetton Buick moved to 3520 Wall Avenue on January 1, 1964.

The firm's 1984 sales of Buicks, Jeeps, and used cars exceeded nine million dollars. The dealership has forty-eight employees with a monthly payroll of $75,000 to $80,000.

Whetton's son Mark is general sales manager. Another son, Alan, has opened his own Buick, GMC Truck, Cadillac, and Pontiac agency in Brigham City. Son-in-law Doug Hammer serves as manager of the Whetton Buick parts department.

Long active in community affairs, Whetton was president of the Ogden Area Chamber of Commerce in 1968. He has been a busy member, even when working much of the time in Las Vegas, of the governing board of Ogden's McKay-Dee Hospital Center. His most rewarding post, in his own estimation, has been the presidency of the McKay-Dee Foundation because of the "good feeling" it gave "to be helping others."

MOUNTAIN FUEL SUPPLY COMPANY

When weather is at its coldest, Mountain Fuel Supply Company delivers more heating energy to its customers than all other available sources combined, including oil, coal, electricity, and wood.

To do this, the firm has nearly 7,250 miles of pipeline backed up by thousands of miles more of lines owned by natural gas suppliers located throughout the Intermountain West. For more than fifty years this network has never failed to provide adequate supplies of natural gas at affordable prices to Mountain Fuel's customers—residential, commercial, and industrial—now numbering 430,000 in Utah and Wyoming.

The company's Ogden service area, with nearly 75,000 customers in Weber, North Davis, and Morgan counties, has a long association with natural gas—an association that goes back before Mountain Fuel began providing gas service in the early 1930s.

Artificial gas was initially manufactured in Ogden in 1872, primarily for street lighting. After natural gas became available to area residents following completion in 1929 of a major interstate transmission pipeline, gas increasingly became the fuel of choice for Ogden area residents because of its cost, convenience, and cleanliness.

Mountain Fuel's area headquarters is at 2940 Washington Boulevard. Personnel there are responsible for serving customers and maintaining a local network of main and service lines. The network represents 1,350 miles of pipeline and includes 114 employees drawing an annual payroll of nearly three million dollars. Mountain Fuel pays nearly $500,000 annually in property taxes to the three counties.

Heading the Ogden operations are James Brown, manager for retail operations, and Jack Boyer,

"Pipeline '29" crossed 200 miles of rugged Utah and Wyoming terrain to bring the first natural gas to the Ogden-Salt Lake City area. The crews often used their combined weight to bend pipeline for welding.

manager of distribution operations. The two are proud that Mountain Fuel's rates remain among the lowest in the nation and that there has never been a major disruption of service in Utah. This service dependability and the low rates have significantly contributed to Ogden's attractiveness for industrial expansion.

The history of natural gas distribution in the Ogden area is complex. It has gone through eight major changes since the first manufactured gas plant was built on Lincoln Avenue, between Twentieth and Twenty-first streets. First coal, then oil, was burned in a closed process, and the escaping gas was captured and distributed to streetlights.

The first major change came in 1893 when the Ogden firm was consolidated with the Salt Lake City Gas Co. Two years later it experimented with the distribution of natural marsh gas from the shores of Great Salt Lake but

pressure was too low.

Union Light & Power Co. took over the artificial gas business in 1897. This became Utah Light & Power Co. in 1899, then the Utah Light & Railway Co. in 1904. The Ogden Gas Co. assumed the operation in 1906 and served until 1928, when it was purchased by Wasatch Gas Co., a subsidiary of the newly formed Western Public Service Corp.

Natural gas was discovered in commercial quantities in 1922 in Baxter Basin, 200 miles east of Ogden and near Rock Springs, Wyoming. Western Public Service, owned by Ohio Oil and other eastern interests, decided Utah's Wasatch Front offered the best potential market and immediately began planning a transmission line over the rugged Wasatch Mountains.

Despite heavy winter snows and spring floods and mud, "Pipeline '29" was completed in August 1929, prompting celebration in Ogden and other cities. Crews laid 334 miles of four- to eighteen-inch, high-tensile-strength steel pipe, using horse-drawn sleds when tractors bogged down.

On May 7, 1935, Western Public Service Corp. stockholders approved the consolidation of its various subsidiaries into Mountain Fuel Supply Company, with headquarters in Salt Lake City. At this time 22,252 Utah customers enjoyed natural gas service.

During World War II, with its resultant population explosion in northern Utah, demand for natural gas exceeded the utility's ability to acquire steel pipes diverted to the war effort. As a result, a freeze was imposed on most new connections. When the war ended and restrictions were removed, there were long lines of applicants seeking service to new or renovated homes, apartments, and businesses.

Lines were extended throughout northern Utah and southwestern Wyoming. New fields were developed in Utah, Colorado, and Wyoming. Mountain Fuel had 45,385 customers in 1945, 82,204 in 1950, 126,081 in 1955, 220,795 in 1965, and about 435,000 in 1985.

Much of the Ogden area's natural gas supply now comes from wells in the Overthrust Belt between Evanston, Wyoming, and Coalville, Utah, just east of Ogden. The original transmission line has been supplemented by two larger pipelines. A new pipeline constructed through Hyrum Canyon near Logan permits Ogden to be served from both the north and south. Connections are maintained with other companies engaged in gas development and transmission to supplement supplies from wells in more than fifty Utah, Wyoming, and Colorado fields.

Mountain Fuel pioneered the underground storage of natural gas so that excess supplies available during periods of light demand are readily available as reserves during cold weather. The first subterranean storage complex was at Chalk Creek, near Coalville. Others have followed at Leroy, Wyoming, and Bridger Lake and

Much of Mountain Fuel's gas supply comes from wells like this one in Wyoming operated by the Wexpro Company. Both Mountain Fuel and Wexpro are now subsidiaries of the Questar Corporation.

Clay Basin in northeastern Utah, and additional storage at Coalville. The firm has also been searching for other alternative sources of supply. A pilot coal gasification plant has been built in West Jordan, Utah, as part of this program.

In Mountain Fuel's 1983 annual report, chairman B.Z. Kastler and president R.D. Cash said, "We feel very bullish about our business and growth opportunities for the future." Cash noted that in difficult times Mountain Fuel has "fared better" than most comparable utilities because of the firm's "growth,

flexibility, and competitiveness."

The most recent corporate change came late in 1984, when Mountain Fuel Supply Company stockholders voted to form the Questar Corporation as a parent holding company to separate more clearly utility and nonutility functions.

Mountain Fuel is now operating exclusively as a retailer of natural gas. Under Entrada Industries Inc., also a subsidiary of Questar, come Wexpro and Celsius Energy, companies primarily devoted to exploration and development; Mountain Fuel Resources Inc., basically a natural gas transmission and storage operation; Interstate Brick Company; and Questar Development Corporation, which handles property development and energy research.

MORTON THIOKOL, INC.

Every time an American space shuttle is launched, more than 6,000 northern Utah residents have special reasons for cheering loudly. They are the men and women who work at the Utah and Wasatch divisions of Morton Thiokol, Inc., at facilities in Ogden, Brigham City, and near historic Promontory.

All of the solid rocket booster motors that help lift the shuttles into orbit have been fabricated by the firm in Utah. Motor cases are taken apart when they are recovered after a launch, returned to the Wasatch Division for re-loading with solid fuel, and shipped back to NASA's shuttle assembly center.

Morton Thiokol also has contracts to build motors for upper stages of communication satellites, the Air Force's HARM and Peacekeeper missiles, and the Navy's Trident and Standard missiles. Experimental motors for other applications are constantly being developed, and motors up to 156 inches in diameter have been tested.

The Utah Division plant near the Ogden Municipal Airport manufactures military illuminating flares and automotive air-bag inflators. Procurement personnel are housed in an adjacent structure that was once headquarters for the Morton Thiokol Government Systems group.

The division's 6,500-plus employees, with an annual payroll of about $180 million, make Morton Thiokol the largest private employer in Utah. Of the firm's $326-million annual expenditures on procurement, $72.7 million, or 22 percent, are spent in Utah for goods and services. The various manufacturing, testing, and office facilities contain more than two million square feet of floor space. The Wasatch Division, overall,

occupies more than 19,000 acres of land.

The firm originally was the Thiokol Chemical Company. When solid fuel motors became the major product, the word "Chemical" was dropped, and in 1982 the Thiokol Company merged with Morton Salt Company to become Morton Thiokol.

Attracted to Utah by the availability of vast open spaces that would enhance the safety of its operations, Thiokol began Utah operations in the state in 1956 with the opening of offices in Ogden and Brigham City. Work began on the large first stage of the Minuteman missile in October 1957 at the Wasatch plant, located fifty-two miles northwest of Ogden and only seven miles from where the Central and Union Pacific railroads met in 1869.

The first Minuteman motor was static fired in 1959, the same year the missile completed its initial test flight. Later contracts were signed to make motors for the Genie missile; the Poseidon submarine-launched ballistic mis-

An illuminating flare, manufactured in Ogden by Morton Thiokol, floats to earth on its parachute as one of the devices is tested.

sile; its successors, the Trident I and II; Minuteman III; the Peacekeeper ICBM; and other military missiles.

The Utah Flare Division was established in 1972 at the Promontory plant. Production of these ordnance items was moved to Ogden in 1980.

Morton Thiokol, Inc., officials are confident that the firm's employment picture looks positive for years to come, thanks to the new and ongoing business of its Wasatch and Utah divisions.

Air bags, designed to enhance safety of automobile occupants, go through severe tests. Inflators for the bags are made in Ogden by the Utah Division of Morton Thiokol.

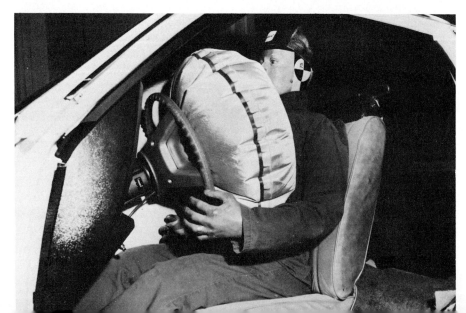

FROERER CORP.

Three generations of Fred Froerers have been instrumental in establishing the Froerer Corp. as one of the most prestigious real estate firms in northern Utah. Fred Froerer, Sr., founded the business in 1925 as a real estate-insurance corporation with J. Francis Fowles. Froerer's Ogden Home Builders Co. became Realty Insurance Company, an independent concern, in 1932.

Fred Froerer, Jr., joined his father in 1939 and, after World War II service in the U.S. Navy, became president of the Froerer Corp. when his father retired.

Now Fred Froerer, Jr., is, as he puts it, "taking it easier" and has passed the management of the company to his sons—Fredrick "Buck" Froerer III, vice-president, legal counsel, and general manager, and Zane B. Froerer, vice-president in charge of investments and sales. The firm's offices are in the Froerer Building, located at 2600 Washington Boulevard.

Eden, in Ogden's Upper Valley, has long been the family's home. Fred Froerer, Sr., was born there and, as a youth, usually had to milk thirty-five to forty cows every morning and evening. He earned tuition money by selling books from door to door, went to Utah State Agricultural College (now Utah State University), and was a star tackle on the "Aggie" football team.

He qualified as a milk tester and worked in Cache Valley dairies for a while. Then he was a school teacher in Brigham City. In 1914 he found his true vocation when he became a sales associate for Carl Rasmussen's Ogden real estate office, remaining there until joining "Frank" Fowles in their early partnership.

Froerer's home building firm had heavy going during the Great Depression but survived, thanks in

Officers of Ogden's Froerer Corp. are chairman and president Fred Froerer, Jr. (center), vice-president, legal counsel, and general manager Fredrick "Buck" Froerer III (right), and vice-president Zane B. Froerer.

part to substantial support from *Ogden Standard-Examiner* publisher A.L. Glasmann.

They developed one of Ogden's first complete subdivisions in the city's East Bench, building many homes on Twenty-seventh Street and Marilyn and Beverly drives.

Fred Froerer, Jr., in his younger days, was the "cleanup boy" for his father's offices on the ground floor of the Kiesel Building. He was graduated from Weber State College and soon acquired his real estate sales license. He was in the Navy as a radio technician and instructor from 1942 until his discharge as an ensign at war's end. He rejoined his father and settled down for his eventful career.

He obtained his real estate broker's license in 1954 and in 1957 became a member of the American Institute of Real Estate Appraisers—the only one in this region and one of only thirty-eight in Utah.

This led to considerable community involvement. He was the

chief negotiator for the Ogden Redevelopment Agency in purchase of property that became the Ogden City Mall and the Ogden Hilton Hotel. He also handled property negotiations on the Ben Lomond Hotel (now Radisson Suite Hotel), and Utah Regional Office Building projects. Thanks to his efforts there was no need on any for court-ordered condemnation. He has also been active on the Kimberly-Clark plant's land acquisition.

Fred Froerer, Jr., has been president of the Ogden Exchange Club, a fund raiser for the Ogden Industrial Development Corporation, a member of the Utah House of Representatives in 1953 and 1957, a member of the Utah State Building Board for two terms, a director of the Ogden Area Chamber of Commerce, and a longtime member of the Ogden Planning Commission and Weber State College School of Business Advisory Board. He is the 1985 president of the Weber County Industrial Development Corporation.

Fred Froerer III has a law degree from the University of Utah and is also active in the community. Zane B. Froerer is one of only thirty CCIMs (Certified Commercial Investment Members) in the state of Utah.

263

WASATCH DISTRIBUTING COMPANY

The half-century-old Wasatch Distributing Company of Ogden is the largest distributor of beer in northern Utah and the third-largest in the state. Each year the more than two dozen vehicles in the Wasatch Distributing fleet deliver the equivalent of more than one million cases to customers in Weber, North Davis, North Summit, Morgan, Box Elder, and Cache counties.

President Rich Peterson lists sales at about $10.5 million annually. The payroll for the firm's thirty-eight employees, payment of substantial taxes, and purchase of supplies represent a sizable contribution to the region's economy.

The history of Wasatch Distributing Company dates back to the 1933 repeal of Prohibition and the legalization—for the first time in more than a decade—of the sale of alcoholic beverages.

The firm was organized by Brig Robinson to distribute Salt Lake City-brewed Fisher Beer. C.R. Arnold and his son-in-law, C.G. Peterson, purchased control in 1949 and took over a warehouse on Grant Avenue, near Twenty-fifth Street, where the Federal Building is now. When Fisher sales dropped as local brews declined in popularity in the face of competition from regional and national companies, Wasatch Distributing took an important step. It acquired the franchise for distribution of Anheuser-Busch products in 1958.

Two years later Wasatch Distributing moved northward to a warehouse and office on Twenty-fourth Street, between Grant and Lincoln avenues. It remained there until 1976 when the downtown Ogden redevelopment project, and the need for even larger facilities, prompted the company's final move to 2361 B Avenue. The original warehouse and offices at the new location occupied 20,000 square feet. A 4,500-foot addition was built in 1978, and another expansion of 15,000 square feet was completed in 1983.

Three important breweries were also added to Wasatch Distributing's product line during this time. The sale of Olympia Brewing Company products began in 1961, Miller Brewing Company beers in 1968, and G. Heilman's brands in 1983. By late 1984 the company's trucks were carrying sixteen different brands of beer, brewed by the four major breweries, and packaged in twelve- and sixteen-ounce cans, twelve-ounce bottles, quart bottles, and half-barrel draft.

C.R. Arnold died in 1976. C.G. Peterson, president and general manager, retired in 1980 after selling the business to his son, Rich, and his daughter, Sheri Peterson Morgan. At that time Rich became president and Sheri took over as operations manager.

Rich Peterson learned the beverage distribution business from the bottom up. As a youngster, beginning when he was only eight years old, he worked in the warehouse, helping route drivers load their trucks. As a teenager he took over sales of a popcorn brand that his father had added to help boost their income. He began working for the company full time in 1968 and handled a variety of assignments before taking over the presidency eleven years later.

In 1968 the firm's annual sales were approximately 165,000 cases (two dozen twelve-ounce cans per case) of beer. That was less than one-sixth of the 1984 level. Capacity in the Twenty-fourth Street warehouse, a site now occupied by the Ogden Hilton Hotel, was

15,000 cases and 300 to 350 kegs. The B Avenue facility has room to store 160,000 cases and 3,000 kegs.

Rich Peterson says the reasons for this tremendous growth come from a wide variety of factors. One has been steady gains in tourism in the four-county Golden Spike Empire of North Davis, Weber, Box Elder, and Morgan counties. Peterson feels there should be even greater growth—particularly in development of Snow Basin, Powder Mountain, and Wolf Creek as year-round recreation centers.

"The population has increased, too," he adds, "particularly as men and women employed in and around Salt Lake City have moved to central and northern Davis County to escape monumental traffic problems in Salt Lake County. More employment at Hill Air Force Base has also been a contribution."

Surveys show that many of these newcomers in the area do not belong to the LDS Church, whose beliefs prohibit the drinking of alcoholic beverages. "Changes in life-styles and personal habits of consumers have also increased the popularity of beer," Peterson

says. "In the old days, 90 percent of our sales were in the form of kegs to taverns. Now only 10 percent of our sales are to taverns.

"It used to be that consumers stopped off for a few beers on the way home from work. Now, thanks in part to better packaging, they pick up a six-pack or twelve-pack and take it home, to the picnic grounds, or to the lakes. They have more leisure time, too," he says.

There have also been technological changes. Wasatch Distributing has a bank of ultra-modern computers to handle paperwork. Advertising on television has made a major change in merchandising, as well.

In the early days of the business, all products were loaded onto trucks, through the back end, by hand. These vehicles had a capacity of 300 to 350 cases. In the mid-1960s placement of loads on pallets was introduced. Trucks with eight side-loading bays carried 650 cases. In recent years tractor-pulled trailers have been employed that have sixteen bays and a capacity of 1,400 cases.

Rich Peterson has an unusual answer to criticism of Utah-sold beer, limited by law to 3.2 percent

of alcohol by weight. He tells critics that "the only difference between Ogden beer and Evanston (Wyoming), beer is seventy miles." Beer sold in the neighboring, no-limit state is, at average, 3.7 percent alcohol.

However, he feels the new "light alcohol"—1 7 to 1.8 percent alcohol—beverages introduced in 1984 will be quite popular "as more attention is given to physical fitness." This was also the reason "light beers"—with about half of the 140 to 150 calories per twelve ounces of regular brews—have been accepted so widely.

"Future sales gains will come primarily at the expense of our competition," the Wasatch Distributing Company president concludes. "Sales of distilled spirits are declining, wine sales have leveled off, and beer sales curves are flat. Campaigns against alcohol abuse and drunk driving are having a growing effect in reducing consumption of all alcoholic beverages."

THE VANESSA-ANN COLLECTION

The Vanessa-Ann Collection has sold more than two million copies of ninety different needlework leaflets and books since it was formed in 1979 by partners Jo Buehler and Terrece Woodruff. But the organization is comparatively unknown in its home town of Ogden, since 99 percent of its sales are outside of Utah. Still, business has doubled each year as the popularity of Vanessa-Ann gains all over the country, and new products are added to the collection.

As a result, the young entrepreneurs have fifteen full-time employees in their headquarters, the seventy-year-old Becker Mansion at 2408 Van Buren Avenue, and at their warehouse in the Ogden Industrial Park. At least twenty other talented women are involved as part-time stitchers or on special projects.

Three little Woodruffs, a pair of Buehlers, and small sons and daughters of other employees busy themselves in the mansion's playrooms or the spacious yard. Occasionally the youngsters are drafted as models and photographed for the books and leaflets produced by Vanessa-Ann for nationwide distribution. That's one reason why the collection has been so successful—its realism. These designers have had, to say the least, hands-on training.

Jo Packham Buehler, a native of Ogden, attended the University of Utah for two years, then was graduated from California State University at Sacramento. Her husband, Scott, a lawyer, is the son of J. Clyde Buehler, co-founder many years ago with the late Norman B. Bingham, of Utah Tailoring Mills, whose made-to-order women's clothing is sold all over the United States.

Although born in Rexburg, Idaho, Terrece Beesley Woodruff also has pioneer Ogden family

Terrece Woodruff, vice-president (left), and Jo Buehler, president.

connections. Her great-grandfather, Charles Woodmansee, was an early-day Ogden merchant. Terrece, called "Tece" by friends, went to Ricks College, then was graduated in fine arts from Utah State University. Her husband, Rocky Woodruff, a certified public accountant, is the financial vice-president of J.B. Parsons Company.

Jo Buehler had little needlework experience until her husband was finishing law school in California. She explains that "I needed a friend and found one who did quilting, cross-stitching, and weaving. To keep her friendship, I took it up, too—and loved it. We took classes together for four years, and I was hooked." When her husband graduated, the couple returned to Ogden and she, for a time, was involved in operating a small retail needlework store, beginning in 1977.

Terrece Woodruff started her professional career as a designer for a California needlework com-

pany, Sunset Designs, then also returned to Ogden with her young family. Friends urged the two to get together because of their common interest in needlework. They met in May 1979 when Buehler called Woodruff to ask her help in a cross-stitch book she was writing. Their conversations led to formation of the partnership.

Over the next several months—although both were pregnant and already had three-year-olds—they wrote, produced, and published four books, entitled *Christmas Pie, Sweet Dreams, Rainbow's End,* and *April Showers.*

Initially they had only 1,000 copies of each printed and lost twenty-five cents per copy because of high printing costs. Success came with numerous reprints. *Sweet Dreams* eventually sold more than 100,000 copies—a best seller!

As they explained in an interview with the national trade publication *Sew News,* the pair felt that needlework patterns already on the market left much to be desired in conciseness and

Karen Gardiner, office manager (left), and Katie Pearce, comptroller.

Nancy Whitley, needlework director (left), and Margaret Marti, editor.

simplicity of illustrations and instructions. "We took a different approach," Buehler says. "There were plenty of books on cross-stitch design, but they gave ideas for pillows and pictures only. You can only put so many pillows and pictures in your house. So we decided to show different kinds of finishing ideas. And we put much more into photography. ... Some companies can get a book to press in twelve weeks. But we take eight months."

For a company name they adopted the middle names of their oldest children—Sara Vanessa Buehler and Lori Ann Woodruff. Justin Buehler is Jo's second child; the other young Woodruffs are Lisa and Shaun.

Initially, Vanessa-Ann patterns were drawn on a dining room table and pilot models were prepared in homes throughout the community. Supplies were stored in a family garage. As sales through wholesalers and stores improved, studios were moved to an old home at 2605 Van Buren. Zoning problems there and the need for more space led to the purchase of the then-vacant Becker Mansion in November 1983.

The emphasis of The Vanessa-Ann Collection is on cross-stitch, but projects include patterns for quilting, applique, embroidery, doll-making, and knitting. Accessories such as children's jewelry, toys, and posters have been added to the line. So have cookbooks, postcards, and calendars.

The leaflets and books are already featured by such national and regional chain stores as Minnesota Fabrics, Mangelsen's, Lee-Wards, Northwest Fabrics, Ben Franklin, and Grand Central-Fred Meyers. Patterns are designed under contract for Bucilla,

Simplicity, Bernat, and Columbia-Minerva. Two books to be printed and sold by Better Homes and Gardens Books were under preparation in the fall of 1984, as well as a volume for Oxmoor House.

Sometimes, working against a deadline, an editor can be found stitching up a doll made from one of the collection's patterns, or one of the partners can be seen ironing or selecting a fabric, colors of floss, buttons, or other trimmings from big sample cases. "We have fun," Buehler and Woodruff agree, "even if we do work long hours."

Susan Whitelock, finishing director (left), and Trice Boerens, design director.

OGDEN CITY SCHOOLS

The Ogden City Schools, now well into its second century, has always had pride in its excellence. Ogden's 600 teachers in 22 schools have good reasons for their pride. When national achievement tests were given recently, every school had scores well above the national average. And dozens of students achieved scores several levels above their grade.

The philosophy of Superintendent William L. Garner and his staff is summarized in the three words, "Futures Are Growing," that have been adopted by the Ogden City Schools as an official motto. These words appear—usually beside a brightly colored sketch of a sliced red apple with a sprightly green leaf—on notebooks, memo pads, blackboards, and in various other applications.

"By growing," explains Eileen Rencher, district public relations director, "we don't mean just the kids. We mean teachers, administrators, parents, and the community, too."

All have come a long way since the days of Charilla Abbot. Miss Abbot was Ogden's first schoolteacher. She had migrated to Utah from New York with her Mormon-convert parents and settled in Ogden on October 27, 1849. In a letter written years later, Abbot told how "the colony wished me to keep school." She was only twenty years old and had a minimum of formal schooling, but she pitched right in.

The school was a small log house, located near the Weber River at the foot of what is now Twenty-ninth Street. The floor was packed dirt. The dozen students sat on backless benches, and books were scarce. The pioneer educator cut a pen from a chicken feather.

Clifford B. Doxey, veteran Ogden teacher, traced the history of his city's schools in detail in a

Ogden's second school was this small frame structure built near the foot of Twenty-ninth Street.

thesis written in 1944. He pointed out that the establishment of schools was a high priority in all Mormon settlements in Utah. This was certainly true in Ogden. The territorial legislature approved a municipal charter for Ogden on February 6, 1851. Mayor Lorin Farr had divided the hamlet into three school districts within a week. He and the council budgeted three dollars to teach each of the 225 students.

New and improved school buildings of adobe and then brick were erected in each district, especially after Louis Moench, later founder of Weber State College, joined the system in 1876. By 1878 there were 1,050 students.

This growth prompted the construction of the Central School (now the Elks Club), on what is now Grant Avenue between Twenty-fifth and Twenty-sixth streets. This was a showplace for years, with its large yard, lawn, trees, and flowers. The two-story structure, with space for 194 double desks

Students in Ogden's old Central School (now the Elks Club) on Grant Avenue between Twenty-fifth and Twenty-sixth streets.

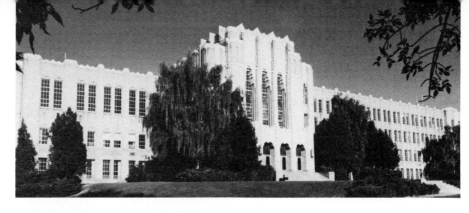

The Ogden High School was acclaimed a classic when it was dedicated on October 29, 1937. Photo by Jon R. Williams

and "plenty of benches in back for the rest," cost $15,000. Classes included rhetoric, mental and moral psychology, civil government, political ethics, physiology, physical geography, bookkeeping, general history, teaching, and music.

Professor Theodore B. Lewis organized a high school in 1890, and classes met in city hall "over the noisy fire station." Parents paid quarterly taxes for their children's tuition until 1890, when Ogden became the first independent school district in the state to provide "free" education to all students, rich or poor, of any religion. Until then several private schools had opened in Ogden because "gentile" parents objected to the Mormon domination of the regular classrooms.

A $100,000 bond issue was passed in 1891 to finance a major construction program. New schools were called the New Madison, Five Points or Lincoln, Pingree, Quincy, Grant, Mound Fort, Chipp, and West Ogden. Their thirty-seven teachers, thirty-one of them women, received salaries averaging seventy-three dollars per month. The annual school operations budget was $50,000. Later buildings were named Dee, Lewis, Polk, Lorin Farr, and Hopkins. A new high school was opened at Twenty-fifth and Monroe in 1908.

Utah's first junior highs or "sub-highs" were inaugurated in Ogden in 1912 by Superintendent John M. Mills and additions were made at Central, Dee, and Lewis to handle the increase. Other major expansions came in 1923 when Weber Academy abandoned its secondary curriculum, and all students below college level had to attend public schools.

A new, $1.2-million Ogden High School, on Harrison Boulevard between Twenty-eighth and Twenty-ninth streets, was opened on

October 29, 1937. Old Central was closed and Monroe High School became a junior high. Superintendent W. Karl Hopkins called the structure on Harrison the "best and most attractive school in the world."

Many changes in the physical plant have been made since that time, including the construction of Ben Lomond High School on Ninth Street, west of Harrison. Population shifts have forced the closure of some schools. In 1981-1982 the junior highs became middle schools to provide a better bridge between elementary and high school, including "some of the best elements of both."

The administration of Superintendent Garner, who had succeeded T.O. Smith in 1969, received a rousing vote of confidence in February 1984. Citizens, by a three-to-one margin, approved a "voted leeway" program, shifting five mills in taxation authority from capital outlay to maintenance and operations. This made possible the carrying out of a $1.2-million

improvement program without raising taxes.

Another milestone was passed when a "career ladder" plan for raising teachers' salaries in accordance with their abilities, as well as seniority, became effective in 1984. This pleased Dr. Garner, who was a teacher before becoming an administrator. He felt that students would be the most important benefactors of better teaching.

"The students come first," he says. "I get joy from watching teachers being successful with students. That's the best thing about my job."

Dr. Garner has also been campaigning for parents to become more involved in the education of their children. "Parents who care about children's education are the backbone of American education," he states. "We educators must recognize that we need the parents on our side."

With that cooperation, he knows that the Ogden City Schools can maintain its long history of excellence.

Mound Fort Middle School is the newest school building in the Ogden City School District. Photo by Jon R. Williams

BIG D CONSTRUCTION CORPORATION

The Big D Construction Corporation of Ogden, a specialist in industrial design and building, is well named. The firm's organizer and president, Dee Livingood, is big in both size and thoughts. His 230 pounds are spread over a six-foot five-inch frame. He and his 126-member staff are usually involved in thirty or more construction projects at a time, many of them in the multimillion-dollar range.

Big D Construction's annual volume of more than twelve million dollars makes it one of the largest and most successful building enterprises in northern Utah. Eighty percent of the contracts that Big D signs are negotiated rather than bid, because of the firm's widespread reputation for speedy, high-standard construction. This means that prospective clients usually come to Big D, rather than being sought out.

"Our forte is speed, and if industries want a complete job, from design to occupancy, done quickly and well, they come to us," Livingood explains. "There have been years when we haven't bid a single job on the open market."

A native of Ogden, Livingood was a teenager in the summer of 1955 when he got his first construction job, working for Peter Kiewitt Company on Hill Air Force Base runways. After graduation from Ben Lomond High School, Livingood became a carpenter's apprentice and married Lorraine Hilton. He took architectural and engineering classes at night and finally, in 1968, formed his own firm. Big D's offices and shops are located at 389 West Second Street, near Defense Depot Ogden.

Livingood quickly recognized the need for a firm that could offer "turnkey" construction services—beginning with the concept and following on with design, con-

Big D Construction Corporation, whose projects are concentrated along the Wasatch Front, is at 389 West Second Street in Ogden.

struction, and finishing. He assembled a dedicated team of craftsmen, including carpenters, concrete specialists, steel erectors, and painters. Only a third of the work on Big D projects is done by subcontractors. "Our job is to fit it all together to make it happen," Livingood says.

The payroll for 1984, when the company had more than forty-five contracts, was well over two million dollars.

Big D projects are concentrated along the Wasatch Front but have included contracts in St. George, Utah; Green River, Wyoming; and Helena, Montana. Big D Construction crews have built several facilities at the Clearfield Freeport Center, have expanded Weber Central Dairy and Great Salt Lake Minerals and Chemical Company plants, have constructed most of the Jetway and Flameco White Motor complexes, and have been involved in several Family Centers throughout Utah.

Close associates from the start have been Dale Satterthwaite, now vice-president and operations manager, and Robert S. Moore, now corporate secretary. Livingood's only son, Jack, joined the corporation as an estimator and is now treasurer. The Livingoods also have three daughters.

Dee Livingood has been active in the Ogden Area Chamber of Commerce and has served as a member of both the Ogden Housing Authority and the city's Seismic Code Committee.

Founder and president Dee Livingood (seated) is surrounded by corporate officers and directors (left to right) Dale Satterthwaite, vice-president; Rob Moore, corporate secretary; and Jack Livingood, treasurer.

WEBER CLUB

The Weber Club of Ogden is the oldest social and civic club in Utah. It was founded on April 6, 1896, just four months and two days after President Grover Cleveland signed a proclamation that made Utah the forty-fifth state in the union.

Articles of incorporation proclaimed that the first objective would be "to promote the general prosperity of all the varied interests of the State of Utah, and especially those of the City of Ogden and its immediate vicinity."

There were seventy-one founding members, all community leaders, with John Scowcroft as president, William Glasmann as vice-president, George H. Matson as secretary, Daniel Hamer as treasurer, and Angus T. Wright, Fred J. Kiesel, and C.K. Bannister as directors. The Weber Club now has more than 625 members, with Thomas G. Barker, Jr., as president for 1983-1985, and James D. Larsen as president for 1985-1986.

Initially, the Weber Club took over the responsibilities of the original Ogden Area Chamber of Commerce, established in April 1887, the first in Utah. In 1912 the club organized the Ogden Publicity Bureau as one of its auxiliaries to promote commercial aspects of the area.

The chamber was reestablished in 1920 to replace the Publicity Bureau, but six years later the organizations were combined. The combination was maintained as the Ogden Area Chamber of Commerce-Weber Club until 1933 when they were formally separated, and each has operated independently since that time.

The first home of the Weber Club was in the old Utah Loan and Trust Co. building at the corner of Washington Boulevard and Twenty-fourth Street—the present site of the Eccles Build-

The home of the Weber Club has been in the former LeRoy Eccles home since 1959. Built in 1918, it is on the southwest corner of Eccles Avenue and Twenty-fifth Street.

ing. When that structure burned, the Weber Club took temporary quarters in the Congress Ballroom on Grant Avenue until the Kiesel Building was completed at Twenty-fourth Street and Kiesel Avenue. The club occupied all of the high-ceilinged sixth floor and had a large ballroom on the fifth floor.

The club moved to the Ben Lomond Hotel in 1928. It later purchased the ornate E.J. Harness home, originally built in 1918 by LeRoy Eccles, and moved there in 1959 after a million-dollar remodeling. In 1982 the building was sold to the Kier Corporation, and the Weber Club leased the lower level for its club rooms.

The Weber Club has been primarily social in nature for the past half-century, providing fine food and beverages and encouraging its members to relax in the company of their associates, guests, and families. It was strictly male at the start, but has recently begun enrolling female members.

Charter member Gus L. Becker, in a 1946 talk, noted that the Weber Club "has seen good times and bad times, has survived the days of Prohibition and crime, moonshine whiskey and home-brewed, so-called beer, has sur-

vived two world wars and the worst depression in history. . . . It has endured all storms . . . and continues to lead the way for Ogden's growth and prosperity."

Thomas G. Barker, Jr., felt the same way during his just-concluded administration as president and pledged that he and his colleagues would do their utmost to assure the Weber Club's continued success as "Utah's oldest and finest social club."

This menu was featured at a banquet held by the founders of the Utah Construction Company at the Weber Club on May 31, 1910. The dishes were named for worldwide Utah Construction projects.

Menu

Chilcoot Cocktail

Meadow Valley Wash in Cup

Sumpter Valley Hobo Trout

O. S. L. Prize Potatoes Rip Rap Style

Sauterne a la Feather River

Oroville Olives Served à la Cement Gravel

Tongue Scraper Radishes

Western Pacific Roosters à la Spring Garden

Rio Grande Potatoes Bridge Timber Style

Sierra Nevada Tunnel Champagne

Spring Lamb à la Leamington Cut-off

Southern Pacific Potatoes Embankment Style

Bridge Trestle Asparagus

Rock Culvert Tomato-Cucumber Salad

Hood River Dinkey Strawberries with Condensed Milk

Manilla Rope Cigars Steam Shovel brand

Bloomer Bar Coffee

OGDEN STANDARD-EXAMINER

The Standard-Examiner *was located for years in the Kiesel Building on Twenty-fourth Street. Business offices were on the main floor, the newsroom on the second floor, and the pressroom was in the basement.*

To state it simply, the *Ogden Standard-Examiner* is a newspaper.

It keeps the 276,000 people living in its circulation area well informed about daily local, state, national, and international affairs.

But the *Standard-Examiner* is much more than just a disseminator of news. It has a rich tradition as an analytical community conscience and is a consistently strong voice for individual and community improvement.

That tradition of community service was established in the rough-and-tumble frontier times by William Glasmann who took

over the six-year-old *Ogden Standard* in 1894.

As a newspaper editor in Ogden's formative years, William Glasmann was fearless, outspoken, and frequently controversial. But above all, he was an enterprising and energetic leader ever ready to promote the economic and cultural growth of his hometown.

It is a tradition carried forward by the third- and fourth-generation descendants of that pioneer newspaper publisher and community stalwart.

Those strong, vibrant roots established almost a century ago have sprouted numerous ventures in the communications fields, with the Glasmann-directed enterprises pioneering advances in theater, radio, broadcast television, cable television, and microwave transmission.

That small frontier publication is today the flagship in a network of newspaper, radio, television, and cable television interests throughout the West and Midwest.

The parent company of that network is the Standard Corporation, now owned by two families. President of the corporation is Wilda Gene Hatch, a granddaughter of William Glasmann and daughter of Abe Glasmann. Her husband, George Hatch, veteran head of KUTV Channel 2, is corporate treasurer.

Equal partners in the enterprise are the children of Blaine V. Glasmann, one of the four sons of William Glasmann. Representing this family is Blaine V. Glasmann, Jr., who is the corporate secretary. His brother, Gordon Glasmann, is vice-president.

Other members of the two families take an active role in the management and operations of the corporation and its subsidiaries.

One of the best known of those subsidiaries is KUTV, one of four Salt Lake City-based television stations. Affiliated with the National Broadcasting Company (NBC), KUTV serves Utah and major parts of surrounding states. By cable television, it reaches as far away as Montana and the Dakotas.

Another subsidiary is the Kansas State Network, which operates six television stations in Kansas, Nebraska, and Missouri. They are KSNW, Wichita, Kansas; KSNF, Joplin, Missouri; KSNT, Topeka, Kansas; KSNK, McCook, Nebraska; KSNG, Garden City, Kansas; and KSNC, Great Bend, Kansas.

In addition to the *Standard-Examiner,* the Standard Corporation also publishes a number of weekly newspapers. These include the *Lakeside Review,* which serves Davis County and the southern part of Weber, the *Sun Advocate* in

Since 1961 the Ogden Standard-Examiner *offices and printing plant have been at 455 Twenty-third Street. The central portion of the modern newspaper facility was formerly the armory of the Utah National Guard.*

Price, the *Emery County Progress* in Castle Dale, three newspapers in Colorado, and two in Idaho at Hailey and Ketchum.

The Standard Corporation helped found the Denver-based Tele-Communications Inc. (TCI), now the largest cable television company in the country. Although the Standard Corporation has no ownership in TCI now, it is involved in some cable television operations with TCI in Illinois and Idaho.

Almost since its beginnings a century ago, the *Standard-Examiner* has been the dominant news medium in the Weber, Morgan, Box Elder, and North Davis areas.

This is due to the well-trained staff of reporters, editors, and photographers who keep *Standard-Examiner* readers accurately and completely informed on local

affairs—whether a high school football game, a Little League tournament, a routine City Council meeting, or a hotly contested zoning hearing.

Standard-Examiner readers are also offered a varied menu of national and international news from major news services.

Today the *Standard-Examiner* is delivered to about 55,000 homes on Monday through Friday afternoons and Saturday and Sunday mornings. That is 63 percent of the homes in the area. This compares with only 8 percent for the two Salt Lake City dailies in the same area.

On Wednesday, the Layton-based *Lakeside Review* delivers 34,000 copies and *Midweek,* a special publication for all non-subscribers in Weber, Morgan, and Box Elder counties, goes to 20,000 homes. This gives the Standard Corporation a total circulation on Wednesdays of 109,000.

The *Standard-Examiner* traces its ancestry back to the *Ogden Junction,* which came off the press on January 1, 1870, with

Franklin D. Richards as publisher and C.W. Penrose as editor. The *Junction's* career was turbulent and its subscription list was sold to the *Ogden Daily Herald,* which eventually became the *Standard* on January 1, 1888, with Frank J. Cannon as publisher.

Cannon turned the paper over to his business manager, William Glasmann, in 1894 when he was elected a territorial member to the U.S. House of Representatives. He was later appointed to the U.S. Senate when Utah became a state in 1896.

Glasmann quickly established the *Standard* as a fearless, driving force for the community's socio-economic growth.

Progress continues to mold the spirit of the *Standard-Examiner.* In recent years a state-of-the-art computer system and additional equipment have been added to make the newspaper more sophisticated and more valuable to its readers. With such planning and foresight, the *Standard-Examiner* looks forward to the next century with anticipation.

WEBER BASIN WATER CONSERVANCY DISTRICT

The Lost Creek Dam and Reservoir are integral units of the Weber Basin Project. Courtesy, the U.S. Bureau of Reclamation

Miles Goodyear immediately planted a garden beside his primitive log trading post when he became the Ogden area's first white settler in 1844. His Indian wife, Pomona, irrigated the plot with water carried in pots from the adjacent Weber River. The Goodyears knew that if there was to be growth and prosperity, the available water resources had to be carefully managed.

This is still true. That's why the Weber Basin Water Conservancy District is so essential to residents of Weber, Davis, Morgan, Summit, and Box Elder counties and to their farms, cities, and industries. Without the district and its complex Weber Basin Project, there would be severe drought

in dry years and disastrous flooding in wet years.

The district's six reservoirs have the capacity to store 469,000 acre feet of water, soon to be increased to 476,900 acre feet. That's more than 156 billion gallons—sufficient to fill the average household water heater nearly four billion times.

Only about 92 percent of the water stored behind the dams can be drawn out for culinary, agricultural, and industrial consumption. The rest must be retained as a wildlife habitat.

Capital investment now exceeds $105 million in federal appropriations. The district and its water users are obligated to repay $81.6 million over sixty years—and more than half has already been repaid. The remainder represents the value of recreational and flood-control facilities that benefit everyone. Replacement costs now would

be four or five times the original amount, according to estimates by manager Keith Jensen.

Construction on the Weber Basin Project began in the fall of 1952 after years of discussion, lobbying, planning, and occasional controversy. The need for upstream storage on the Weber River and its tributaries, including the Ogden River, had long been recognized. Many small dams had been built to divert streamline flow into irrigation ditches, power plants, and municipal waterworks. The Davis and Weber Counties Land Co. built a dam in East Canyon in 1896. The first Echo Dam was constructed about 1926, and the initial Pineview Dam in 1934-1935.

But these were not enough to meet the skyrocketing demand, especially during dry cycles, or to provide adequate flood protection during heavy rains or after above-average snowmelt. The requirement for more reliable water management became particularly acute during World War II, when the expansion of defense facilities in Weber and Davis counties brought tremendous increases in population.

The first steps toward the formation of an area-wide, water-oriented organization were taken in 1945 at meetings in the Davis County Courthouse in Farmington. They were called by Joseph W. Johnson, county assessor, and DeLore Nichols, county agricultural agent, who were to play key roles in the movement for many years.

Davis County provided $5,000 and Morgan County $500 to finance a study of the various problems and potential solutions by E.O. "Ole" Larson, a U.S. Bureau of Reclamation engineer and later its regional director. Larson had been working on Utah

274

water and irrigation research since the early 1920s. Weber County joined forces with its neighbors after a lack of moisture in 1946 threatened crops, and too much precipitation the next winter caused extensive flooding.

The movement was climaxed on March 22, 1949, with the formation of the Weber Basin Conservancy District and passage, five months later, by Congress of the Weber Basin Bill. When President Harry S Truman signed the act on August 29, 1949, secretary/manager E.J. Fjeldsted of the Ogden Area Chamber of Commerce called the action "one of the greatest events in the history of this area."

Dozens of individuals and organizations were involved in the successful campaign. Names most prominent in the district's history include DeLore Nichols, Joe Johnson, David Scott, Fred Abbott, D.D. Harris, Ez Fjeldsted, Harold Clark, Ed Sorenson, Phil Sorenson, Ed Watson, Doren Boyce, Elmer Carver, Thomas East, Judge J.A. Howell, Harold Welch, W.R. White, Harold Ellison, E.J. Skeen, Clinton D. Woods, Rex Greenhalgh, Francis M. Warnick, Senators Arthur V. Watkins and Elbert Thomas, and Representatives W.K. Granger, William Dawson, Reva Beck Bosone, and D.D. McKay.

At hand during all of the efforts was the feasibility study of engineer Win Templeton that concluded: "Our area must have irrigation, municipal, and industrial water for continued growth. ... The only practical means of developing the needed supplies is through participation in the Weber Basin Project."

Congress voted initial funding in July 1952. The repayment contract signed by the district, then placed at nearly fifty-eight million dollars, was the largest in

Sailing is a popular recreation on reservoirs of the Weber Basin Water Conservancy District. Courtesy, the U.S. Bureau of Reclamation

the history of U.S. reclamation and irrigation projects.

A contract signed on November 3, 1952, permitted the drilling of test wells to determine the extent of underground water supplies and to check the load-bearing characteristics at dam sites. With the Ogden-born Utah Construction Company doing much of the work, building of the actual structures came rapidly, with the first phase completed by the end of 1957. Other facilities followed, and expansion still continues. Contracts were let in late 1984 for the enlargement of the Smith and Moorehouse Dam in Summit County to increase storage capacity.

The Weber Basin Water Conservancy District now operates the Pineview, Wanship, Willard, Lost Creek, East Canyon, and Causey dams and reservoirs. It has two small power plants that generate electricity to operate eleven pumping stations. There are 78.9 miles of canals, tunnels, and major pipelines, plus scores of miles of distribution laterals. Nine wells have been drilled, and three water-treatment plants have been built.

Irrigation water is provided to 78,475 acres. Every city in the

district's five-county territory uses Weber Basin water to supplement local supplies. Industries, many using thousands of gallons of water daily, have expanded tremendously. Weber Basin reservoirs are among the most popular in the Intermountain West for recreation, especially boating and fishing.

Ez Fjeldsted left the Ogden Area Chamber of Commerce to serve as the district's first manager from 1950 to 1965. Wayne M. Winegar, former Davis County commissioner, served as manager from 1965 to 1979. He was succeeded by Keith Jensen, former Weber County commissioner and a member of the district's board for twenty years. Policy is established by a nine-member board, now appointed by the governor, that meets regularly at the district's newly remodeled headquarters just off Mountain Road and east of Hill Air Force Base.

Jensen is carrying out the Weber Basin Water Conservancy District board's directive to continue to seek new water supplies— buying water rights as they become available and developing unused sources—because current resources are virtually all "sold" to users. "We have been able to stay ahead of the demand for culinary supplies." Jensen concludes, "Operations have proven that the district is the logical way to manage water, rather than through competing entities."

PATRONS

The following individuals, companies, and organizations have made a valuable commitment to the quality of this publication. Windsor Publications and the Ogden Area Chamber of Commerce gratefully acknowledge their participation in *Ogden: Junction City*.

The Amalgamated Sugar
  Company*
American Fence Company*
American Nutrition, Inc.*
Anderson Lumber Company*
Bavarian Chalet-German
  Restaurant
Big D Construction Corporation*
E. Rich Brewer
The Brockman Company
Browning Company*
Buckner-Radmall Insurance
  Counselors
Burton-Walker Lumber Company*
Case, Lowe and Hart, Inc.*
Chevron Corporation
Coca-Cola Bottling Company of
  Ogden*
Commercial Security Bank*
Credit Bureau of Ogden
First Security Corporation*
Froerer Corp.*
Shirley Eldredge Glasmann
Golden Spike Empire
Great Salt Lake Minerals and
  Chemicals Corp.
Kent M. Hardy, M.D.
Helgesen & Waterfall, Attorneys
  at Law
Robert H. Hinckley, Inc.*
Daniel C. Hunter, Jr., M.D.
IBEC - Ricoh Copiers
Jade Tree, Inc.
Jetway Division of Abex
  Corporation*
Junction City News
The Kier Corporation*
Ladies Literary Club

Leavitt's Chapel of Flowers
  Mortuary, Inc.
  Aultorest Memorial Park
  Corporation*

Living Scriptures*
J. Ralph Macfarlane
Mr. and Mrs. Karl O. Macfarlane
McKay-Dee Hospital Center*
Morton Thiokol, Inc.*
Mountain Bell*
Mountain Fuel Supply Company*
Noel Nellis, M.D.
NICE Corporation*
Claire A. Nielsen, C.P.A.
Northern Utah Glass
Ogden Air Logistics Center-Hill
  Air Force Base, Utah
Ogden City Schools*
Ogden First Federal Savings
Ogden Hilton Hotel-Dave
  Hartvigsen
Ogden Standard-Examiner*
Ogden Weber Area Vocational
  Center
Overland West, Inc.*
Petersen Motor Co., Inc.
Richard O. Petty, D.D.S.
The Pillsbury Company
St. Benedict's Hospital*
St. Joseph's Church*
TRW Inc.*
Union Station
Utah Power and Light Company*
The Vanessa-Ann Collection*
Volvo White Truck Corporation
Wasatch Distributing Company*
Weber Basin Water Conservancy
  District*
Weber Club*
Weber County Commission
Weber County School District*
Weber State College*
Western Zirconium*
Jim Whetton Buick*
W.R. White Company*
Williams International*

*Partners in Progress of *Ogden: Junction City*. The histories of these companies and organizations appear in Chapter VI, beginning on page 200.

BIBLIOGRAPHY

The assistance of librarians, archivists, and people of the community has been much appreciated in this project. Especially helpful have been:

Barbara Parsons Bernstein, Russell B. Farr, John E. Lamborn, Brad Larson, Grove Pashley, Mr. and Mrs. L.S. Rowse, Adele Smith, Jean M. Christensen, Mary Patterson, William W. Terry, Julie Rasmussen, Dorothy Draney, and Susan Lowery.

Alexander, Thomas G. "Ogden's Arsenal of Democracy, 1920-1955." *Utah Historical Quarterly* XXXIII (Summer, 1965): 236-247.

Arrington, Leonard J., and Alexander, Thomas G. "Supply Hub of the West: Defense Depot Ogden, 1941-1946." *Utah Historical Quarterly* XXXII (Spring, 1964).

Arrington, Leonard J. "Reclamation in Three Layers: the Ogden River Project, 1934-1965." *Pacific Historical Review* XXXV #1 (February, 1966): 15-34.

Arrington, Leonard James. *Utah's Biggest Business: Ogden Air Materiel Area at Hill Air Force Base, 1938-1965.* Salt Lake City: Utah State Historical Society, 1965.

Art Publishing Company. *Ogden City, Utah, Picturesque and Descriptive.* Neenah, Wisconsin: Art Publishing Co., 1889.

Barnes, Lyle J. *Ogden's Notorious "Two-Bit Street."* Master's Thesis, Utah State University, 1969.

Browning, John. *John M. Browning, American Gunmaker: An Illustrated Biography of the Man and His Guns.* Garden City: Doubleday, 1964.

Chamber of Commerce. *Ogden and Opportunity.* Ogden: Chamber of Commerce, n.d.

Chamber of Commerce. Ogden, Utah. *Ogden, the Junction City of the West.* Ogden: E.A. McDaniel, 1888.

Chamber of Commerce. *Occupational Survey, Ogden Area, September, 1946.* Ogden: Chamber of Commerce, 1946.

Church of Jesus Christ of Latter-day Saints. Ogden Eighth Ward. *Minutes of the Ogden 8th Ward Sunday School, 1908-1936.* Holographic Manuscript.

Cline, Gloria Griffen. *Peter Skene Ogden and the Hudson's Bay Company.* Norman: University of Oklahoma Press, 1974.

Corcoran, John Dennis. *An Appraisal of the Governments of Ogden City and Weber County.* Master's Thesis, University of Denver, 1942.

Deseret News. *Guide to Salt Lake City, Ogden and the Utah Central Railroad.* Salt Lake City: Deseret News.

De Voto, Bernard. "Good Places to Grow In." *Lincoln and Mercury Times* VIII (March-April, 1956): 1-3.

Erastus Bingham Family Corporation. *The Descendants of Erastus Bingham and Lucinda Gates.* Ogden: The Erastus Bingham Family Corporation, 1970.

Farr, John. *My Yesterdays.* Salt Lake City: Granite Publication Co., 1957.

Federal Writer's Project. Utah. *A Partial Bibliography of Source Material on Weber County and Ogden City, Utah.* Ogden: The Ogden Historical Society, 1938.

First Security Bank of Utah. *Ogden—Gateway City.* Salt Lake City: First Security Bank of Utah, Idaho and Wyoming, n.d.

Haefeli, Leo. "A Stroll Through Ogden." *Tullidge's Quarterly Magazine* I (1881): 475-484.

Hansen, Alma Wayment. *A Historical Study of the Influence of the Railroad Upon Ogden, Utah, 1868-1875.* Provo: Master's Thesis, Department of History, Brigham Young University, 1953.

Historical Records Survey. *A History of Ogden.* ed. by Dale Morgan. Ogden: Ogden City Commission, 1940.

Historical Records Survey. *Inventory of the County Archives of Utah: No. 29 Weber County.* ed. by Dale Morgan. Ogden: Historical Records Survey Project, 1940.

Hunter, Milton R. *Beneath Ben Lomond's Peak: A History of Weber County 1824-1900.* Salt Lake City: Deseret News Press, 1944.

Jameson, Jesse H. "Ogden: Junction City for the Pacific Railroad." *SUP News* VI (August 1959): 3, 16.

Kelly, Charles. *Miles Goodyear: First Citizen of Utah, Trapper, Trader, and California Pioneer.* Salt Lake City: Western Printing Co., 1937.

Kotter, Richard E. "The Transcontinental Railroad and Ogden City Politics." *Utah Historical Quarterly* XLII #3 (Summer, 1974): 278-289.

League of Women Voters of Weber County, Utah. *Weber County ... Yesterday, Today and Tomorrow.* Ogden: League of Women Voters, 1975.

Morgan, Dale Lowell. "Miles Goodyear and the Founding of Ogden." *Utah Historical Quarterly* XXI #3, 4 (July-October, 1953): 195-218, 307-329.

Mountain States Telephone & Telegraph. *75th Anniversary, Ogden, Utah.* Ogden: Mountain States Telephone, 1955.

Ogden City Corporation. *Welcome to Ogden, Utah - A Mountain Wonderland.* Ogden: Ogden City Corporation, 1965.

Ogden Standard Examiner. "Ogden in Profile." *Ogden Standard Examiner,* April 5, 1966.

Pardoe, T. Earl. *Lorin Farr, Pioneer.* Provo: Brigham Young University Press, 1953.

Provisional League of Women Voters. *Know Your Town.* Ogden: Provisional League of Women Voters, 1963.

Richards. Jesse, "Ogden's Industrial Development." *Union Pacific Magazine* III #12 (1924): 5, 31-35.

Sadler, Richard W., and Critchlow, William J., III. "Miles Goodyear's Fort Buenaventura." (Unpublished manuscript for the Utah Department of Parks and Recreation, copyright, 1978.)

Shurtliff, Luman Andros. *Journal of Luman Andros Shurtliff.* n.p., 1936.

Stanford, Joseph. *Historical Sketch of Ogden City.*

Tillotson, Elizabeth M. *A History of Ogden, 1940-1960.* Historical Records Survey, 1962.

Tullidge, Edward Wheelock. *Tullidge's Histories Vol. 2.* Salt Lake City: Press of the Juvenile Instructor, 1889.

Tullidge's Quarterly Magazine. "Ogden and Its Representatives." *Tullidge's Quarterly Magazine* II (1883): 187-228.

Utah Federal Writers' Project.

Partial Bibliography of Source Material on Weber County and Ogden City, Utah. Ogden: Ogden Historical Society, 1938.

Weber Club. *A Glimpse of Ogden.* Ogden: Weber Club, n.d.

West, Chaucey W. "Ogden, the Gateway of the West." *Utah Magazine* I #3 (May' 1935): 19, 45.

Western Galaxy. "Ogden City." *Western Galaxy* I (1888): 439-459.

Wright, Martha R. "Junction City Sets Pace." *Utah Magazine* VIII (March, 1946): 22.

The Carnegie Free Library was an Ogden landmark for over two-thirds of a century. Neo-classical in design, it was the first building in Utah used solely as a library and was noted for its excellent collection of Western Americana. Courtesy, Ogden Chamber of Commerce

INDEX

GENERAL INDEX

Italicized numbers indicate illustrations

BOOKS IN THE WINDSOR HISTORY SERIES

trated History of Rapid City, by David B. Miller

TENNESSEE
Chattanooga: An Illustrated History, by James Livingood
Metropolis of the American Nile: Memphis and Shelby County, by John E. Harkins

TEXAS
Beaumont: A Chronicle of Promise, by Judith W. Linsley and Ellen W. Rienstra
Corpus Christi: The History of a Texas Seaport, by Bill Walraven
Dallas: An Illustrated History, by Darwin Payne
City at the Pass: An Illustrated History of El Paso, by Leon Metz
Houston: Chronicle of the Supercity on Buffalo Bayou, by Stanley E. Siegel
Waco: Texas Crossroads, by Patricia Ward Wallace
Where the West Begins: Fort Worth and Tarrant County, by Janet L. Schmelzer

UTAH

Odgen: Junction City, by Richard C. Roberts and Richard W. Sadler
Salt Lake City: The Gathering Place, by John S. McCormick

VIRGINIA
Norfolk's Waters: An Illustrated Maritime History of Hampton Roads, by William Tazewell
Richmond: An Illustrated History, by Harry M. Ward

WASHINGTON
King County And Its Queen City: Seattle by James R. Warren
South on the Sound: An Illustrated History of Tacoma and Pierce County, by Rosa and Murray Morgan
A View of the Falls: An Illustrated History of Spokane, by William Stimson

WEST VIRGINIA
Charleston and the Kanawha Valley: An Illustrated History, by Otis K. Rice
Huntington: An Illustrated History, by James E. Casto
Wheeling: An Illustrated History, by Doug Fetherling

WISCONSIN
The Fox Heritage: A History of Wisconsin's Fox Cities, by Ellen Kort
Green Bay: Gateway to the Great Waterway, by Betsy Foley

CANADA
Calgary: Canada's Frontier Metropolis, by Max Foran and Heather MacEwan Foran
Edmonton: Gateway to the North, by John F. Gilpin
Hamilton: Chronicle of a City, by T. Melville Bailey
Kitchener: Yesterday Revisited, by Bill Moyer
Where Rivers Meet: An Illustrated History of Ottawa, by Courtney C. J. Bond
Regina: From Pile O'Bones to Queen City of the Plains, by William A. Riddell
Saint John: Two Hundred Years Proud, by George W. Schuyler
Saskatoon: Hub City of the West, by Gail A. McConnell
Toronto: The Place of Meeting, by Frederick H. Armstrong
Winnipeg: Where the New West Begins, Eric Wells

THIS BOOK WAS SET IN
CENTURY AND GARAMOND TYPES,
PRINTED ON
70-LB. MEAD ENAMEL OFFSET
AND BOUND BY
WALSWORTH PUBLISHING
COMPANY

WEBER RIVER